Success for All Students

Promoting Inclusion in Secondary Schools through Peer Buddy Programs

Carolyn Hughes

Vanderbilt University

Erik W. Carter

University of Wisconsin—Madison

PEARSON

Boston   New York   San Francisco
Mexico City   Montreal   Toronto   London   Madrid   Munich   Paris
Hong Kong   Singapore   Tokyo   Cape Town   Sydney

We dedicate this book to all the students, teachers, administrators, and family members who are working and interacting every day to create schools that are communities of belonging, acceptance, caring, and tolerance for all. Your courage and imagination are our inspiration.

Series Editor: Virginia Lanigan
Marketing Manager: Amy Cronin Jordan
Editorial Assistant: Scott Blaszak
Production Supervisor: Joe Sweeney
Production Editor: Greg Erb
Editorial-Production Service: Walsh & Associates, Inc.
Composition and Prepress Buyer: Linda Cox
Manufacturing Buyer: Andrew Turso
Cover Administrator: Kristina Mose-Libon

For related titles and support materials, visit our online catalog at www.ablongman.com.

Library of Congress Cataloging-in-Publication Data

Hughes, Carolyn, 1946–
    Success for all students: promoting inclusion in secondary schools through peer buddy programs / Carolyn Hughes, Erik W. Carter.
       p. cm.
    Includes bibliographical references and index.
    ISBN 0-205-42420-1
    1. Peer counseling of students—United States. 2. Student service—United States. 3. Counseling in secondary education—United States. 4. Students with disabilities—Education (Secondary)—United States. I. Carter, Erik W. II. Title.

LB1027.5.H37 2006
373.14'047'0973—dc22   2004060043

Printed in the United States of America

10 9 8 7 6 5 4 3 2 1   11 10 09 08 07 06 05

CONTENTS

FOREWORDS

Carolyn Hughes and Erik Carter have written a wonderful book for teachers and administrators who want to use service–learning as a technique for building community in their school and facilitating students' personal development. Service–learning is a powerful tool for teachers because it helps them address important goals for many students at the same time. When students help others, they often come to care about them, to have an interest in their well-being, and to be able to put themselves in others' shoes. This personal connection and chance to be of service helps students define themselves as strong, competent people. Doing service that makes a real difference in someone's life whom they come to care about also encourages students to think of themselves as members of their community with a commitment to improving that community. This process, then, encourages personal development and citizenship engagement. It also helps students engage constructively with their own school. When students are teamed with others in important work, they are more likely to come to school and to be interested in what is happening there, which contributes to their sense of community involvement.

This process of personal and social engagement also contributes directly to helping students attain academic goals. Students who care and are involved in their communities become curious and have real questions about issues they confront. Students whose interest is engaged and whose assumptions are challenged develop an increased capacity for problem solving and critical thinking. And real questions answered in part while engaged in real experiences lead to deeper understanding of subject matter.

But service–learning is not always easy for teachers and schools to implement. Instead, it presents some serious challenges that can be political, professional, or practical. This book provides the supporting arguments, the evidence, and the tools for addressing these challenges.

Sometimes colleagues or administrators resist service–learning because they are not convinced it is worth the trouble. Hughes and Carter provide a clear rationale for service–learning and how it can help schools meet current demands of No Child Left Behind and other federal policy. Because they have tried their model and done extensive research on its impact on teachers and students, educators have the scholarly data to persuade others of the value of establishing peer buddy programs in their schools. Their research demonstrates the power of peer buddy programs on student engagement, motivation, and academic success.

This book also provides ample support for teachers nervous about their ability to carry out such a program with students. First, the peer buddy program model is clearly described to allow replication. Second, the book is rich with examples of how the model is used with a variety of students. Third, there are step-by-step guidelines and, where appropriate, checklists and forms to help teachers design projects, facilitate reflection activities, and assess results.

Because the authors know that even educators who are committed to service–learning and know how to implement it with their students are sometimes daunted by the challenge of practical logistics, they provide extensive directions for making a service–learning peer buddy program work vis-à-vis the realities of everyday life. There is clear practical advice about building political support for the program, recruiting participants, matching students with buddies and supporting their efforts, and providing continuing support for faculty and staff involved in the program. Because the peer buddy program is developed to allow service within the school environment, it also helps faculty build strong service–learning programs that are not limited by the complex logistics of transportation and timing that make community-based programs a challenge.

This book is the complete package for faculty and administrators who are concerned about engaging students in the school community in order to improve student outcomes. Hughes and Carter have provided the theory, the scholarship, and the practical tools to help educators succeed in establishing peer buddy programs that work.

Janet Eyler
Vanderbilt University

Have you had that dream where you showed up in your old high school hallway with your pajamas on—or with nothing on—while everyone else was fully clothed? Do you remember at least once when you were chosen last or almost last by the team captain for a playground game? Can you remember when everyone else around you was asked to dance and you were left standing alone, trying to disappear? Maybe you recall covering up your failing grade on a quiz when the teacher handed back papers. Nightmares from our school days center on being rejected, failing, not belonging, and not fitting in. Such memories can remain toxic in our minds for years.

Belonging and membership are key themes that many have voiced in the unfinished battle for inclusive schools. No matter how much children are nurtured and loved by their family, when children enter school, they need and typically seek membership and warm accepting relationships there as well. Norm Kunc (2000) calls the basic human need to belong "a right" that is glaringly absent in today's schools:

> Belonging—having a social context—is requisite for the development of self-esteem and self-confidence . . . . Despite the essential importance of belonging . . . it is interesting to note that . . . schools provide little nurturance or assistance. (p. 83)

In agreement with Maslow's hierarchy of human needs, Kunc (2000) has long argued that fulfilling the basic need of belonging and love allows children to develop the higher order need of self-esteem. Experiencing the sense of belonging to groups with typical-age peers and having friendships gives children and adolescents the security needed to focus on achievement, mastery, recognition, and respect. "Providing a person with a sense of belonging is pivotal for that person to excel" (p. 82). Belonging and acceptance must not be made conditional on achievement.

In our society, segregated special instruction classes (in the form of resource rooms, self-contained classrooms, remedial reading groups, ESL classes) predominate as the approach to address differences in achievement and behavior. Many students in these classes do not develop a sense of self-worth because their need to belong is made contingent on achievement. They cannot earn their way out of the special classroom.

> Consequently, the students in segregated classrooms learn not only that they are not good enough to belong but also that *they will never be good enough to belong,* because their disability, and the subsequent reason for their banishment, can never be removed. (Kunc, 2000, p. 89)

In a similar vein, Thomas Hopkins, an adult with cerebral palsy, commented on his high school experience in the 1970s:

> I say I am the man from Mars because all my life I've felt different from "normal" people. . . . Maybe there is a magic . . . in being around typical kids, because that's where

you pick up the clues and the skills that make ordinary living possible—those things that aren't taught, per se, in inclusive settings but are part of the atmosphere of a real-world environment. I didn't get that, so I never really learned how to make friends, how to fool around and hang out, or how to talk to and tease girls, I never really learned how to be a "guy": how to pick up on the way my generation had of saying things like "hip" or "cool" or "bad" meaning "good," or whatever it was that gave people my age their own language. (Hopkins & Rosenberg, 1998, p. 376)

Even though Thomas graduated in 1979, students with and without disabilities graduating from high school today make similar comments about the need to belong and to have friends. What is the solution to these common experiences of being on the outside that so many students with disabilities have? Most solutions will not be simple, and they will address two themes: (a) make inclusion with appropriate supports a reality for students with disabilities throughout their school years, and (b) develop programs of peer support to encourage interactions, reinforce learning, and promote positive relationships between students with disabilities and their peers.

If read and used, this book on peer buddy programs can be part of the solution. It is a guidebook that sets forth clearly defined steps for planning programs of peer support and putting them into place. This book not only builds upon the authors' history with actual peer buddy programs in middle and high schools, its contents rest firmly upon convincing evidence of the power of peer support. Readers will find ready-to-use guidance on laying the groundwork for a program, developing the program procedures, recruiting students, training and supporting the peer buddies, and evaluating and sustaining these programs. The book is organized to provide specific advice in each chapter to teachers, school counselors, and administrators on the roles these individuals may play. Case studies give direction through example, and quotes from peer buddy program participants motivate and direct readers in their planning.

If you and your colleagues are interested in promoting positive relationships between students with disabilities and their peers, read this book and use its guidelines to set up a peer buddy program in your own school. There is little time to wait; you probably have students who could benefit right now.

Martha E. Snell
University of Virginia

References

Hopkins, T.L., & Rosenberg, R.R. (1998). The man from Mars. In L.H. Meyer, H. Park, M. Grenot-Scheyer, I.S. Schwartz, & B. Harry (Eds.), *Making friends* (pp. 375–381). Baltimore: Paul H. Brookes.

Kunc, N. (2000). Rediscovering the right to belong. In R. Villa & J.S. Thousand (Eds.), *Restructuring for caring and effective education* (pp. 77–92). Baltimore: Paul H. Brookes.

PREFACE

This book is written for anyone who is concerned about the conditions in today's secondary schools. A quick survey of current newspaper and magazine articles and editorials, television newscasts and program specials, and formal and impromptu community gatherings tells us that this group includes just about everyone. We frequently hear or read about (a) high student dropout rates; (b) low academic performance; (c) lack of student discipline; (d) increasingly challenging cultural, linguistic, economic, and academic diversity; and (e) poor postsecondary student outcomes, including high unemployment and limited civic engagement, as characteristic of today's middle and high schools. Current education legislation, such as the Individuals with Disabilities Education Amendments (IDEA) of 1997 (PL 105-17) and No Child Left Behind (NCLB) Act of 2001 (PL 107-110), has been introduced to address some of these problems by promoting access to general education curricula and raising academic standards and performance expectations for all students. Additional educational initiatives addressing contemporary secondary education include (a) developing "communities of caring" in which students treat each other with respect and compassion, (b) providing community service opportunities to develop students' citizenship skills and engagement, and (c) promoting experiential learning to engage students in relevant, real-life problems and opportunities.

Although we do not pretend—by any means—to address all the problems that may exist within today's secondary schools, this book is an attempt to target at least some of them by promoting inclusive, compassionate communities for *all* students, including students with disabilities, within secondary school environments in which all students are actively and successfully engaged as concerned citizens. Based on our extensive experience in secondary schools—in particular, high schools—we propose a unique means toward achieving these goals by involving students in service–learning peer support programs that promote more unified, positive educational experiences for both general and special education students. Started as a grassroots initiative with just a few students in one high school in Nashville, Tennessee, the Metropolitan Nashville Peer Buddy Program—the prototype for the educational initiative proposed in this book—grew to be a districtwide program subsequently adopted nationally across many schools.

Participants in the Peer Buddy Program enroll in a 1-credit service–learning course designed to increase access to general education curricula and activities by students with disabilities. As peer buddies, students provide social and academic support to their classmates with disabilities by (a) helping them acquire skills needed to succeed in the general education environment and (b) adapting the environment to be more welcoming, accepting, tolerant, and accommodating to individual differences and needs. The peer buddy model addresses challenges to inclusion characteristic of secondary schools, such as 50-minute class scheduling and departmentalized classes and faculty, by introducing peer buddies as support to students across classes, activities, and environments. The notion of promoting inclusion through peer buddy programs is timely in relation to recent legislation, such as IDEA 1997 and NCLB, that seeks to increase access to general education and raise performance standards for all students, including students with disabilities and members of other underrepresented groups. School staff, parents, politicians, and others argue that insufficient resources are available to address these educational initiatives. Peer buddies can help teachers and administrators who are attempting to achieve legislative goals by serving as a helping hand to promote the success of students with disabilities in general educational curricula and activities.

Peer buddy programs have been described as a win-win situation that offers benefits to all participants. *Students with disabilities* learn new social, academic, employment, and life skills while expanding friendships and activities with their general education peers. *General education students* improve their academic performance, increase their disability awareness, enhance their personal growth, and develop career interests through this service–learning experience. *General and special education teachers* benefit by increasing their opportunities for communication and collaboration with each other as they help support students across school environments and activities. *Administrators and school counselors* gain assistance in meeting the requirements of legislative mandates to increase inclusion and raise academic performance, while promoting students' citizenship skills and community awareness. *Parents* find that their goals of increased friendship, academic performance, community service, and character development for their children are addressed through peer buddy relationships and experiences. Although our primary focus in this book is secondary (middle and high) schools because our experience is in these environments, the benefits, philosophical basis, and practices of peer buddy programs extend to all grade levels, including preschool and elementary school.

Our book consists of eight chapters divided into three sections. Section I (Chapters 1 and 2) provides a legislative, philosophical, and research basis for peer buddy programs. In addition, we describe variations of peer buddy programs, such as a single-classroom model versus a districtwide model. Section II (Chapters 3 to 5) provides explicit steps for starting up a peer buddy program, such as identifying key participants, recruiting and training peer buddies, and establishing program expectations. Section III (Chapters 6 to 8) addresses how to maintain and evaluate a peer buddy program by providing support to participants, expanding the program into the community and other settings, and working with others as a team. The book's content is relevant to anyone wanting to start up a peer buddy program whether on a small-scale, individual classroom level or on a school- or districtwide level. To make the process of beginning and maintaining a peer buddy program come alive, we include case studies and first-person quotes (using pseudonyms) of a variety of program participants representing different perspectives and roles. Forms and checklists are provided to guide users through the program implementation process, and learning activities challenge readers to put their thoughts into action in designing their own peer buddy programs. Suggestions for individual participants who are serving different roles within a peer buddy program, such as administrator, teacher, or parent, are provided in boxes with identifying graphic icons. In addition, research findings and relevant legislative initiatives are included in boxes throughout the chapters. Finally, resources for implementing peer buddy programs, such as organizations and publications, are listed in the appendix. All suggestions and materials have been field-tested firsthand by program participants in the Metropolitan Nashville Peer Buddy Program across a variety of schools and students, ensuring their relevance and usefulness.

The challenges in secondary education today are tremendous. We do not suggest that a peer buddy service–learning program alone can turn a low-performing or troubled school into an exemplary school environment. We do propose, however, that a peer buddy program, in combination with school reform or other inclusion efforts, can be instrumental in building *community* within a school in which *all* students feel welcomed, accepted, and included.

Acknowledgments

We have many people to thank whose ideas, insights, hard work, and support contributed to the development of this book. First, we would like to acknowledge the exemplary work of the editorial and production staff at Allyn and Bacon. We are grateful to Virginia Lanigan, our editor, for her encouragement, support, and assistance throughout the writing process. Thank you also to Scott Blaszak, editorial assistant, for his clear answers to our frequent questions. Second, we wish to thank the reviewers who provided valuable feedback on previous drafts of this book and who challenged us to expand our own view of the metropolitan Nashville Peer Buddy Program: Kimberly Fatata-Hall, Nova Southeastern University; Janice Ferguson, Western Kentucky University; Constance J. Fournier, Texas A&M University; Linda Schwartz Green, Centenary College; Beth R. Handler, University of Lousiana at Lafayette; C. Bobbi Hansen, Universtiy of San Diego; Amy J. Malkus, East Tennessee State University; Kathleen M. McCoy, Arizona State University; and Cheryl A. Young, University of North Carolina Charlotte. Third, we are flattered that Janet Eyler and Marti Snell, international leaders in their respective educational fields, were each willing and eager to write a foreword for our book. Fourth, we appreciate the U.S. Department of Education, Office of Special Education and Rehabilitative Services (Grant Nos. HO23N10017 and H158Q960004), NICHD (Grant P30HD15052), and the Tennessee Developmental Disabilities Council, which supported us in providing technical assistance to the Peer Buddy Program.

Fifth, many people contributed to the development and implementation of the Peer Buddy Program over the years. Thank you to the numerous undergraduate and graduate students who have contributed time working on the Peer Buddy Project—including Paulo Alcantara, Emily Bradford, Melissa Brock, Xinsheng Cai, Susan Copeland, Karen Curry, Kristine Derer, Greg Fischer, Stephanie Fowler, Joy Godshall, Stacey Hall, Mindy Harmer, Bridget Houser, Tanya Hughes, Bogseon Hwang, Dan Killian, Jin-Ho Kim, Gretchen Kleeb, Sarah Lorden, Jennifer McCall, Sarah Pitkin, Judith Presley, Michael Rodi, Stacey Scott, Mark Strong, Cherwanda Williams, and others too numerous to mention. A special acknowledgment is extended to Carol Guth, project coordinator, without whose hard work, inspiration, and dedication this project would not have been the success it was.

Finally, we extend our immense gratitude to the scores of students, peer buddies, teachers, administrators, and family members who participated in and contributed their time to the Peer Buddy Program. We especially thank the students, staff, and parents of McGavock High School who created the Peer Buddy Program. Your faith in a buddy system to support inclusion is what this book is all about.

References

Individuals with Disabilities Education Act Amendments of 1997, PL 105-17, 20 U. S. C. § 1400 *et seq.* (1997).
No Child Left Behind Act of 2001, PL 107-110, 115 Stat. 1425 (2002).

"He's My Best Friend!": Why Start a Service–Learning Peer Buddy Program?

1 Benefits of Inclusion of ALL Students

In this chapter, you will learn about . . .

- Federal legislation and philosophical trends that support inclusion and student interaction.
- Benefits of inclusion and community for general and special education students, teachers, administrators, and family members.
- How service–learning can promote inclusion.
- How service–learning peer buddy programs promote citizenship for all students.

Why? . . .

Increasing access to general education and including all *students, such as students with disabilities, in the mainstream of everyday school life are a primary focus of recent federal legislation and school reform efforts. This chapter provides a rationale for establishing peer buddy programs to increase inclusion and promote interaction among general and special education students in secondary schools. Peer buddy programs, a type of service–learning activity, are described and suggested as a way to increase inclusion. Benefits to ALL participants in service–learning peer buddy programs are cited in research and described through the words of actual participants.*

CASE STUDY BOX: *Reflecting on Our Mission*

It was early September and Mr. Bryant, the new assistant principal at King High, was beginning to notice that daily life for students in special education classes was very different from that of their general education peers. Throughout the day, he could see general education students scurrying around the building, attending a variety of academic and vocational classes, and catching a word with their friends as they passed in the halls. In contrast, special education students at King seemed to spend most of their time in one wing of the school, often not even entering the halls between classes. At sports events, extracurricular activities, and community happenings, general education students were seen in droves. Special education students, however, were notably absent. To Mr. Bryant, it seemed like there were two schools within a school: special education and general education. He wondered if students from the two "schools" even knew each other. Maybe it would be even more surprising if they did. After all, even special and general education teachers rarely had the time or opportunity to interact with each other.

Some special education students did, of course, take classes with their general education peers. Although teachers liked having these students in their classes, Mr. Bryant knew that many already felt stretched to the limit with an increasingly economically, culturally, and aca-

(continued)

CASE STUDY BOX *Continued*

demically diverse range of students. Many teachers felt that they didn't have the time or resources to add another student to their class who might have special needs. Were special education students really a part of these classes? Mr. Bryant wondered. As he looked around the general education classrooms, students with disabilities still seemed to be members of a separate school—visitors for the day in someone's class, watching but not really participating in the social and academic activities of their classmates. And general education students seemed to be missing out too because they didn't even seem to know some very interesting members of their classes.

Reflecting on his observations, Mr. Bryant looked at the school's mission statement posted in the main office: "The mission of King High School is to provide a positive learning experience that prepares all students to be productive citizens in a diverse society." It sounded hollow as he read it aloud. Are we really preparing *all* of our students to be productive citizens? Is our school really a *community* that includes all students as interactive partners? Or do we have separate groups of students—and even teachers—within our school? If so, how can we show students what community and citizenship really mean? Sure, Mr. Bryant was new to the school, but it just seemed like too many students were at the margins of high school life. Could King High do a better job of bringing all students and teachers together into one school community? Determined to answer his questions, Mr. Bryant set out to talk with members of his staff.

The Importance of Inclusion and Student Interaction

Few topics evoke as strong a reaction among educators as the issue of inclusion. The manner in which students are educated really does affect everyone—students, teachers, administrators, families, and community members. Traditionally, special education students have spent their school days in separate classrooms, apart from their peers in general education. As inclusive practices are pursued in more and more schools, stakeholders are wrestling with some of the following questions: What are the benefits to members of a school community when students with disabilities are educated alongside their general education peers? How can school personnel and general education students help support the inclusion of students with disabilities in general education environments? *Peer buddy programs—in which general education students interact with and support special education students—are an effective strategy for increasing inclusion and access to the general education curriculum.* These programs are described more completely later in this chapter and the remainder of the book. In this chapter, we (a) outline the legal, philosophical, and research-based arguments supporting inclusion and access to the general education curriculum, (b) overview challenges to inclusion in typical middle and high school settings, and (c) introduce service–learning peer buddy programs as means to promote inclusion.

Legislative and Policy Initiatives Supporting Inclusion

In the 1970s, Congress passed landmark legislation mandating that students with disabilities receive a free appropriate public education (Education for All Handicapped Children Act of 1975). Since then, we have been witnessing a remarkable shift in the location of educational services for special education students—from separate to neighborhood schools, from special education to general education settings, from the periphery to the mainstream of school life. This evolution in educational placement reflects a larger school reform effort to merge general and special education to meet the needs of *all* students. Within the context of school reform, the roles of administrators and general and special education teachers constantly are being refined. Schools are restructuring to accommodate and educate an increasingly diverse student population—ethnically, culturally, economically, and academically. These changes have been driven, in part, by legislative and policy initiatives, as described below.

Individuals with Disabilities Education Act

"Disability is a natural part of the human experience and in no way diminishes the right of individuals to participate in or contribute to society." The Individuals with Disabilities Education Act (IDEA) Amendments of 1997 (PL 105-17) open with these words, emphasizing the importance of improving educational outcomes for students with disabilities. A major step toward meeting this goal involves ensuring that all students have access to the general education curriculum to the maximum extent possible.

"Improving educational results for children with disabilities is an essential element of our national policy of ensuring equality of opportunity, full participation, independent living, and economic self-sufficiency for individuals with disabilities."

Individuals with Disabilities Education Act Amendments of 1997

Authors of the 1997 IDEA Amendments argued that educational services for students with disabilities are most effective when services and supports, whenever appropriate, are provided in the general education classroom and when school personnel hold high expectations for these students. In fact, the IDEA Amendments place the burden on educators to provide justification for the extent to which students with disabilities are *not* participating with their peers in general education activities.

General education participation for students with disabilities is consistent with the Individuals with Disabilities Education Act Amendments of 1997, which state: "To the maximum extent appropriate, children with disabilities, including children in public or private institutions or other care facilities, are educated with children who are not disabled, and special classes, separate schooling, or other removal of children with disabilities from regular educational environments occurs only when the nature or severity of the disability is such that education in regular classes with the use of supplementary aids and services cannot be achieved satisfactorily."

Individuals with Disabilities Education Act Amendments of 1997

IDEA 1997 also clearly states that just physically being present in a general education classroom does not ensure access to the general curriculum and the myriad activities in which general education students are involved. Students also need individualized supports, adaptations, and instruction. To achieve this end, the Amendments stress the importance of ongoing collaboration among educators, actively involving both general and special education teachers in the development and continuing review of students' educational programs.

No Child Left Behind Act

A primary intent of the No Child Left Behind (NCLB) Act of 2001 (PL 107-110) is to promote higher academic standards, educational excellence, and improved outcomes for *all* students. NCLB is characterized by its emphasis on greater school accountability for students' achievement, more options for parents, improved teacher quality, and increased flexibility and local control. This legislation has important implications for how educational services are to be provided to students with disabilities and their general education peers. The accountability measures outlined in NCLB require that special education programs and services more closely align with state and local standards. This requirement to involve students with disabilities in states' accountability systems highlights the importance of involving students with disabilities in the general education curriculum so that students can achieve statewide content standards. Moreover, educators and administrators are held accountable for the achievement of *all* students, because schools must document progress in educating all subgroups of students, such as English language learners, members of ethnic groups, students from high poverty backgrounds, and students with disabilities.

Increased inclusion of students with disabilities in general education curricula and activities is implicit in NCLB. Authors of the Act contended that "for too many years, too many children in special needs classes have been left behind academically, without a chance to succeed in school and prepare for life" (House Education and Workforce Committee, 2002). Consequently, additional resources and supplemental services, such as tutoring, are provided to schools to promote the inclusion and success of special education students within general education contexts and standards. Peer buddies—students who are succeeding within the general education curriculum—are an obvious resource to improve outcomes for students with disabilities.

President's Commission on Excellence in Special Education

The President's Commission on Excellence in Special Education was formed in 2001 to address the need for reform of the special education system. Among the Commission's recommendations was that schools should treat students with disabilities as general education students first, rather than view them as separate from general education. In addition, the Commission argued for a proactive emphasis on educational outcomes for all students versus a more traditional approach requiring students to "fail" before getting services. Further, the Commission articulated that, in providing services, the responsibility for educating students with disabilities should be shared by all teachers. As stated in the Commission's report, general and special education must "share responsibilities for children with disabilities. They are not separable at any level—cost, instruction, or even identification" (p. 9). The Commission also emphasized the importance of frequent social interaction among general and special education students—including minority students—to improve students' employability and postsecondary outcomes.

Special education and general education are treated as separate systems but, in fact, *share* responsibility for the child with disabilities. In instruction, the systems must work together to provide effective teaching methods and ensure that those with additional needs benefit from strong teaching and instructional methods that should be offered to a child through general education.

President's Commission on Excellence in Special Education (2002)

Transition Legislation

Young adults with disabilities continue to lag far behind graduates without disabilities in the areas of employment, postsecondary education, community participation, and quality of life (e.g., Wagner, Cameto, & Newman, 2003). If postschool outcomes are an indicator of the effectiveness of school services, it is clear that the educational needs of many students with disabilities are not being met. The IDEA Amendments of 1997 sought to strengthen transition services for adolescents with disabilities, defining transition services as a coordinated set of activities designed within an *outcome-oriented* process. This shift to a focus on outcomes is consistent with current educational reform movements (e.g., NCLB). Local educational agencies are accountable for the effectiveness of transition services and must develop strategies that promote accountability for results. Moreover, transition services, consistent with all special education services, are to be closely aligned with the general curriculum. The emphasis in IDEA on maximizing students' participation in inclusive school, work, and community settings also is apparent in other disability-related legislation, such as the Americans with Disabilities Act of 1990 (PL 101-336) and the Rehabilitation Act Amendments of 1992 (PL 102-569).

The Americans with Disabilities Act of 1990 promotes the involvement and meaningful participation of students with disabilities in public programs and activities, stating "no qualified individual with a disability, shall by reason of such disability, be excluded from participation in or be denied the benefits of services, programs, or activities of a public entity, or be subjected to discrimination by such entity" (Section 12132).

Americans with Disabilities Act of 1990

Philosophical Support for Inclusion

Family members, educators, adult service providers, and individuals with disabilities have fought hard to have children and youth included in the mainstream of school, work, and community life. These advocates have articulated a strong philosophical commitment in support of inclusive practices, one that reflects values such as normalization, self-determination, and community participation (Villa & Thousand, 2000). The normalization principle emphasizes the importance of enabling individuals with disabilities to have lives that are as similar to that of their peers as possible. The self-determination movement stresses the importance of empowering individuals with disabilities to speak for themselves and act on their choices and preferences to promote full and equal participation in everyday school and community life.

Philosophical support for inclusion also is found among general educators and advocates of school reform. For example, the National Association of Secondary School Principals (NASSP) endorsed the concept of inclusion articulated in the 1997 IDEA Amendments. The NASSP proposed that knowing, accommodating, and building friendships with a diversity of peers benefit both general and special education students in inclusive schools (National Association of Secondary School Principals, 2000). Benefits of inclusion for general and special education teachers identified by NASSP include co-teaching opportunities, sharing of resources and support services, and joint staff development.

In addition, challenges facing secondary schools today, such as high dropout rates, violence, and school failure, have prompted educators to propose building a sense of community in schools in which supportive relationships are cultivated for *all* students, teachers, and parents (Schaps, 2003). Caring communities in which all participants share common purposes and ideals are advocated as a means of character and citizenship development and fostering a sense of tolerance, acceptance, and belonging among increasingly culturally, economically, and academically diverse school populations. Proponents of inclusive school communities argue that "schools that nurture positive relationships among students and among students and teachers are more likely to realize the payoff of more engaged students achieving at higher levels" (Scales & Leffert, 1999).

Research Basis for Inclusion

Over the past decade, research documenting the positive and pervasive impact of inclusion on students, educators, and others has accumulated steadily. These benefits are reported for (a) general education students, (b) students with disabilities, (c) general education teachers, (d) special education teachers, (e) administrators, and (f) parents, as derived from studies of inclusion in secondary schools (Copeland et al., 2002; Freeman & Alkin, 2000; Hughes et al., 2001). Findings from these researchers are described below. Comments from participants in the Peer Buddy Program in Nashville, Tennessee, are included to illustrate these benefits.

General Education Students

Educators and parents sometimes express concern that inclusion may hold general education classmates back academically. Fortunately, research shows that general education students actually benefit academically and socially when peers with disabilities are included in their classes, particularly when general education students provide support to or interact with their peers (e.g., Cushing & Kennedy, 1997; Dugan et al., 1995). Benefits to general education students include higher grades, improved academic performance, enhanced personal growth, increased awareness of disability issues, development of new friendships, and interest in pursuing careers in special education.

"Peer buddy . . . huh? That was my first reaction to this program. Of course, I had heard about the program from former peer buddies, but I didn't know what to expect. Like many others, I had already made my assumptions about these students. Since that time, I have come to realize that these assumptions were incorrect. I thought that students with disabilities were helpless, but this is not the case. As the first couple of weeks went by, I began to see that many of the students were not much different than me. A lot of the students enjoy many of the same games and activities that I do. As time has gone by, the majority, if not all, of the students and I have become good friends, especially the guys. The peer buddy program has been a wonderful experience for me. It has allowed me to make new friends who have slight differences, but with more similarities than you could imagine!"

Jamie Randall
Peer Buddy

"[Being a peer buddy] changed the way I thought about people with disabilities, because I actually sat down with them and got to know them."

Sue Ann Draper
Peer Buddy

Students with Disabilities

Many exciting, wonderful things happen in school—getting a part in a school play, dissecting frogs in biology, conducting a research project with classmates, going to the homecoming dance. In many middle and high schools, however, special education students have limited opportunity to participate in the myriad activities that make up school life. In addition, because of their typically limited involvement in the general curriculum, students may have little opportunity to develop meaningful social relationships with their general education peers. General education participation and inclusive settings expand opportunities for interacting and developing friendships with a variety of peers while students participate together in joint activities. Studies show that students also learn new skills—including social, academic, employment, and life skills—especially when interacting with a peer buddy (Fisher & Meyer, 2002; Harrower, 1999).

"They are my best friends! My peer buddies introduce me to their friends, and now I have lots of friends."

Delray Montego
Special Education Student

"I like having someone in biology class who knows the material and can explain things I don't understand."

Terina Jamison
Special Education Student

"Here are recognized school leaders who care about the students with disabilities and offer them encouragement—'I know you can do this!' In the halls at class changes, peer buddies are somebody special education students can identify with, someone who knows them, calls their name, and can help them."

Mr. Sykes
Principal

General Education Teachers

Having special education students in class can be very gratifying. Teachers who have included these students in their classes report greater personal satisfaction and professional growth as a result of teaching a more diverse group of students. Studies show that although some teachers initially may feel apprehensive toward inclusion, many more welcome the opportunity (Copeland et al., 2004). Not only do teachers themselves enjoy interacting with students with disabilities, they also enjoy watching general and special education classmates grow personally and socially as they interact with each other. Although including special education students in a class may make additional demands on teachers' already full loads, general education students can be a big help. Teachers report that peer buddies in the classroom are like a "second set of hands" when making accommodations and adapting instruction for students with disabilities. In addition, peer buddies can help their special education peers become an active, contributing part of the classroom and school communities.

"Special education students add a different viewpoint and way of seeing things to the classroom. The special education students want to please you and are very cooperative, so they become good role models for their general education peers."

Mr. Burgess
General Education Teacher

Special Education Teachers

Many special education teachers themselves feel isolated throughout the day and may have little opportunity to interact with other adults. These teachers report benefiting from opportunities to collaborate with general education teachers while working together cooperatively to support the inclusion of students with disabilities in general education classes (Copeland et al., 2002). Special education teachers find that, in doing so, they learn new content-area skills, are exposed to new curricula and materials, and enjoy associating with teachers of different backgrounds outside the special education field. They also report personal satisfaction in seeing the growth that students with disabilities experience when included in general education classes, such as academic gains, social skill development, and increased friendships. Special education teachers report that peer buddies are invaluable assets for welcoming and supporting students with disabilities in the general education environment and serving as a liaison for teachers to the general education class.

"This year I have a student in my class who has severe autism. When Candice first came into my room, she appeared to have no interest in others and only initiated interactions when she wanted to eat or go to the restroom. Then Candice developed a friendship with her peer buddy, Carrie. Now she watches the door for Carrie every day. When they are together, Candice makes eye contact with her buddy frequently, laughs often, and even initiates conversation. We never saw her do these things before! Candice also has increased her vocal repertoire from 4 to 11 words. We have been truly amazed with the difference peer buddies have made in the lives of our students."

Ms. Radon
Special Education Teacher

"Many of my students were afraid to leave the classroom or their teachers. Peer buddies provided them with a natural and age-appropriate way to participate in high school activities."

Ms. Acton-Brown
Special Education Teacher

Administrators

School administrators today have to dance to the beat of many different drums. They are the ones ultimately responsible in their schools for compliance with the least restrictive environment (LRE) requirements of the 1997 IDEA Amendments—specifically by including students with disabilities in the general education curriculum and activities to the maximum extent possible. The NCLB Act of 2001 also has expanded the responsibilities of school administrators in meeting the demand of achievement of academic standards by *all* students. Further, administrators must ensure that rigorous academic programs are available to all students. Happily, inclusive practices enable administrators to promote high standards and other related educational requirements and goals. Including students with disabilities in general education classes allows these students to access the general education curriculum and standards-based instruction. Teacher quality, another provision of NCLB, also is enhanced as special and general education teachers collaborate to implement a standards-based curriculum for all students. Peer buddies who support special education students can aid the fusion of general and special education by assisting teachers in unifying their efforts. In addition, when peers support access to the general education, school staff are addressing a mission of many secondary schools: to promote citizenship and community service.

"The peer buddies are tomorrow's leaders. Some day they will make decisions about who will work in various corporations and businesses. These students are more likely to take a chance on hiring individuals with disabilities, based on their relationships with their partners through the peer buddy program."

Ms. Sword
Principal

Family Members

What do family members of students with disabilities think of inclusion? Many times, it is parents or other family members who push schools to include their children in general education (Garrick Duhaney & Salend, 2000). These family members are aware of the many benefits typically associated with inclusion, such as higher expectations for students and access to a more varied curriculum. In addition, parents whose children have peer buddies in their general education classes report that their children experience more enthusiasm for school, feel more a part of the community inside and outside of school, and improve their academic performance and sense of self-esteem. Parents of peer buddies also cite increased self-esteem, citizenship skills, and interest in others among the benefits experienced by their children (Carter & Hughes, 2003).

"When we went into the basketball game and sat in the spot where we usually do, I heard someone from across the gym screaming, 'PORTIA! PORTIA! PORTIA!' I looked up to find that one of the peer buddies was standing and waving her arms in the air and screaming for Portia. Portia was delighted and ran over to sit beside Tisha, who was screaming for her. Had there not been a peer buddy program, this would not have happened!"

Ms. McCormick
Grandparent of a Special Education Student

"It is quite pleasant for me to have my daughter out on the weekends and have peer buddies speak to her and go out of their way to see what she's up to. She feels, I think, much less isolated than she did."

Mr. Ryder
Parent of a Special Education Student

The implications of legislation, philosophical arguments, and research supporting inclusion are substantial. Collectively, they emphasize the importance of (a) educating students with disabilities alongside their general education peers; (b) holding high expectations for all students, including those with disabilities; (c) providing appropriate and effective educational supports to individuals with disabilities; and (d) building caring, accepting, and tolerant school communities that include *all* students. Because schools are inherently social places, inclusion is a vital influence on the lives of adolescents with disabilities, positively impacting self-esteem, social support, academic performance, and peer norms and values. It is through relationships with their peers that adolescents find companionship, develop intimacy, formulate future goals, and begin to determine "who they are" (Bukowski, Newcomb, & Hartup, 1996).

Full participation in secondary schools refers not only to academic classes, but also to the full range of everyday activities that occur within a school. The Individuals with Disabilities Education Act Amendments of 1997 state that "in providing or arranging for the provision of nonacademic and extracurricular services and activities . . . each public agency shall ensure that each child with a disability participates with nondisabled children in those services and activities to the maximum extent appropriate to the needs of that child."

Individuals with Disabilities Education Act Amendments of 1997

Challenges to Secondary School Inclusion

To what extent are students with disabilities being included within typical middle and high school settings? Despite growing support for inclusive practices, many adolescents with disabilities remain outside the mainstream of everyday school life. For example, 33 percent of students with emotional and behavioral disorders, 45 percent of students with multiple disabilities, and 51 percent of students with mental retardation spend more than 60 percent of their school day outside of the general education classroom (U.S. Department of Education, 2002). In addition, African American, Hispanic, and Asian American students with disabilities spend a greater percentage of time outside the general education class than do their white or Native American counterparts. For example, 32 percent of African American students spend more than 60 percent of the day outside the general education class versus 15 percent of white students. Students with disabilities also become more isolated from general education as they transition from elementary to high school. Across all disabilities and ethnicities, 19 percent of students ages 6 though 11 spend more than 60 percent of the school day outside the general education class versus 28 percent of students ages 12 through 17 and 41 percent of students ages 18 through 21. Further, adolescents with disabilities not only remain on the fringes of academic activities, they also participate less often in everyday school activities such as clubs, extracurricular activities, sports, student government, and community service projects.

Why does separation for students with disabilities persist in secondary schools despite the many benefits of inclusion? Unfortunately, the typical school day presents a variety of challenges to teachers and administrators wanting to increase students' access to general education. By recognizing and anticipating potential barriers, however, school staff are better positioned to minimize roadblocks to inclusion. *Moreover, peer buddy programs represent an effective strategy for circumventing many of these challenges.* Among the challenges to inclusion and access to general education are (a) scheduling, (b) curricula, (c) attitudes, (d) classroom- versus community-based instruction, and (e) demands on teachers. These barriers have been identified in research conducted by ourselves and others (e.g., Copeland et al., 2004; Pivik, McComas, & LaFlamme, 2002) and are confirmed by participants in the Metropolitan Nashville Peer Buddy Program (e.g., Hughes et al., 2001). A summary of the challenges to secondary school inclusion follows.

Scheduling

In elementary and preschool settings, students typically spend the majority of their school day in a single classroom, alongside the same teacher and cohort of peers. As students transition to secondary school settings, however, classmates and teachers change from one period to the next as students rotate classrooms every 50 or 90 minutes. Rotation scheduling often makes it difficult for students to have sustained access to the same group of peers for more than a short period of time. For example, a high school student may attend as many as six different classes each day, coming into contact with more than 180 different classmates. Some students may thrive on the variety in class composition inherent in such a schedule, but others may experience loneliness and isolation (Osterman, 2003).

Curricula

As students progress through the educational system, the focus on academic performance becomes more pronounced, especially with the growing emphasis on competency testing in NCLB and as a graduation requirement (Schloss, Smith, & Schloss, 2001). Academic tasks dominate the instructional focus of secondary school curricula, and content addressed in class becomes increasingly complex over time. As students age, the gap between academic skills possessed by students with disabilities and those held by their general education peers widens. However, secondary teachers may expect that all students enrolling in their classes should have prerequisite skills and that curricula should not have to be modified for individual students. Or, classroom teachers may struggle with how to provide appropriate support to and adaptations for students with disabilities and still meet the instructional needs of other students. For example, students in a chemistry class may be constructing models of complex molecules. Their teacher, however, may be unsure how to modify the activity to actively involve a student with mental retardation or visual impairments.

Attitudes

The success of inclusion depends on the support of participants within the school community. Although attitudes toward students with disabilities have improved dramatically over the past thirty years, some students, teachers, or administrators may hold negative attitudes toward students with disabilities. For example, students with disabilities may be teased by their peers, or teachers may hold lowered expectations of students with disabilities. Attitudes clearly impact behavior and can influence the manner in which students are educated or treated by others. Attitudes and beliefs also are strongly influenced by knowledge and past experience in relation to an issue. Students and teachers often report that they possess limited knowledge about disabilities, such as how to communicate with a student with limited verbal skills, or have had little opportunity to interact with people with disabilities in their everyday lives.

Classroom- versus Community-Based Instruction

Many students with disabilities benefit from instruction provided in community or employment settings. Special education students, particularly those with more severe disabilities, may spend one or more class periods per day receiving instruction in the community, learning to use public transportation or making purchases at a community business. Time spent off-campus, however, is time spent outside of general education classrooms, curricula, and activities. For example, a student may spend each afternoon working at a local print shop as part of her employment training. Although this experience provides her with opportunities to develop career skills, it limits her opportunities to access the general education curriculum and spend time with her same-age peers. Finding the right balance between classroom- and community-based instruction is a challenge for secondary educators.

Demands on Teachers

Increased demands placed on general and special education teachers, coupled with limited resources, further amplify the challenges associated with including students with disabilities in secondary classrooms. For example, general education teachers typically experience large classroom rosters; pressure to cover specific course content; demands of competency testing; increasing ethnic, economic, and academic diversity among students; and limited time to collaborate with other teachers. Similarly, special education teachers often report being overwhelmed with paperwork—including developing and monitoring Individualized Education Programs (IEPs)—as well as growing caseloads. Unfortunately, these substantial demands may place the goal of including students with disabilities in general education lower on a teacher's list of priorities.

Many challenges exist in providing students with disabilities with access to the general education curriculum. These potential barriers, however, are not insurmountable. Teachers and administrators must commit to finding ways to promote the full participation and inclusion of all students in their school. *Service–learning peer buddy programs offer a promising solution for addressing many of the challenges just described.* In the following sections, we present an overview of the growing service–learning movement and introduce peer buddy programs as a type of service–learning experience designed to promote secondary school inclusion.

Overview of the Service–Learning Movement

In addition to high academic standards, the importance of civic engagement often is acknowledged to be an integral goal of students' educational experiences. Too many students are not fully engaged in learning, do not see the relevance of what is learned in school to the world outside of the classroom, or fail to complete high school. Moreover, when students do leave high school, they often are uninvolved in civic activities such as voting and volunteering in their communities. Service–learning activities have been advocated as a means to reverse these trends by involving students actively in giving back to and interacting with their communities.

What Is Service–Learning?

Service–learning refers to educational activities in which students participate in organized service experiences that address actual societal needs and are integrated into students' academic curricula (Eyler & Giles, 1999). That is, an equivalent emphasis is placed on both *service* and *learning*. For example, as part of a middle school science class, students may analyze a community environmental issue, present their findings to community members, and engage in a cleanup project. Or, students in a mathematics class may use newly learned skills to plan and build a wheelchair ramp. Service–learning typically is differentiated from community service, which is not linked to the school curriculum and does not include explicit learning objectives or organized reflection. Moreover, benefits are expected to be experienced both by recipients of the service project *and* students who are providing the service. For example, positive impact from participating in service–learning activities has been found for students in the areas of academic learning, career exploration, attitudes toward schooling, civic responsibility, and personal/social development (Billig, 2000).

Roots of Service–Learning

The principles on which service–learning are built are not new. The public purpose of education, the importance of involving students in hands-on learning, and the value of preparing students for citizenship all have been advocated since at least the early 1900s. Participation in service–learning has spread rapidly over the past fifty years. During the 1990s, legislative action served as a catalyst for the swift expansion of service–learning programs across the nation (e.g., National and Community Service Act of 1990; National and Community Service Trust Act of 1993).

Recent surveys indicate that almost half of all public high schools have organized service–learning activities as part of the school curriculum and more than 80 percent of all public high schools have students participating in community service activities through the school (e.g., Skinner & Chapman, 1999). Growing support for service–learning also exists among students parents, teachers, administrators, and national organizations. Furthermore, some states and districts require that students participate in service activities as a condition for graduation or promotion, while others strongly encourage and support service–learning projects as a means for achieving educational goals and promoting student achievement.

Key Components of Quality Service–Learning

Although service–learning activities vary widely, several components are regarded as critical features of service–learning projects (e.g., National Commission on Service–Learning, 2002). These features are summarized as follows:

- *Service projects are organized in relation to an academic course or curriculum.* Service–learning activities are linked explicitly with curricular objectives, content, and standards. Projects are not treated as an "add-on" to the curriculum, with little or no connection to academic instruction. Rather, they are woven into the school and class curricula.
- *Service projects have clearly stated instructional objectives.* Service activities should have a clear purpose and focus. The educational goals of service–learning projects are laid out in advance and experiences are designed thoughtfully to support students in meeting instructional objectives.

"In other classes, we learn innumerable amounts of facts that we later forget. But having a service–learning opportunity like being a Peer Buddy has given me life skills that I will carry with me forever."

Jules Marlowe
Peer Buddy

- *Service projects address genuine community needs in a sustained manner.* Authentic needs, within or beyond the walls of the school, are identified and tackled through service–learning activities.

- *Organized reflection activities enable students to draw lessons from service activities.* Service–learning typically is differentiated from traditional volunteering by its emphasis on reflection throughout all stages of the service project. For example, teachers may engage service–learning participants in classroom discussions, presentations, or directed writing projects, such as reflective journals.

What Is a Service–Learning Peer Buddy Program?

There are many types of service–learning experiences available for secondary students, such as helping a community complete a needs assessment or organizing a cleanup day at a daycare center. One type of service–learning opportunity for young people is participation in a peer buddy program. *Peer buddy programs* are designed to promote the general education participation of students with disabilities and provide service–learning opportunities for secondary school students. General education participants ("peer buddies") typically receive academic credit for spending a minimum of one class period per day with their classmates with disabilities, although interactions may extend beyond the school day. Structured activities in which peer buddies are involved include supporting students with disabilities in general education classes, helping their peers become included in the mainstream of everyday school life, assisting peers in performing activities in the community or at employment training sites, and developing friendships. In addition, peer buddies are required to reflect on their experiences and complete written assignments that integrate their practical experiences into their academic curricula. In turn, special education participants give peer buddies the opportunity to expand their social and citizenship skills, enhance their self-esteem, learn more about themselves and their capabilities, and explore possible career options.

> "There is much discussion about high school students participating in service projects, and this is a great thing for the students to do. The peer buddies are giving something back to the community. The buddies see they can help their partners with disabilities become active participants in their communities. All the students enjoy the program!"
>
> *Ms. Reed*
> *Principal*

> "The Peer Buddy course is truly a learning experience for all students. The special education students develop other friendships outside of the classroom. As for the general education students, they too develop friendships."
>
> *Mr. Swanson*
> *Guidance Counselor*

Why is a service–learning peer buddy program an effective strategy for achieving a more inclusive school community? First, peer buddy programs offer teachers an effective resource for addressing many of the challenges to inclusion present in secondary schools. Peer buddies (a) act as liaisons to the general education curriculum and environment, (b) lighten demands on teachers when accommodating students, and (c) provide instructional and social support to their peers with disabilities. Peer buddies are invaluable to both general and special education teachers who are struggling with how to meet the needs of *all* students in general education classes. Second, peer buddy programs tap into a resource widely available on any school campus—general education peers. General education students show that they are willing, available, and able to provide effective support to their classmates with disabilities and that doing so is a reciprocal process. Peer buddies indicate that they derive as much benefit from providing support as their peers do. Third, peer buddy programs can be implemented *on-campus*, providing students with service opportunities without having to grapple with issues related to transportation, liability, and financial costs. Although peer buddy support and interaction also can occur off-campus, much support can be provided right at school, making peer buddy service–learning an attractive option for busy secondary school students. Finally, *peer buddy programs work!* Our work with the Nashville Peer Buddy Program in high schools in Nashville, Tennessee, has shown the success of the peer buddy model in promoting inclusion and fostering successful outcomes for students, teachers, administrators, and parents time and time again. And that is why we have entitled this book *Success for All Students: Promoting Inclusion in Secondary Schools through Peer Buddy Programs.*

Summary

Inclusive school practices have the potential to benefit *all* students. At first glance, the challenges associated with inclusive programming may appear daunting. Peer buddy programs, however, are an effective strategy for achieving a more inclusive school community and promoting service–learning opportunities for students. In the remainder of this book, we will outline exactly how to plan, implement, and evaluate a peer buddy program in your classroom, school, or district. Although our focus is on secondary schools, the philosophy and practices of peer buddy programs are just as appropriate and applicable to elementary school programs as well.

Learning Activities

- Take a few minutes and reflect on the mission statement of your school or a school with which you are familiar. What are the implications of that statement for how educational services are provided for general education students? For students with disabilities? To what extent do educational programs and curricula in the school promote the values espoused in the mission statement?
- How involved are students with disabilities in the mainstream of school life in your school or a school in which you have recently spent time? Many teachers are unaware of just how isolated some students really are. Make a list of the activities and settings in which general education students are involved in school. Over one or two school days, casually observe these different activities and settings and note the extent to which students with disabilities are participating in these activities. What factors do you think hinder (or support) their participation? Do the same for other students in the school, such as English language learners or members of ethnic groups.
- If you are an in-service teacher, think about the classes that you currently teach. If you are a preservice teacher, think about the methods classes and practica you have taken. Which of your own teaching practices support inclusion? How would your instructional procedures change by the addition of students with disabilities in the classroom? What concerns do you have about including students with disabilities in general education classes?
- Think about your school (or one nearby you) as a community. Are *all* students included within that community or are there subgroups, perhaps English language learners or students enrolled only in vocational education classes, who do not seem to be a part of

the larger community? If you are an administrator, what could you do to ensure that *all* students feel a part of the school community?

■ List the different ways that general education peers might provide support to students with disabilities. What might be the benefits of peer-delivered support as compared to support provided by an educational assistant or special education teacher? What are some possible drawbacks?

■ Does your school or one in which you are involved have a service–learning program? Could peer buddies be a part of that program? Jot down the pros and cons of starting a peer buddy service–learning program in a school. What additional information or resources do you need to begin such a program?

Case Study Box: *Making Our Mission Come Alive*

Much had changed in the two years since Mr. Bryant first arrived at King High School. After some initial prodding, school staff devoted some time to examining their instructional practices and the degree to which those practices promoted the school's mission. Teachers and administrators began to realize that there was much more they could do to meet the needs of all students and create a school community that included all students. But where should they begin?

The teachers had come to recognize the benefits and importance of including students in general education classes. Not only was inclusion consistent with the philosophy of the school, but it also was clear that it was mandated by recent legislation. But, they still were left wondering how to do it. One of the teachers had heard about Richmond Schools, a neighboring school district that had started a peer buddy program. Richmond Schools were addressing the dual purpose of supporting general education access and promoting students' roles as citizens—the same goals that King High School was hoping to achieve. General education peers in the Richmond Schools' peer buddy program provided support to students with disabilities in general education classrooms. Special education students received instructional assistance and peer support, while general education students received service–learning credit and were improving their citizenship skills. King High School staff agreed that such a program was worth trying out.

Mr. Bryant was pleased. So far, the peer buddy program had been introduced only on a small scale—just a handful of classrooms and a couple dozen students. But the impact was already promising! Teachers were more willing to include special education students in their classes knowing that they had support provided by peer buddies and the backing of the administration. General education peers were learning new skills and growing personally in their roles as peer buddies. Special education students were succeeding in the general curriculum and making new friends. King High was beginning to feel more like a community than a cluster of subgroups. Next semester, the peer buddy program would be expanded to several more classrooms. Although there was much left to do, Mr. Bryant was already grinning from ear to ear!

References

Americans with Disabilities Act, 42 U.S.C. § 12101 *et seq.* (1990).

Billig, S. H. (2000). Research on K-12 school-based service-learning—The evidence builds. *Phi Delta Kappan, 81*(9), 658–664.

Bukowski, W. M., Newcomb, A. F., & Hartup, W. W. (Eds.). (1996). *The company they keep: Friendship in childhood and adolescence.* New York: Cambridge University Press.

Carter, E. W., & Hughes, C. (2003, October). *Promoting peer interaction in secondary schools: Effective interventions.* Presentation at the meeting of the International Council for Exceptional Children, Division on Career Development and Transition. Roanoke, Virginia.

Copeland, S. R., Hughes, C., Carter, E. W., Guth, C., Presley, J., Williams, C. R., & Fowler, S. E. (2004). Increasing access to general education: Perspectives of participants in a high school peer support program. *Remedial and Special Education, 26,* 342–352.

Copeland, S. R., McCall, J., Williams, C. R., Guth, C., Carter, E. W., Fowler, S. E., Presley, J. A., & Hughes, C. (2002). High school peer buddies: A win-win situation. *TEACHING Exceptional Children, 35*(1), 16–21.

Cushing, L. S., & Kennedy, C. H. (1997). Academic effects on students without disabilities who serve as peer supports for students with disabilities in general education classrooms. *Journal of Applied Behavior Analysis, 30,* 139–152.

Dugan, E., Kamps, D., Leonard, S., Watkins, N., Rheinberger, A., & Stackhaus, J. (1995). Effects of cooperative learning groups during social studies for students with autism and fourth-grade peers. *Journal of Applied Behavior Analysis, 28,* 175–188.

Education for All Handicapped Children Act of 1975, PL 94–142, 20 U.S.C. 1400 *et seq.* (1975).

Eyler, J., & Giles, D. E. (1999). *Where's the service in service–learning?* San Francisco: Jossey-Bass.

Fisher, M., & Meyer, L. H. (2002). Development and social competence after two years enrolled in inclusive and self-contained educational programs. *Research & Practice for Persons with Severe Disabilities, 27,* 165–174.

Freeman, S. F. N., & Alkin, M. C. (2000). Academic and social attainments of children with mental retardation in general education and special education settings. *Remedial and Special Education, 21,* 3–18.

Garrick Duhaney, L. M., & Salend, S. J. (2000). Parental perceptions of inclusive placements. *Remedial and Special Education, 21,* 121–128.

Harrower, J. (1999). Educational inclusion of children with severe disabilities. *Journal of Positive Behavior Interventions, 1,* 215–230.

House Education & the Work Force Committee. (2002, October 10). *"No Child Left Behind" emphasizes results, expanded options for children with special needs.* Retrieved October 23, 2003 from http://edworkforce.house.gov/issues/107th/endgamekit/fsspecialed.htm

Hughes, C., Copeland, S. R., Guth, C., Rung, L. L., Hwang, B., Kleeb, G., & Strong, M. (2001). General education students' perspectives on their involvement in a high school peer buddy program. *Education and Training in Mental Retardation and Developmental Disabilities, 36,* 343–356.

Individuals with Disabilities Education Act Amendments of 1997, PL 105–17, 20 U. S. C. § 1400 *et seq.* (1997).

National Association of Secondary School Principals (NASSP). (2000, February 3). *Statement of the National Association of Secondary School Principals on special education.* Retrieved September 15, 2003, from http://www.principals.org/advocacy/ps_sped_ed.cfm

National and Community Service Act of 1990, PL 101–610, 42 U.S.C. 12401 *et seq.* (1990).

National and Community Service Trust Act of 1993, PL 103–82, 107 Stat. 785 (1993).

National Commission on Service–Learning. (2002). *Learning in deed: The power of service-learning for American schools.* Newton, MA: Author.

No Child Left Behind Act of 2001, PL 107–110, 115 Stat. 1425 (2002).

Osterman, K. F. (2003). Preventing school violence. *Phi Delta Kappan, 84*(8), 622–627.

Pivik, J., McComas, J., & LaFlamme, M. (2002). Barriers and facilitators to inclusive education. *Exceptional Children, 69,* 97–107.

President's Commission on Excellence in Special Education. (2002). *A new era: Revitalizing special education for children and their families.* Washington, DC: U.S. Department of Education, Office of Special Education and Rehabilitative Services.

Rehabilitation Act Amendments of 1992, PL 102–569, 29 U. S. C. §§ 701 *et seq.* (1992).

Scales, P., & Leffert, N. (1999). *Developmental assets: A synthesis of the scientific research on adolescent development.* Minneapolis: Search Institute.

Schaps, E. (2003). Creating a school community. *Educational Leadership, 60*(6), 31–33.

Schloss, P. J., Smith, M. A., & Schloss, C. N. (2001). *Instructional methods for secondary students with learning and behavior problems* (3rd ed.). Boston: Allyn and Bacon.

Skinner, B., & Chapman, C. (1999). *Service learning and community service in K-12 public schools.* Washington, DC: U.S. Department of Education, National Center for Education Statistics.

U. S. Department of Education. (2002). *Twenty-fourth annual report to Congress on the implementation of the Individuals with Disabilities Education Act.* Washington, DC: Author.

Villa, R. A., & Thousand, J. S. (2000). *Restructuring for a caring and effective education: Piecing the puzzle together* (2nd ed.). Baltimore: Paul H. Brookes.

Wagner, M., Cameto, R., & Newman, L. (2003). *Youth with disabilities: A changing population: A report of findings from the National Longitudinal Transition Study (NLTS) and the National Longitudinal Transition Study-2 (NLTS2).* Menlo Park, CA: SRI International.

2   What Does a Peer Buddy Program Look Like?

In this chapter, you will learn about . . .

- One district's peer buddy program to promote inclusion, access to the general curriculum, and service–learning opportunities for students, as an illustrative example.
- Options for tailoring a peer buddy program to meet the needs of a school community.
- Using the remainder of this book to start a peer buddy program in a classroom, school, or district.

Why? . . .

Peer buddy programs can take a variety of forms in secondary schools—from school- and districtwide programs to informal activities within classrooms. First, we provide an overview of the Metropolitan Nashville Peer Buddy Program to illustrate one model of an effective peer buddy program. Next, we describe variations of peer buddy programs in different schools. Finally, we overview how to use the rest of this book to guide you or others through the process of beginning a peer buddy program in a classroom, school, or district.

CASE STUDY BOX: *The Peer Buddy Program: A Win–Win Situation*

Tyrell never had much of an opportunity to get to know special education students at McGavock High School. Sure, he often passed these students in the hallway on the way to his classes or saw them eating together at a table in the corner of the lunchroom. But none of them were on the football team with him, enrolled in any of his classes, or participating in any of the extracurricular clubs of which he was a member. To be honest, Tyrell was a bit curious about what life was really like for special education students at his school. After all, his aunt had taken special education classes and so had his cousin. But with all the demands of high school life, he just never got around to finding out.

Allan had always dreamed of becoming a body builder. Asking the coach about enrolling in a weightlifting class was an almost weekly occurrence. Coach Fischer always replied with a hesitant "maybe next semester, Allan." Coach Fischer didn't think he knew enough about teaching students with disabilities—and, with twenty-five other students enrolled in his class, he hardly felt he had the time to provide the individualized support he thought Allan would need. Of course, Allan could always come to class if an educational assistant would join him, but Allan said that would just be too embarrassing. Besides, who would help Allan in the boys' locker room if he were to need it? Allan would just have to wait until next semester.

CASE STUDY BOX *Continued*

Ms. Gladstone was very aware of the challenges to inclusion in general education encountered by students with disabilities at McGavock High. Like other special education teachers in her school, she desperately wanted to find a way to increase the social and academic participation of her students. But how? She brainstormed with a colleague from a local university about the possibility of having general education peers help support students. After all, general education students were literally everywhere at McGavock and, when given the chance, were often eager to help out their classmates with disabilities. Since an important goal for many of Ms. Gladstone's students was to increase their social interaction in general education settings, who better to involve in that effort than general education peers?

Teachers, administrators, guidance counselors, and university staff all worked together to develop a program at McGavock High School that would allow general and special education students to interact regularly with each other. Out of that collaboration, a peer buddy program was created! General education students, called peer buddies, received course credit for spending at least one class period each day interacting with and supporting their classmates with disabilities. Tyrell became Allan's peer buddy and provided the one-to-one support that Allan needed to participate fully in the weightlifting class. It truly was a win-win situation for everyone—Allan made a new friend and learned new skills that were important to him, Coach Fischer received the additional support that he felt he needed in the form of a peer buddy, Ms. Gladstone was able to expand one of her students' general education involvement, and Tyrell learned more about himself and others as a result of his experiences.

Some peer buddies, like Tyrell, supported their peers with disabilities in nonacademic classes such as gym, chorus, and art. Others provided support in academic and career education classes or at community-based instruction sites. Since the peer buddy program began, it no longer was uncommon to see students with disabilities eating with peers in the lunchroom, "hanging out" in between classes, participating in school clubs, and attending sports events and school dances. Best of all, peer buddies were introducing their own friends to their partners with disabilities, enlarging each student's circle of friends.

The peer buddy program may have started with just one teacher in one classroom in one high school, but the idea spread quickly. Before long, all eleven comprehensive high schools in the school district offered the peer buddy program to students. The program looked a little different in each school, as teachers adjusted activities based on the unique circumstances of their school community. Still, the overall goals remained the same—to promote inclusion, access to general education, and service–learning opportunities for students.

Peer buddy programs can be a "shot in the arm" for a school. As the case study shows, peer buddy programs can (a) connect general and special education students, (b) expand students' time spent in general education activities, (c) promote the citizenship of students, and (d) help build a caring school community. Although programs in different schools share common goals, no peer buddy program has to look the same. Many factors within a school influence the shape a particular program will take. In this chapter, we (a) describe the origins and growth of a peer buddy program in Nashville, Tennessee, (b) illustrate some of the ways a peer buddy program can be tailored to address the goals and circumstances of a school or classroom, and (c) provide an overview of how to use the remainder of this book to customize and implement a peer buddy program in a school. This information is useful for teachers or administrators already involved in a school, pre-service teachers planning on entering the teaching profession, or parents of students likely to be involved in a peer buddy program.

"A student with autism, with little or no interaction with people, today during lunch moved to a table to sit with peer buddies. I was sitting there—my jaw just dropped wide open!"

Mr. D'Angelo
Special Education Teacher

Case Example: The Metropolitan Nashville Peer Buddy Program

In starting up any kind of a new program, it is helpful to have an example of one that already has been established. Doing so is useful in avoiding some of the pitfalls that others may already have addressed. The case study above is a snapshot of the experiences of one school district—Metropolitan Nashville Public Schools in Nashville, Tennessee—in establishing a peer buddy program. We now describe the expansion of the Metropolitan Nashville Peer Buddy Program from its beginnings with just a few teachers in one high school to a districtwide program. This story will be helpful to anyone wanting to start a peer buddy program on a classroom, school, or district level to (a) promote general education participation, (b) provide service-learning opportunities, (c) offer general and special education teachers a support resource, and (d) help all students meet high academic standards through access to the general curriculum.

Beginning a Program: One High School's Story

When the peer buddy program in Nashville originated, McGavock High School was the largest high school in the state with over 2,700 students, more than 300 of whom were receiving special education services. Special education students, particularly those with more severe disabilities, spent most of their school day in self-contained or resource classrooms. Although special education students ate lunch in the cafeteria and attended some general education classes, they had limited contact with general education students. Lack of available support to assist teachers in adapting curricula and making individual student accommodations limited students' access to the general curriculum. Both general and special education teachers at McGavock were concerned that one segment of the school population was not a part of the larger school community. These teachers felt that not only were *all* students missing out by not knowing each other and sharing classes together, teachers also expressed that they themselves wanted to have classes that were more academically diverse. Administrators agreed that a school was not "whole" until all its parts were included and that a range of skills, perspectives, and backgrounds was challenging and beneficial to everyone. McGavock High School currently did not seem to reflect the sort of cohesive community that school staff had hoped to foster.

In response to these concerns, teachers, administrators, students, and university staff brainstormed together how they could develop a peer buddy program. The result was a credit course in which general education students could enroll as a service–learning opportunity. All stakeholders in the school had a role to fulfill in activating the program. Peer buddies enrolled in the program spent at least one class period each day interacting with and supporting their classmates with disabilities across a variety of settings inside and outside of school. Teachers shared information with peer buddies about disability awareness, instructional and motivational techniques, and including students in daily school activities. Administrators and guidance counselors played a critical role in getting the initial word out about the program to the student body through a variety of avenues such as closed circuit television and school assemblies.

School staff developed a process for enrolling students in the program. Students interested in becoming peer buddies met with guidance counselors and special education teachers in an initial screening process. Once enrolled, peer buddies then helped to recruit additional students into the program.

As peer buddies, general education students served as positive role models while supporting their special education peers in academic and career education classes. Joint extracurricular activities included student council, cheerleading, school chorus, basketball games, lunch, shopping, and visiting each other's homes. Peer buddies helped their special education peers complete class projects, such as research reports and science experiments, as well as communicate with teachers and classmates. Peer buddies also introduced their partners to their own friends, expanding the number of peers with whom special education students developed relationships.

"Students with disabilities used to sit at their own tables in one corner of the cafeteria. They wouldn't talk to anyone and now they go outside and talk to everyone. They are much more comfortable now! I feel good that I'm doing something to change students who didn't normally speak to other people."

Brandon Scruggs
Peer Buddy

Expanding the Program

The peer buddy program was an instant success at McGavock High School. As word of the program spread, other teachers became interested in expanding the peer buddy program to their high schools. With support from grants awarded by the state Developmental Disabilities Council and the U. S. Department of Education, the program soon was replicated across all eleven high schools in the district.

What has been the impact of the peer buddy program? During funding, more than 300 special education students and over 120 general education peer buddies participated in the program each year. Importantly, students still continue to participate at these same annual rates even after state and federal funding has been withdrawn. Teachers and parents report that special education students speak up for themselves more, feel better about themselves, and are developing important academic, social, recreational, and employment skills (e.g., Copeland et al., 2002). Special education students report that they are involved in more activities, such as going to the library, lifting weights, and going downtown, when accompanied by their peer buddies; that they have made new friends at school; and that they feel more comfortable starting conversations and meeting new classmates (Hughes et al., 1999; Hughes et al., 2001). Peer buddies comment that they are more aware of diversity issues, are better at communicating, have increased their tolerance and understanding of themselves and others, have more appreciation of individual differences, and have made new friends (e.g., Carter, Hughes, Copeland, & Breen, 2001; Copeland et al., 2004). Administrators and guidance counselors notice that both general and special education students flourish in a peer buddy program. Students develop pride in themselves as they meet new challenges and realize that they have succeeded and are appreciated by others.

"At the Junior-Senior Prom, the special education students are surrounded by their friends (peer buddies and others) telling them 'You look so nice.' And at the Honors Assembly at the end of the year, these students get the loudest applause and recognition."

Ms. Chinn
Principal

Program Variations

In setting up a program, it is critical to have goals in mind. Doing so allows you to design a program that addresses your goals while you continuously evaluate progress toward these goals. What are the goals of a peer buddy program? As we have discussed so far in this book, these goals are multiple. We want to provide service–learning opportunities to general education students to build their community awareness and citizenship skills. We want to create caring climates in schools in which *all* students are equal, visible, and participating members. We want to increase access to the general education curriculum and achievement of high standards by *all* students. We want to lessen the load of teachers and provide opportunities for them to collaborate with each other.

Although core goals are common across peer buddy programs, there are variations in how programs are designed and implemented across schools. Variations that we have observed relate to (a) extent of program (classroom, school, or district level), (b) participants, (c) settings, and (d) grade level.

"The peer buddy program is not only designed for the special education students, but also for the peers because they are learning about their potential!"

Ms. Curry
Special Education Teacher

"Ann got to see other students working together, and she had the opportunity to participate with them. Not only that, but the general education students had a chance to work with Ann. This is a win-win situation!"

Mr. Rees
General Education Teacher

Extent of Program (Classroom, School, or District Level)

We have observed that the best approach to starting a peer buddy program in any school or district is on a bottom-up basis. Even in a districtwide program, it is individual teachers, staff, and students who are on the front line implementing the program. Therefore, it is best that the impetus for a program comes directly from front-line people or closely related stakeholders to ensure ownership of and commitment to the program. For those interested, a program eventually can be expanded to additional schools or across an entire district, if there are individuals at each school who are desirous of and truly willing to commit the time and effort it takes to start a peer buddy program. The Metropolitan Nashville Peer Buddy Program described above started at one high school with just a handful of teachers and administrators, and then expanded to all eleven comprehensive high schools in the district, *but only when at least one teacher at each additional school showed an interest in starting a program in his or her school.*

The task of starting a school- or districtwide peer buddy program may seem daunting to an individual teacher. A teacher may be more interested in having peer buddies for a just a few students in her classroom or in a handful of classrooms. Fortunately, peer buddy programs can take different forms as they meet the goals of inclusion, general education access, community building, and service–learning in a school. For example, a culinary arts teacher could arrange for several general education classmates to work cooperatively as a peer group to help a special education student prepare meals in the class's kitchen and complete required reading and written assignments. As in any peer buddy model, participating general education students should be given guidance and ongoing support by the culinary arts or special education teacher and should be required to reflect on their experiences as a service–learning opportunity. Or, a biology teacher could have her entire class participate in a service–learning project involving planning, starting, and maintaining a community garden. Peer buddy class members could help their special education classmates decide which plants are best for the climate and soil type of their garden, how the plants should be arranged in the garden, how to plant the seeds or set out young plants when it is time to plant, and how to care for the plants as they grow. Likewise, special education teachers can arrange for peer buddies to attend a drama or American history class to help a student learn her lines in a play or to develop an argument to use in a class debate. Same-age peers are less noticeable or intrusive than are teachers or educational assistants when entering a general education class as supports. Finally, student teachers and practicum students can ask peer buddies to regularly attend a keyboarding or English class with one or two of their special education students to help these students complete assignments. Or, peer buddies could help these students decorate for a party or practice Salsa steps in their Spanish club.

"Students with disabilities feel more confident having peer buddies. They help them keep up in class!"

Mr. Riordan
General Education Teacher

Promoting Peer Interaction and Service–Learning

Several programs designed to promote both inclusion and service–learning in secondary schools are described in the research literature. Participants from both general and special education have experienced multiple benefits from involvement in these programs, including increased self-esteem, social skills and problem-solving skills; improved attitudes toward others; more opportunities to serve others; and additional opportunities for contact with their peers.

(continued)

- High school students with severe disabilities worked with their general education peers in a social studies class on a service–learning project in which school supplies were collected for an elementary school in El Salvador (Kleinert & Owens, 2003).
- Junior high school students with learning disabilities receiving special education services in resource classrooms worked together with their general education peers to implement service activities at a local retirement center and elementary school (Yoder, Retish, & Wade, 1996).
- High school students with severe disabilities partnered with their general education classmates to design and create a community garden as part of a semester-long service–learning project (Burns, Storey, & Certo, 1998).
- Junior high school students with learning disabilities and behavioral disorders worked with their general education peers to provide peer tutoring to younger students with disabilities in reading and math (Brill, 1994).
- General and special education high school students collaborated together to collect aluminum cans and raise money for a local charity, while simultaneously learning about the environment, money management, and service (Gent & Gurecka, 1998).

Participants

Peer buddy programs can be implemented with a variety of students, both as recipients and providers of support. For example, peer buddies have provided support to students with a range of disabilities, such as autism, mental retardation, learning disabilities, and emotional and behavioral disorders. After all, limited access to the general curriculum is a critical concern for *all* students with disabilities (Individuals with Disabilities Education Act Amendments of 1997). Although many peer-mediated programs have been directed toward providing support to students with high-incidence disabilities such as learning disabilities, students with moderate to severe disabilities also have reaped substantial benefits from involvement in peer buddy programs.

"I want to get good grades so I can pass to the next grade. I like when peer buddies show interest in helping me with my work."

Som Poori
Special Education Student

Peer buddy programs also can include a range of students as providers of support. High-achieving students are not the only ones who can make great peer buddies. Students who are not "academically promising" or involved in many extracurricular activities also can benefit from the program. For example, students who are at risk of dropping out have found a reason for attending school because they know their special education partner enjoys working with them each day. Some of these students have made the best peer buddies in a program by empathizing with their peers and treating them as equals. Moreover, the opportunity to be a peer buddy does not have to be limited just to general education students. *Teachers successfully have included students with learning disabilities, emotional and behavioral disorders, or mild mental retardation, for example, in assisting peers with more severe disabilities in completing academic assignments or employment tasks.* When provided with opportunities to assist others, rather than always being on the receiving end of support, students with disabilities have increased their self-confidence and learned important life skills.

"Many students benefit from being a peer buddy—not just the 'best' students. Some seniors found a positive reason to stay in school by being a peer buddy. Administrators can assist with suggesting students who would benefit from being in the program."

Ms. Covington
Principal

Settings

Peer buddy programs typically are introduced initially in a school to increase special education students' participation in general education classes. Teachers also report how helpful peer buddies are in promoting students' participation in activities throughout the school day—pep club, Future Teachers of America, intramural sports, chess club, school assemblies, lunch, and extracurricular activities (see Chapter 7). Some schools have a "Lunch Bunch" where peer buddies bring their own friends to eat with special education peers in the cafeteria. Peer buddy programs also can be applied to community-based training or employment settings. Special education students who receive instruction off-campus—such as learning to ride the bus, working part-time in a restaurant or department store, or purchasing items in a store—do not need to be apart from their general education peers. Peer buddies can provide support to students in off-campus settings. When service–learning activities are incorporated into community-based instruction, the experience becomes an inclusive one that meets the educational needs of all participants.

"We have opportunities to work in the community—we work at Kroger and the Susan Gray School. Having a peer buddy who works with the special education students makes the students feel great and provides them with additional support."

Ms. Ortega
Special Education Teacher

Grade Levels

The peer buddy programs with which the authors of this book are most familiar occur at the secondary level—middle and high schools. These settings may be among the most challenging in which to conduct peer buddy programs because of departmentalization of teachers and classes, 50- or 90-minute class changes, and limited opportunity for schoolwide discussion or community building. In many ways, preschool or elementary school settings are ideal for implementing peer buddy programs because typically there is less movement among students and teachers throughout the school day, allowing the opportunity for relationships among students to develop naturally. Indeed, the same principles and philosophy that support inclusion and access to general education curricula on the secondary level apply to younger students. Early childhood and elementary age "buddies" can be just as effective in promoting inclusion as older students. For readers interested in introducing peer buddy programs among a younger school population, we highly recommend adapting suggestions in this book to specific age levels and settings.

Peer buddy programs are flexible tools for achieving important educational goals, including access to general education, social acceptance, community building, and citizenship. Whatever the circumstances of a classroom, school, or district, there are effective ways of adapting peer buddy programs to meet the specific needs of a school community. In the next section, we describe how this book can provide a blueprint for tailoring peer buddy programs to particular situations.

How to Use This Book

You are now familiar with the concept and goals of a peer buddy program. Next, it is necessary to know how to get a peer buddy program started, whether on an individual student or schoolwide level. The purpose of this book is to provide a complete, step-by-step guide to pre- or in-service teachers, school counselors, administrators, parents, and others for establishing, implementing, and evaluating peer buddy programs. An overview of the organization of the book and means to adapt its suggestions to specific school environments follows.

Organization of the Book

Section I.   Section I of this book has provided a broad overview of peer buddy programs. Specifically, in Chapter 1, we presented legislative, philosophical, and research arguments for inclusion and proposed service–learning peer buddy programs as a means to promote inclusion and community membership in schools. In this chapter (Chapter 2), we described the Metropolitan Nashville Peer Buddy Program as a case example, as well as variations that peer buddy programs can take.

Sections II and III.   In the remainder of this book, we present (a) recommended steps for setting up a peer buddy program; (b) roles of peer buddies in inclusive, extracurricular, and community-based settings; and (c) strategies for evaluating and sustaining programs long-term. Our suggestions are based on our extensive experience in implementing and evaluating peer buddy programs across multiple schools and settings. The chapters in Sections II and III are arranged as a series of steps to follow to guide you through starting your own program. Pick and choose the steps that are most applicable to your situation. As we have suggested, peer buddy programs can be adapted to meet the goals of a particular classroom, school, or district.

Section II contains strategies to guide you in planning and starting up a peer buddy program. Specifically, in Chapter 3, we address the initial steps that should be taken to lay the groundwork for a new peer buddy program. Building a solid base of support for a program is an essential first step when beginning any new school program. Investing time and effort in getting other administrators, teachers, and school counselors in the school community "on board" from the very beginning will pay off with large dividends later on. Once these initial steps have been addressed, it is time to begin getting students involved. In Chapter 4, we outline a process for identifying students who may benefit from involvement in a peer buddy program. We present several approaches for recruiting and screening general education students to become peer buddies. We also describe strategies for matching general education peer buddies with special education students. When general education students have been recruited, they will need to be oriented to their new roles as peer buddies. In Chapter 5, we present a plan for preparing general education peer buddies to interact with and provide effective support to their classmates with disabilities. Specifically, we describe an orientation session that introduces peer buddies to disability issues, roles, instructional strategies, and other information and resources that they will need to provide meaningful support. We also present guidelines for establishing procedures that maximize program benefits for participating students and teachers.

"At first, I was nervous about being a peer buddy. I did not know what to expect. I asked myself many questions. 'Will the students like me?' 'How will they react to me?' 'Will I be a good peer buddy?' But after I experienced being in the program, I enjoyed the students. I believe that they have enjoyed my help as well. I would encourage other students to get involved in this program."

Jameel Acres
Peer Buddy

Section III addresses effective strategies for sustaining peer buddy programs. When the roles and responsibilities of participants, teachers, and other school staff are clearly laid out, everyone is much more likely to enjoy and benefit from the experiences. In Chapter 6, we present tips for providing ongoing support to general education peer buddies throughout the semester or school year. These tips are designed to make sure that peer buddies are comfortable in their roles, that they have access to the information and resources they need, and that opportunities for learning and growth are maximized. In Chapter 7, we address some of the issues that teachers, school counselors, and administrators may encounter when implementing peer buddy programs in different settings. For example, we discuss possible variations peer buddy programs can take when applied in inclusive classrooms, during community-based instruction, during noninstructional school activities (e.g., lunch, extracurricular clubs, afterschool activities), or in special education classrooms. In Chapter 8, we present ideas for evaluating, sustaining, and expanding a program. You will want to know that your program is meeting the goals that you set out for it. We describe how an advisory board can provide valuable feedback and guidance regarding program implementation. Ideas for recruiting participants, structuring meetings, and gathering program suggestions also are presented.

"To have a good, dependable peer buddy working with special education students is a must. In my classes, peer buddies have worked well. With thirty to thirty-two students and three to four special education students, it is not possible to keep a close eye on everyone. Darrell was just the type of peer buddy needed for my class."

Mr. Potter
General Education Teacher

Customizing a Peer Buddy Program

As you read through Sections II and III, you will see that we have provided a practical resource for pre-service teachers, school staff, or others wanting to begin a peer buddy program. Chapters 3 through 8 clarify the steps and provide the information and resources you will need to start and maintain a peer buddy program as a credit class on a school- or districtwide basis.

In addition, we provide options and guidance for designing peer buddy experiences on a much smaller scale—for example, to support just a few students with disabilities or within just a handful of classrooms. These recommendations are especially appropriate for individual general and special education teachers or for pre-service teachers completing student teaching or practicum experiences, as well as teachers who do not yet have a credit class for peer buddies established in their school or district. In addition, we provide more detailed information for teachers implementing peer buddy activities in a single classroom in Chapter 7.

Whether peer buddy programs are implemented schoolwide, districtwide, or classroom by classroom, everyone has a part to play in making sure that programs are meeting the goals of the school community. To provide additional information about the specific roles each member of the school community should play in implementing a program, we have included icons that signal these roles. These icons are as follows:

Administrators play a vital role in providing resources and support needed to ensure that every educational program in a school is a success. The importance of administrator involvement to the success of a peer buddy program is no exception. If you are a principal, assistant principal, department chair, or other school administrator, check out the information that accompanies this icon for steps you can take to support a peer buddy program in your school.

The role of **school counselors** in getting a peer buddy program off the ground also is crucial. If you are a school counselor, look for this icon to read about additional ways that you can support a successful peer buddy program.

Teachers—whether general education, special education, student teachers, or practicum students—will have the closest day-to-day contact with participating students and will play an instrumental role in ensuring that peer buddy programs run smoothly. If you are a teacher, do not overlook the additional tips we provide to you whenever this icon appears. In addition, this icon lets you know that alternative strategies are available for setting up a peer buddy program in a single classroom. The readings in this type of box describe how peer buddy activities can be implemented *without* developing a peer buddy credit class. After all, for some teachers or practicum students, the option of developing a credit course just may not be available given time or resource constraints.

Parents can be valuable partners in any school program. The potential influence of parents on the success of a school program and the lives of students is powerful. Each time you see this icon, look for additional information about the roles that parents can play in making sure that their children get the most out of their involvement in peer buddy programs, either as peer buddies or as students receiving support.

Compiling This Book

The content of this book is derived, in large part, from our experiences in implementing a peer buddy program across eleven comprehensive high schools in Nashville, Tennessee, over a five-year period. Over the years, we have worked closely with scores of teachers, administrators, school counselors, students, and parents to develop a program that *really works* when it comes to increasing the social, academic, and civic involvement of secondary students. In addition, the Metropolitan Nashville Peer Buddy Program has been adapted and replicated nationally across many schools in numerous districts, both urban and rural, with a wide diversity of student populations. The implementation strategies and resources described throughout this book have been developed in cooperation with multiple stakeholders in a variety of school communities. We have taken great care to incorporate into this book the wonderful feedback of these and other persons provided to us during in-services, trainings, conference presentations, advisory board meetings, and technical assistance visits. In addition, we have conducted a number of studies to evaluate outcomes associated with peer buddy programs. The findings of these studies have provided us with additional insight into program benefits and strategies that increase students' academic and social participation. We share these findings throughout the book.

Our goal has been to develop a resource that is both user-friendly and comprehensive. To this end, we have included a number of features that will help you apply the steps for starting a peer buddy program outlined in this book.

- Throughout the book, we have included reproducible forms that can be used "as is" or modified based on the specific circumstances of your school, district, or classroom. These forms have been field-tested by teachers, students, school counselors, and administrators implementing peer buddy programs across a number of schools and are intended to be a practical resource to assist you in getting your program running as smoothly as possible.
- Case studies and first-person quotes are interspersed throughout each chapter. Each case study illustrates practical ideas educators, administrators, and students have used to make their peer buddy program a success. Quotes are included to provide you with first-hand perspectives of participants actively involved in peer buddy programs.
- We have included boxes addressing current research and legislation related to topics such as general education access, service-learning, peer support strategies, and peer interaction. This information is intended to keep you up to date on recent initiatives that relate to implementing peer buddy programs.
- At the end of each chapter, we present brief *Learning Activities* to guide you in putting your thoughts into action in relation to implementing peer buddy programs.
- Finally, we have compiled an appendix detailing resources related to (a) service–learning programs and (b) strategies for promoting inclusion and student interaction. If you have further questions not answered in the chapters, consult the appendix for additional information sources.

Summary

Peer buddy programs are effective tools for increasing access to general education, providing service–learning experiences to students, and creating inclusive, caring school communities. Establishing a peer buddy program requires the active involvement, collaboration, and support of students, teachers, administrators, school counselors, parents, and others. We suggest to you that it is worth the effort. School communities have much to gain when general and special education students have opportunities to learn and interact together.

Learning Activities

■ How does the situation at your school, practicum site, or another school setting compare to the description of McGavock High School in the beginning of this chapter before school staff there began implementing a peer buddy program? What are the similarities? What are the differences? How inclusive is the school setting with which you are familiar?

■ What aspects of the Metropolitan Nashville Peer Buddy Program seem most practical for your school situation or classroom? What do you think should be changed to meet the needs at your school? List particular issues you would like to address in starting your own program.

■ Are there already informal peer buddy activities being implemented somewhere within your school or a school you have visited recently? If so, what degree of success have such activities enjoyed? Think about how you would tap into these activities to begin expanding support available to all students in a school.

■ In starting a peer buddy program in your classroom or school, how would you address issues of diversity, including economic, academic, and cultural differences among students? What barriers can you identify that need to be addressed to promote inclusion of all students and building of community within the school setting?

References

Brill, C. L. (1994). The effects of participation in service–learning on adolescents with disabilities. *Journal of Adolescence, 17,* 369–380.

Burns, M., Storey, K., & Certo, N. J. (1998). Effect of service learning on attitudes toward students with severe disabilities. *Education and Training in Mental Retardation and Developmental Disabilities, 34,* 58–65.

Carter, E. W., Hughes, C., Copeland, S. R., & Breen, C. (2001). Differences between high school students who do and do not volunteer to participate in a peer interaction program. *Journal of the Association for Persons with Severe Handicaps, 26,* 229–239.

Copeland, S. R., Hughes, C., Carter, E. W., Guth, C., Presley, J., Williams, C. R., & Fowler, S. E. (2004). Increasing access to general education: Perspectives of participants in a high school peer support program. *Remedial and Special Education, 26,* 342–352.

Copeland, S. R., McCall, J., Williams, C. R., Guth, C., Carter, E. W., Fowler, S. E., Presley, J. A., & Hughes, C. (2002). High school peer buddies: A win-win situation. *TEACHING Exceptional Children, 35*(1), 16–21.

Gent, P. J., & Gurecka, L. E. (1998). Service learning: A creative strategy for inclusive classrooms. *Journal of the Association for Persons with Severe Handicaps, 23,* 261–271.

Hughes, C., Copeland, S. R., Guth, C., Rung, L. L., Hwang, B., Kleeb, G., & Strong, M. (2001). General education students' perspectives on their involvement in a high school peer buddy program. *Education and Training in Mental Retardation and Developmental Disabilities, 36,* 343–356.

Hughes, C., Guth, C., Hall, S., Presley, J., Dye, M., & Byers, C. (1999). They are my best friends: Peer buddies promote inclusion in high school. *TEACHING Exceptional Children, 31*(5), 32–37.

Individuals with Disabilities Education Act Amendments of 1997, PL 105–17, 20 U. S. C. § 1400 *et seq.* (1997).

Kleinert, H., & Owens, J. (2003). *Inclusive service learning.* Kentucky Peer Service Learning Project. Retrieved May 13, 2004, from http://www.ihdi.uky.edu/kypslp/ServiceLearningPP4-24-03.pdf

Yoder, D. I., Retish, E., & Wade, R. (1996). Service learning: Meeting student and community needs. *TEACHING Exceptional Children, 28*(4), 14–18.

PART TWO

"How Do I Start?": Setting Up a Peer Buddy Program

CHAPTER

3

Laying the Groundwork

In this chapter, you will learn about . . .

- The importance of building a solid base of support when planning a peer buddy program.
- Strategies for increasing awareness about the program among administrators, school counselors, teachers, parents, and others.
- Issues related to deciding whether to develop a peer buddy credit course.

Why? . . .

Building support is an important first step when laying the groundwork for a peer buddy program. Starting a program requires the active involvement and support of teachers, administrators, school staff, students, and parents. Commitment to the program is critical even for one single teacher starting a program with only a few students. This chapter provides an overview of the initial action that should be taken when first establishing a peer buddy program and includes discussion of issues related to developing a credit course.

CASE STUDY BOX: *The Importance of Support*

As a new special education resource teacher at Spence Middle School, Ms. Ortiz felt a mix of excitement and apprehension about her first school year. Her student teaching experience had been really positive—her supervising teacher was a great mentor and Ms. Ortiz had learned many ways to increase students' success in general education activities at Spence. For example, Ms. Whittsen, her supervising teacher at Hadley Middle, had had an ongoing peer buddy program where peers assisted students with disabilities in their general education classes and befriended them at lunch and during other school activities. Ms. Ortiz liked to share personal stories about the positive impact the peer buddy program had on students—like how Jared had excelled during the bridge building project in science and how Selma had belted out "The Star-Spangled Banner" at the homecoming football game. It came as no surprise that starting a peer buddy program at her new school was one of the first things on Ms. Ortiz's "to-do" list.

Shortly after the school year began, Ms. Ortiz was ready to get her peer buddy program off the ground. After all, she thought, if it worked at her student teaching placement at Hadley, it should work anywhere. Eagerly, Ms. Ortiz began by approaching the general education teachers in her wing of the school to inform them that she soon would be sending students with disabilities to their classes along with some "peer buddies." The teachers, who since the beginning of the year already had been given several new directives from the school district, were reluctant to get involved in yet another program—especially one that they had never heard of before. Moreover, they already were concerned about how many students they

(continued)

CASE STUDY BOX *Continued*

had in their classes, in particular, those who had "special needs." One by one, the teachers politely, but firmly, turned down Ms. Ortiz's "offer."

At the end of what seemed like a particularly rotten day, Ms. Ortiz sat alone at her desk. What was she doing wrong? Why was the peer buddy idea such a hit at her old school, but such a flop at Spence? Frustrated, Ms. Ortiz called her mentor, Ms. Whittsen, to ask for advice. Soon, she realized that the peer buddy program that appeared to run so smoothly during her student teaching had been around for a long time before she ever arrived at Hadley Middle. Ms. Ortiz had had no idea what was involved in getting the program off the ground! Ms. Whittsen revealed that a lot of time initially had been invested explaining the program to teachers and students, gaining their support and laying the groundwork for an effective, collaborative program. She said that for others to get involved, they had to believe that there would be benefits to the program. If Ms. Ortiz expected the same success, she would need to start spending time building a base of support among her faculty colleagues, too.

Importance of Establishing a Base of Support

As we indicated in Chapter 2, it has been our experience that the most successful peer buddy programs are those introduced from the "bottom up." Few educational programs are well received when imposed on school staff without first obtaining their support and consent (Eisner, 2002). Peer buddy programs are no different. Whether a peer buddy program will occur in just a few classrooms or across an entire school or district, it is critical to gain the interest and backing of other members of the school community before proceeding.

Why do we stress the need for building a solid base of support *before* starting a peer buddy program? First, a peer buddy program is a collaborative venture requiring the help of many within the school community. For example, school counselors typically sign up students who are taking the peer buddy credit course; administrators officially sanction and help publicize the program; general education teachers provide accommodations for students with disabilities in their classrooms; special education teachers arrange for and help peer buddies assist their peers in accessing general education; and parents often provide the impetus and support for inclusion to occur. Second, getting others on board in support of a peer buddy program expands available resources, experiences, ideas, strengths, and skills. Third, widely enlisting the support of others helps a program reach its full potential and broadens its impact within the school community.

> "The school administration is needed to help encourage general education teachers to welcome students with disabilities in their classes with the assistance of peer buddies. They also are needed to get more students involved in the program."
>
> *Mr. Maldaur*
> *Special Education Teacher*

Of course, support does not have to be garnered from everyone at school all at once. A teacher or administrator may decide to begin small and expand a program's base of support gradually as the program grows. In the next section, we walk interested readers through four steps for building support for a program: (1) identifying key players, (2) promoting the program, (3) describing benefits for all participants, and (4) enlisting support.

Even if you are a pre-service **teacher** or a single teacher planning peer buddy activities for just one or two classrooms, you will still want support from others in the school community. The number of people whose help you enlist will be smaller, but the importance of gaining their support is not diminished. The support of the principal and involvement of other special education teachers, general education teachers, and educational assistants is still critical to the success of your program.

Step 1: Identifying Key Players

The first step in acquiring support for a peer buddy program is to determine exactly whose support you should seek. When first getting a program started from scratch, you may be unsure of whose support you will need and at what point you will need it. To guide you in this process, we recommend that you consider enlisting the support of (a) administrators, (b) teachers, (c) school counselors, and (d) parents.

Administrators.   Administrators are critical in ensuring that the educational and social needs of all students in a school are addressed (Rodriquez & Romaneck, 2002). They are the driving force behind a school's mission to promote inclusion, service–learning, and community building. The vision of a principal is contagious, influencing the attitudes of teachers, students, staff, and parents and shaping the campus climate. The support (or lack of support) of an administrator can mean the difference between an educational program that thrives and one that never really gets off the ground. Moreover, administrators also have unique responsibilities in starting up a peer buddy program—spreading the word to school staff about the benefits of the program, offering guidance with scheduling and grading issues, and brainstorming solutions to potential challenges.

> "Students with disabilities are included in special education for exposure, stimulation, and opportunity to achieve and comprehend. We need to provide opportunities for special education students to take high standard curriculum courses."
>
> *Mr. Crowell*
> *Principal*

Because administrators typically are the "gatekeepers" to a school, they are a key to making a peer buddy program a reality. Therefore, the principal or assistant principal usually is the first person whose support you should seek. What difference can the support of a principal make? In one high school we have worked with, a special education teacher began a peer buddy program with great intensity and excitement, but without seeking the support of his principal. The number of peer buddies involved in the program increased rapidly and it soon became an extremely popular class among students. However, the growth in the number of peer buddies was accompanied by a drop in the number of students who signed up to be office assistants, which inconvenienced office staff. The principal responded by limiting the number of students who could enroll in the peer buddy program. Had the support of the principal been sought and had he been informed of the benefits of the program before it was introduced, the conflict possibly could have been avoided. In contrast, in another high school, the principal was involved actively early on in the planning of a peer buddy program. As the program developed and peer buddies began to enroll, the principal quickly became one of the most vocal advocates of the program among students and teachers.

 As an **administrator,** your words and actions set the tone for the rest of the school and strongly influence the school climate. Conveying to your school staff that you value a peer buddy program that promotes inclusion, community building, and service–learning can have a huge impact on students' and staff's willingness to become involved. As an administrator, you already may be sold on the idea of a peer buddy program in your school. Your challenge may be to get your teaching staff on board with you. Think about the hesitations that teachers may have about the changes likely to accompany inclusion. Brainstorm ways that a peer buddy program can allay these concerns.

Teachers.   Teachers often are responsible for the day-to-day activities associated with peer buddy programs. Special education teachers usually coordinate the schedules of and provide guidance to peer buddies who are assisting students with disabilities throughout the school campus. Educational assistants also may help direct peer buddies in supporting special education students in activities on- or off-campus. General education teachers, in cooperation with special education teachers, are responsible for peer buddies who are working with their classmates with disabilities in science, history, culinary arts, or other classes. A core group of just a few teachers often is enough to get a program initially up and running. But as the program grows, more and more teachers are likely to be impacted by the program. Therefore, it is important to identify teachers who are willing to work closely with you in getting the program off the ground.

 A great way to get the word out about a budding program is to talk to general education **teachers** who already have students with disabilities enrolled in their classes. These teachers often are looking for effective strategies for supporting students in the general education curriculum. Let teachers know that peers are an excellent source of natural support that is far less stigmatizing to the student than a teacher or educational assistant. Moreover, peer buddies can also assist teachers in meeting both the educational and social needs of students with disabilities. Once teachers have had a peer buddy in their classrooms, they will spread the word to other teachers about the positive difference a peer buddy program can make.

School Counselors.   School counselors are critical to starting up any peer buddy program. They are the staff members most closely involved in helping students develop their programs of study and enroll in their classes. Because counselors know the student body of a school so well, they are experts at identifying students best suited to participating in a peer buddy program. Keep in mind that in many secondary schools, students are assigned to counselors according to grade level, alphabetical order, or other identifiers. It is important to determine which counselor is the best contact in a school when looking for support in building a new program.

In some schools, **school counselors** may be the best people to develop and oversee a peer buddy program. Because, as a counselor, your schedule may be more flexible than a teacher's, it may be easier for you to fit the responsibilities of supporting a peer buddy program into your daily routines. Talk with your administrator about the specific role you can take in a program. You may be the push that gets the program going.

"The peer buddy course at our school is an important course for a number of reasons. It helps support the inclusion of special education students into the general education population. Also, the peer buddy course allows general education students to learn more about students with disabilities. As a result of this experience, some students may even consider special education as a career option. My primary role in the intake of students into the peer buddy course is to focus on seniors. Other guidance counselors focus on underclassmen. Before the other guidance counselors and I recommend the peer buddy course to students, we always make sure that they have flexibility in their schedules. For the past few months, the students' interest in the program has increased drastically at our school."

Ms. Henry
Guidance Counselor

Parents.   A strong school–parent partnership is an important ingredient in any successful school program—you may find out that it is actually parents who are pushing to have peer buddies for their children. Enlisting the support of parents prior to and throughout implementation of a peer buddy program is invaluable. Communication with parents about a peer buddy program can be accomplished through parent newsletters, presentations at PTA meetings, conversations at open houses, parent–teacher conferences, articles in the school newspaper, or postings on the school website. Parents care about the peer relationships of their children and will be eager to communicate about a peer buddy program. Many also will play an important role in ensuring that peer buddy relationships extend beyond the school day into their homes and communities.

"Bryant has had wonderful experiences with the peer buddy program. He has made some really good friends—met some fantastic people. Jerome, who is currently a peer buddy, is an old friend of Bryant's. They do many things together outside of school. Bryant has spent the night at Jerome's home, they go to Boy Scouts together, and Jerome even accompanies Bryant on trips to the orthodontist. Bryant also joins Jerome and other friends frequently for lunch in the cafeteria."

Mr. Tulley
Parent of a Special Education Student

Step 2: Promoting the Program

Administrators, teachers, and other school staff likely are familiar with the topics of school reform and inclusion. They are less likely, however, to be aware of how peer buddy programs can promote service–learning, community building, and accessing general education. Your next task will be to promote the goals of a peer buddy program to members of your school community. The first section of this book provided you with an overview and purpose of a peer buddy program. If you already have an idea about the goals of your program and plans for what the program should look like, go ahead and share your thoughts with others. A well-thought-out and clearly explained purpose and plan can go a long way in convincing others of the worth of a program. On the other hand, if you are not exactly sure what the program should look like in your school, share examples of program variations as described in Chapter 2 and throughout the rest of this book. You can then work collaboratively with administrators and teachers to decide which program variations would best serve the students in your school.

A faculty meeting is a great avenue for getting the word out to teachers about a new or existing program (see box). Other outlets for sharing program information include faculty newsletters, flyers placed in teacher mailboxes, postings on bulletin boards, or casual conversations in the hall or teachers' lounge.

Promoting Your Program at Faculty Meetings

Faculty meetings are great opportunities to (a) get updated on the latest school happenings, (b) strengthen staff cohesion and build morale, and (c) share ideas about educational practices that work. Principals often use faculty meetings to discuss effective practices being implemented within the school. Why not use a faculty meeting as a chance to get the word out about your school's peer buddy program? Check with your principal about getting the program on the agenda for your next meeting. Then prepare a presentation focused on the purpose of the program and an overview of how it would fit into your school's programs. Encourage staff members at the meeting to think about how a peer buddy program would benefit themselves, their students, and the school. Helping staff understand and value a program is critical to shoring up their support. Use the Faculty Meeting Outline (Table 3.1) and the following strategies to guide you in preparing your presentation.

- A brief presentation is best—you do not want your colleagues to nod off. Do not talk at great length—your primary goal is to pique interest and enlist support.
- Faculty meetings often are used by administrators to revisit the school mission. As you present an overview of the peer buddy program, connect program goals directly to your school's mission—goals such as building citizenship and providing service. Keep in mind that the mission statement of a school helps staff set priorities and make decisions about where to devote time and effort.
- Not every faculty meeting involves the entire school staff. Often, teachers meet by grade level or department, such as social studies or math. These meetings are a great place to talk to teachers about how a peer buddy program would fit within their department or cluster to meet student goals.
- Adapt or expand the Faculty Meeting Outline for use during longer in-service trainings or staff development sessions, particularly when your program is more developed.

Step 3: Describing Benefits for All Participants

With so many other issues vying for the attention of administrators and teachers, why would staff want to invest their time and resources into yet another program? Clearly explaining the potential benefits of peer buddy programs for all participants can help staff realize that their efforts would be well spent. Staff may not realize that peer buddy programs can help (a) enhance educational outcomes for all students, (b) sup-

TABLE 3.1 Faculty Meeting Outline

- *Briefly describe your peer buddy program or ideas for a potential program.* Effective strategies for describing the program include:
  - Sharing a short video of the program or slide show using presentation software.
  - Having a peer buddy or student with a disability share a brief testimonial about his or her experiences with the program.
  - Asking other teachers to share specific ways that the program has been implemented effectively in their classrooms.
- *Explain the value of the program* by describing potential benefits for students, teachers, and others in the school community. Examples of these benefits are listed in Table 3.2.
- *Give examples of different ways that teachers can be involved,* from informal to more formal roles that accommodate their level of interest and available time. Examples include:
  - Identifying and recruiting potential peer buddies within their classes.
  - Spreading information about the program to students in the classes they teach and school clubs or sports teams they sponsor.
  - Having a peer buddy provide support in their classrooms.
  - Enrolling students with disabilities and peer buddies in their classrooms.
- *Provide clear information about whom to contact for additional information* or distribute a brief form designed to gauge teachers' interest in becoming involved (see Figure 3.1, *Teacher Interest Form*).
- *Offer to answer any questions* that school staff might have about the program.

port teachers and administrators in responding to school reform efforts, (c) promote inclusive practices for all students, and (d) build a cohesive school community. A summary of the benefits reported by participants in peer buddy programs is provided in the box at the bottom of this page and in Table 3.2. These benefits can be shared with people you talk with about the program. Selling them on the idea that the program is not only good for students but also for teachers and administrators should be an important part of your marketing pitch.

Who Benefits from a Peer Buddy Program?

The specific appeal of a peer buddy program may differ from person to person. Some teachers may resonate more with benefits related to increasing students' inclusion in general education settings, while others are drawn more to the service–learning opportunities associated with such programs. In Table 3.2, we summarize findings of research studies describing the benefits of peer buddy programs as experienced by teachers, students, and participants. Communicate to members of your school community that these are some of the benefits they can expect to see from participating in a peer buddy program.

"Increasing awareness is necessary and very important. This can be done by informing the guidance counselors, particularly the senior counselor, and the teachers. I have been extremely active because I wanted to be. I feel that administrators should be closely involved in supervision and follow-up. They should also play a big role in the screening process."

Ms. Monaco
High School Principal

TABLE 3.2   Benefits Associated with Peer Buddy Programs

For general education students. . .
- Develop new friendships
- Increase their advocacy skills and awareness of disability issues
- Gain additional knowledge about people in general and those with disabilities
- Learn enhanced interpersonal skills
- Experience personal growth and a sense of accomplishment
- Develop an interest in pursuing a career in human services
- Increase their expectations of peers with disabilities
- Learn from students with disabilities who are positive role models
- Have fun

For students with disabilities. . .
- Develop new friendships
- Gain opportunities for social interaction with peers
- Acquire important academic, social, and life skills
- Spend time with age-appropriate role models
- Receive effective peer support in general education settings
- Increase their independence and self-confidence
- Have fun

For teachers. . .
- Receive additional assistance from peer buddies in individualizing instruction for students with disabilities
- Experience professional growth and personal satisfaction
- Provide socializing opportunities for all students
- Experience increased diversity in the classroom

For administrators. . .
- Improve the school climate by supporting practices that foster a caring school community
- Align school practices with school reform efforts and legislation related to inclusion

For parents. . .
- Experience increased enthusiasm for their children's schooling
- Appreciate their children's growth and expanded social interactions and friendships

Sources: Copeland et al. (2004); Copeland et al. (2002); Helmstetter, Peck, & Giangreco (1994); Hughes et al. (2001); Longwill & Kleinert (1998).

Step 4: Enlisting Support

Once you have communicated clearly your program ideas with other members of the school community, step back, listen, and absorb their feedback. Explore the idea of a peer buddy program with others, allowing them to provide their ideas and assist you in navigating around potential roadblocks and challenges. Encouraging the input and advice of others can assist you in refining your plans for a program. Next, shore up their support by asking them to assist you in getting the program up and running. One strategy may be to gather a core group of school staff together to begin brainstorming and planning for the program. Another strategy would be to distribute a form to teachers asking them to indicate their level of interest in participating in the program. We have provided an example of such a form (Figure 3.1). Remember—as we said previously, acquiring support is not a one-time endeavor. Rather, you will want to establish a standing source of support.

FIGURE 3.1 Teacher Interest Form

Teacher: _____ Date: _____ Grade level(s): _____

Course(s) taught: _____ Room number: _____

☐ YES! I am interested in being involved in the peer buddy program in one or
more of the following ways:

    ☐ I would like to have peer buddies support students with disabilities in my
classroom.
    ☐ I would like to have peer buddies support students with disabilities in the
club or school activities that I sponsor.
        Club(s): _____
    ☐ I would like to help with identifying students who might make a good
peer buddy.
    ☐ Other: _____

☐ PERHAPS NEXT SEMESTER! I am just not able to be involved in the peer
buddy program at this time. However, I would be interested in talking further
about the program next semester.

☐ NO, I am not currently interested in being involved in the peer buddy program.

Questions and/or comments: _____

_____

_____

_____

_____

Return this completed form to _____ in Room _____
or place in my faculty mailbox.

Developing a Credit Service–Learning Course

As we described in Chapter 2, peer buddy programs can look different from one school
to the next, ranging from small volunteer programs to classes taken for credit, depend-
ing on the goals and needs of a school. In some cases, a pre-service teacher or an individual teacher or staff member may introduce a program on a fairly informal basis
with just a few students. In other cases, a schoolwide program involving many participants may become established. When implementing a peer buddy program across an
entire school or district, we recommend incorporating a credit service–learning course
into the school's curriculum to allow peer buddies to spend at least one period each
day with their peers with disabilities. Secondary school environments pose a unique
challenge to educators wanting to promote inclusion and build community. Limited
flexibility in students' daily schedules and time conflicts with activities such as community-based instruction and career education pose substantial challenges to interaction among students. The addition of a credit course circumvents these scheduling

barriers by providing daily class time in which peer buddies and their classmates with disabilities can participate. Moreover, a credit course provides students with structured service–learning opportunities and the ongoing support and guidance of a supervising teacher.

A credit course is not always necessary or may not even be the best option in a particular school. For example, if you, as one **teacher**, are implementing a peer buddy program in just a single classroom, the effort required in establishing a credit course may not be justified. Instead, you may just want to recruit one or two general education students to provide support during that one particular class period. Even when a credit course is implemented, it should not be the *only* avenue for general education students to promote the inclusion of their peers with disabilities. Students also should have opportunities to hang out between classes, during lunch, and when participating in extracurricular and other school activities.

Obtaining New Course Approval

The manner in which new courses are incorporated into a school's curriculum varies from district to district. It will be important to do some research to find out exactly how new courses get approved in a particular school. Speak with an administrator or contact the local education agency and state department of education to find out about established policies and procedures for applying for a new course offering. Sometimes approval can be granted at the school level; other times it must be approved at the district or state level. Also, find out if a school already has an existing course that can accommodate the goals of a peer buddy program. For example, many districts and states already have service–learning, peer tutoring, or peer counseling courses approved for students within which peer buddy activities could be incorporated.

Although the process of applying for a new course may vary from school to school, it typically involves the completion of a new course application or development of a course syllabus. At a minimum, the information provided in these documents should include an overview of the peer buddy course, a list of learning objectives, a description of required assignments and activities, and an overview of any requirements for enrolling in the course. In Figure 3.2, we provide a sample course application that can be modified to reflect your expectations for participating students and the requirements of your school, district, or state.

"Before we had a peer buddy in class, I assigned different students to work with Brenda. Then when we got a peer buddy who came to class every day, it took the pressure off Brenda's classmates. Brenda has been very happy to have her peer buddy's assistance."

Mr. Anglin
General Education Teacher

Course Credit Issues

If the peer buddy program will be listed as a credit course, you will have to decide under which department the course will be listed. Districts and states vary with regard to how electives or service–learning courses are treated. Some schools allow for general elective courses, while others require that courses fall under a particular department.

FIGURE 3.2 Sample New Course Application

Sample New Course Application

Name of proposed course: *Peer Buddy Class* or *Peer Tutoring*

Describe briefly the nature of the course:
This course is designed to provide students with sufficient knowledge and skills to enable them to serve as peer supports for students with disabilities who are members of their school community. The curriculum will focus on the following areas: inclusion, exceptionalities, technology, curriculum, instructional techniques, and behavior management.

Total number of hours of instruction:
90/semester, 180/year

Total units of credit available through course/program:
1/2 to 2 full credits

Check one area of the curriculum in which the elective credit is awarded:
☐ Arts   ☐ Foreign Language   ☐ Science   ☐ Vocational Education
☐ Business   ☐ Language Arts   ☑ Social Studies   ☐ Wellness & P.E.
☐ Computer Technology   ☐ Math   ☐ Special Education   ☐ General Elective

Prerequisite(s):
Recommendation by school counselor, teacher interview

Anticipated enrollment in course:
5 to 25 students per school

Grade level(s) eligible to enroll:
Tenth to twelfth grade

Justification for course/program (reason for including this course in the school program):
Students will acquire a wide variety of skills that will enable them to be effective change agents, both as peers and as parents, human service providers, and leaders in the future. Students will learn the characteristics of individuals with disabilities and develop skills necessary to support and interact with them in mutually reinforcing ways. Students will, therefore, have the opportunity to acquire the orientation and skills they need to participate in a community where people with considerable diversity live and work.

Resources used to develop the course:
Hughes, C., & Carter, E. W. (2005). *Success for all students: Promoting inclusion in secondary schools through peer buddy programs.* Boston: Allyn and Bacon.

Goals of course/program (student learning goals):
(1) To enhance the participation of students with and without disabilities as peer buddies, friends, and good citizens.
(2) To diminish the negative attitudes that students may have regarding their peers with disabilities.
(3) To arrange daily experiences for students without disabilities to interact with their general education peers.

(continued)

FIGURE 3.2   Continued

Major units of instruction of course/program:
(1) Teach general education students how to support and interact appropriately with their classmates with disabilities.
(2) Teach students that school and community should be barrier-free environments for all students.
(3) Teach students to understand various types of disabilities and how these disabilities affect people.
(4) Encourage students to develop positive attitudes toward peers with disabilities.
(5) Demonstrate to students how their peers with disabilities can be contributing members of and participants in the community.
(6) Provide students with different perspectives related to interacting with students with disabilities by having buddies read materials written by individuals with disabilities and their family members.
(7) Provide students with daily opportunities to interact with their classmates with disabilities.

Proposed instructional methods and activities:
(1) Students will participate in group and individual discussion seminars with assigned teacher.
(2) Students will participate in school activities or field-based training opportunities with peers with disabilities one period each day.
(3) Students will complete weekly reading and homework assignments.
(4) Students will maintain a reflective journal of their experiences with their classmates with disabilities.
(5) Students will complete one afterschool project per semester.

Procedure for evaluating student progress:
(1) Information from assignments and lectures will be assessed by written and oral tests.
(2) Field-based experiences will be assessed on the basis of correct application of curriculum content.
(3) Pre- and post-tests will be administered to students to determine if they have learned factual information regarding the characteristics of individuals with disabilities.
(4) Parents of students participating in the course as well as the parents of students with disabilities will be asked to complete a questionnaire regarding school success and observed attitude changes.
(5) Students will give a written evaluation of the course and teacher.

State standards relating to this course:
(1) Have competence in the fundamentals of learning and communication.
(2) Have sufficient information to realize his or her life goals.
(3) Know and practice the basic requirements of responsible citizenship.
(4) Know the principles, habits, and attitudes conducive to good physical and mental health.
(5) Establish and maintain satisfactory relationships with other persons.
(6) Acquire career information and economic competence.

Peer buddy courses with which we are familiar primarily have been considered social studies or career education classes.

In light of the many benefits associated with peer buddy programs, it is not surprising that many general education students want to be peer buddies for multiple semesters. After all, many students will have developed new relationships with their classmates with disabilities and are seeing their peers and themselves grow and develop new skills. Service–learning can become "addictive"! Some schools, however, have to limit the number of times that students can enroll in a peer buddy course. Often, this is a practical decision because students can take only a limited number of electives. Just because students can no longer enroll in a credit course does not mean that they cannot still support their peers. Alternative means of peer buddy participation are presented in Chapter 7, Implementing Peer Buddy Programs Inside and Outside the Classroom.

Instructor Issues

In some states, the department within which the course falls can influence which teacher is assigned to the course. Because general education students will be receiving academic credit for the peer buddy program, the proposed teacher for a course may need to be endorsed to teach in that particular subject area. For example, if the course is listed as a social studies elective, the teacher of record for the peer buddy course may need to have a general education social studies credential. The No Child Left Behind Act of 2001 stresses the importance of ensuring that teachers are certified in the subject areas in which they teach.

In most of the schools with which we have worked, special education teachers have taken primary responsibility for coordinating peer buddy courses. In doing so, these teachers are listed as the instructor of record for all peer buddies signing up to take the class. This choice relates, in part, to the flexibility special education teachers typically have with regard to scheduling and their familiarity with the needs of special education students. Peer buddy courses also can be co-taught successfully with a general education teacher.

Participant Issues

In developing your peer buddy credit course, you also will need to make decisions about which and how many students you want to have involved. For example, in some schools, peer buddies must be in tenth grade or higher. Younger students often have little room in their programs of study for electives due to graduation credit requirements. Limiting the course to older students, however, decreases the total number of students assisting special education students and makes it increasingly difficult for younger students with disabilities to be paired with peer buddies who are in their classes. At least initially, it may be wise to limit the program to just a handful of peer buddies to work out any logistical issues before opening up the program to a larger group of students. In any case, whatever enrollment criteria you decide on should be included in the course description included in the school's course catalog. A sample course catalog description you may choose to follow is provided in Figure 3.3.

"I got into the peer buddy program quite by accident. As a transfer student, I had some extra hours left over, so the guidance counselor suggested being a peer buddy rather than an office worker. I had worked with some children with disabilities at a horseback riding program, but I hadn't been around students my own age. So, I was definitely in for a serious culture shock the first time I walked into the class. Little by little, I began to get to know the different students. I also began to learn about their different disabilities. When I learned that Latrone had autism and James had muscular dystrophy, I immediately went to the library and checked out books on the subject. But the life skills that I have learned can't be found in books! By spending time with the different students, I learned that they aren't any different from me on the inside. As teenagers, we're all dealing with parents, hormones, and trying to figure out what to do with the rest of our lives! Each of the students has taught me different things that influence my daily life. By working with these students, I have not only helped them learn life skills, but I have acquired brand new skills myself!"

Sharon Sengbouttara
Peer Buddy

FIGURE 3.3   Sample Course Catalog Description

Peer Buddy Course

Course Description

This peer buddy course is designed to enable students to develop peer relationships while acting as peer buddies and positive role models for students with disabilities. The peer buddies will learn about various types of disabilities and learning challenges; instructional techniques for students with disabilities; and ideas on how to help increase the social skills, interactions, and general education participation of their peers with disabilities in the day-to-day activities at their school and in their community. The course can be taken as an elective for X credit(s) per semester, one class period per day.

Qualifications

Students must meet the following criteria: (a) an interest in the peer buddy program, (b) an adequate GPA, (c) good attendance, (d) a recommendation from a teacher or guidance counselor, and (e) their program of studies allows for an elective course.

Requirements

Students acting as peer buddies will report daily to an assigned special or general education teacher. The peer buddy, teacher, and student with a disability will discuss and decide on an activity or assignment in which the peer buddy and student will participate. The peer buddy will be required to keep a daily journal, complete weekly and/or six-week written assignments, complete reading assignments, and maintain good attendance.

Course Objectives

- Students will develop teaching and study skills.
- Students will practice academic and social skills.
- Students will become advocates and learn valuable advocacy skills.
- Students will be provided with realistic career exploration for education or human service professions.
- Students will experience impressive extracurricular opportunities to include on college applications or resumes.
- Students will gain in self-esteem by knowing they have enriched others' lives.

Summary

Sharing the goals of a prospective program with other members of the school community is an important step when starting up a peer buddy program. Administrators, teachers, school counselors, and parents all have a role in building a peer buddy program. Advertising the benefits of participation in a peer buddy program will increase the likelihood that others will want to be involved. As your program expands, remember to keep key players in your school aware of the progress of your program and the gains students are making as participants. You also can consider if you want to develop a credit course for peer buddy participation.

CASE STUDY BOX: Working Together to Make It Work

As the new semester approached at Spence Middle School, Ms. Ortiz decided to take a few steps back and ponder the advice Ms. Whittsen, her former supervising teacher, had given her. If Ms. Ortiz wanted her peer buddy program to be successful, she was not going to be able to go it alone! Since a primary goal of the program would be to get special education students more involved in general education curricula and activities, it made sense to involve general education teachers in deciding the best way to go about meeting that goal.

Ms. Ortiz shared her goals and vision for the program with her principal and a small group of teachers. Together, they spent some time brainstorming ideas about how best the program would fit at Spence Middle. Many of the teachers expressed that they were willing to have students with disabilities in their classes, but that they were concerned about providing them with support while instructing the rest of the students in the class. When they learned that a peer buddy could assist in providing this support, a genuine sigh of relief was audible throughout the group.

Together, this small group of educators began developing a plan for getting a peer buddy program going. They submitted an application for a credit course to their district office. While waiting for approval, they began identifying and developing informal ways of creating peer support opportunities across the school day. Ms. Ortiz was thrilled with the progress that was being made—what a difference a little support seemed to make!

Learning Activities

- Identify other education programs in your school that appear to be thriving, such as a service organization or an afterschool club. Talk to the teachers and administrators involved in these programs about what it took to get them off the ground. How did they enlist the support of administrators, counselors, teachers, and parents? Find out what recommendations they may have for you as you begin planning your peer buddy program.
- What goals do you hope to accomplish by establishing a peer buddy program? Which of these goals (or other goals) do you think will resonate most with different members of the school community? The answers to these questions will provide you with strategies for designing and spreading the word about your program.
- In what ways might parents be involved in designing and implementing a peer buddy program? What are some of the potential challenges and benefits of involving parents?
- What do you see as the benefits and drawbacks of establishing a credit course? If you are unable to initially establish a credit course in your school, what other ways of getting a peer buddy program established might work?
- Sit down with a group of students in your school. How do they feel about becoming peer buddies? What benefits do they see related to assisting their peers with disabilities? What challenges do they envision as far as scheduling opportunities to interact with their peers? Ask the students to brainstorm about ways to promote the program to potential participants at school.

References

Copeland, S. R., Hughes, C., Carter, E. W., Guth, C., Presley, J., Williams, C. R., & Fowler, S. E. (2004). Increasing access to general education: Perspectives of participants in a high school peer support program. *Remedial and Special Education 26*, 342–352.

Copeland, S. R., McCall, J., Williams, C. R., Guth, C., Carter, E. W., Fowler, S. E., Presley, J. A., & Hughes, C. (2002). High school peer buddies: A win-win situation. *TEACHING Exceptional Children, 35*(1), 16–21.

Eisner, E. W. (2002). The kind of schools we need. *Phi Delta Kappan, 83,* 576–583.

Helmstetter, E., Peck, C., & Giangreco, M. (1994). Outcomes of interactions with peers with moderate or severe disabilities: A statewide survey of high school students. *Journal of the Association for Persons with Severe Handicaps, 19,* 277–289.

Hughes, C., Copeland, S. R., Guth, C., Rung, L. L., Hwang, B., Kleeb, G., & Strong, M. (2001). General education students' perspectives on their involvement in a high school peer buddy program. *Education and Training in Mental Retardation and Developmental Disabilities, 36,* 343–356.

Longwill, A. W., & Kleinert, H. L. (1998). The unexpected benefits of high school peer tutoring. *TEACHING Exceptional Children, 30*(4), 60–65.

No Child Left Behind Act of 2001, PL 107–110, 115 Stat. 1425 (2002).

Rodriguez, J. C., & Romaneck, G. M. (2002). The practice of inclusion. *Principal Leadership, 2*(8), 12–15.

4 Recruiting Participants

In this chapter, you will learn about . . .

- Encouraging student participation in a service–learning peer buddy program.
- Ways to recruit peer buddy program participants.
- Strategies for screening peer buddies.
- Tips for matching peer buddies and special education students.

Why? . . .

Once the groundwork for a new peer buddy program has been laid, it is time to begin recruiting students. Careful consideration should be given to identifying students who potentially may benefit from participating in a service–learning peer buddy program. After all, it is the participating students who, to a large extent, determine the success of a program. In this chapter, we outline steps for (a) identifying general education and special education students as participants in a peer buddy program, (b) recruiting and screening potential participants, and (c) matching peer buddies to their special education peers.

CASE STUDY BOX: *Recruiting Students at Roosevelt High*

As a consulting special education teacher, Ms. Williams could not wait to get a service–learning peer buddy program started at Roosevelt High School! She had read in a teacher publication about the success of such a program and was eager to begin involving special education students with their peers in general education classes, extracurricular activities, and other school programs at Roosevelt. Such involvement, she was convinced, was critical to equipping both general and special education students for their adult lives after leaving high school, as well as developing a caring and compassionate community at school. Ms. Williams secured the support of her principal and fellow teachers and made certain that the peer buddy course was listed in Roosevelt's course catalog. Now, she thought, it would simply be a matter of opening her door when peer buddies knocked. But alas, after several weeks of waiting, not a single student signed up for the peer buddy course!

With the fall semester already well underway, Ms. Williams was feeling a bit anxious. At a loss for ideas, she asked Mr. Haymaker, the school counselor, to encourage any students who still had an open class period in their schedules to sign up for the peer buddy course. She just didn't want another semester to slip away without students at Roosevelt experiencing the benefits of service–learning, inclusive education, and general education participation. By the

(continued)

CASE STUDY BOX *Continued*

next afternoon, three general education students already had been enrolled by the guidance counselor.

James was the first student to enroll in the program and immediately Ms. Williams was certain she had found the perfect peer buddy. James had a younger sister who had a disability, and he seemed to get along so naturally with his classmates with disabilities. His role would be to interact with and assist a student in a physics class—adapting assignments, clarifying activities, and introducing the student to peers. The honeymoon was short-lived, however, as Ms. Williams soon realized that James's attendance was erratic. As awesome as James was when he interacted with his classmates with disabilities, it was impossible to predict when he would show up for school. Because his special education partner really had come to depend on James for help and camaraderie in his physics class, Ms. Williams knew she would have to find a more consistent source of support.

The other two general education students who enrolled in the peer buddy program did not seem to fare much better, although for quite different reasons. Almost immediately, Ms. Williams knew that Sarah would be a challenge. She had a "reputation" for stirring things up in her other classes. After talking with the counselor, Ms. Williams discovered that Sarah had enrolled in the peer buddy program because few teachers in school wanted her in their classes. The last thing Ms. Williams wanted was for a peer to teach the students new ways to get into trouble!

As with James, Abby also looked promising at first. But after a few weeks, Ms. Williams realized that Abby had agreed to become a peer buddy for altogether different reasons than she initially shared with the guidance counselor. It turned out that Abby's new boyfriend was in the same world history class as the special education student Abby was paired with. Soon it was apparent to Ms. Williams that Abby was more interested in flirting with her new boyfriend than fulfilling the peer buddy role she had signed up for.

A bit frustrated and a little deflated, Ms. Williams decided she would need to rethink her approach to recruiting and selecting peer buddies. She decided a more personal approach, at least initially, might be the best way to identify peer buddies for participation in the program. So, with the help of the guidance counselor and several other teachers, she began to brainstorm ways of encouraging student participation in Roosevelt's new service–learning peer buddy program.

Encouraging Student Participation

Ms. Williams's experience illustrates the importance of planning and implementing recruitment strategies that motivate student participation as well as being thoughtful and deliberate regarding students who may enroll in a peer buddy program. The right peers can make the difference between a program that is mediocre and one that is wildly successful. Therefore, it is critical to plan carefully the strategies you will use to identify and recruit participants. In this chapter, we present (a) practical strategies for identifying and recruiting general education students as peer buddies, (b) tips for screening prospective general education students, and (c) methods for matching general and special education peers.

Why Do General Education Students Participate?

As you plan how you will recruit students, it is useful to consider some of the reasons why general education students decide to become involved in peer buddy programs. Many students who are motivated to participate already have had experience interacting with people with disabilities (Carter, Hughes, Copeland, & Breen, 2001). Some likely were peer buddies in elementary school, attended summer camp with peers with disabilities, or worked at an afterschool job with a co-worker with a disability. Others may have a family member, relative, or close friend with a disability. Often, these students are interested in supplementing their experiences during the school day. For other students who have an interest in eventually pursuing a career in education or other human services fields, involvement in a peer buddy program may be a viewed as a valuable way to learn what such a career might be like on a daily basis. Still others may never have had experiences with people with disabilities, but are looking for a service–learning experience that presents new challenges and opportunities with an unfamiliar group of students.

"Why I Became a Peer Buddy": Students' Reasons for Joining a Peer Buddy Program

"I have thought about being a special education teacher and I wanted to determine whether this is a field I may want to pursue by working firsthand with students. I hope that I gain experiences that might better prepare me for a career in this field later in life."

"I have a brother with disabilities and I like to work with people with disabilities and to interact with them, because they are really no different than me."

"I have a learning disability myself and I feel like I can help other students and can understand their challenges. It is a chance to get to know students and find out about disabilities other than what I have."

"My older brother worked with students with disabilities while he was in high school. He always would come home and tell me about his experiences and so I decided to do the same thing."

"I love to work with people—disability or no disability! I just thought it would be a good experience for me."

"What I like best about the peer buddy program is getting to know everyone. I have made some lifelong friends!"

Peer Buddies
Metropolitan Nashville Peer Buddy Program

Although you may assume that students want to become peer buddies because they are mainly interested in spending time with classmates with disabilities, students may choose to participate in peer buddy activities for altogether different reasons. For example, students may enroll as peer buddies because they have friends already involved in the program whose lead they are following or with whom they want to spend time. Others report that they like the added attention and recognition they get from working with teachers, administrators, and other adults as a result of participating in the program. Or, some students may just need an extra credit or an added service–learning course in their program to graduate. Regardless of the initial reason students find themselves drawn into a peer buddy program, most find it a rewarding experience even if for different reasons than they first anticipated. For example, although a student initially may enroll in the program because she thinks it will be an "easy A," she may develop meaningful friendships and learn important life lessons.

Planning and Developing Recruiting Strategies

It is important to plan ahead your recruitment strategies. When starting up a new peer buddy program, active recruitment is necessary (Hughes & Carter, 2000). We suggest that you start slowly and be selective for the first few semesters as you establish the course expectations and reputation of the program. Starting off too quickly can overwhelm teachers and leave peer buddies without the assistance needed to interact effectively with their classmates with disabilities. Moreover, a fast start can result in students perceiving the program to be just an easy grade with few responsibilities. Starting more slowly provides time to experiment with program ideas, such as having students complete a community needs assessment together or plant a community garden, while you develop procedures that make the most sense for your students and school.

After the first year, however, you can expect that the peer buddies will do a large part of the recruiting for you. For most students, the program overwhelmingly is a positive experience, and students usually are eager to tell their friends and classmates about their experiences as a peer buddy (Hughes et al., 2001). For example, a popular and conscientious softball player whom we know enrolled as a peer buddy at the urging of her coach. After an entire semester of hearing stories about the relationships she developed and the enjoyment she derived from interacting with special education peers, several of her teammates also decided to sign up for the course the following school semester. This phenomenon of peers recruiting peers—evident across all of the schools we have worked with—highlights the importance of identifying and enrolling quality peer buddies right from the start.

Ways to Recruit Peer Buddies

How *do* you recruit students to a new program, especially if you are new to a school yourself? Secondary school students are notorious for having a full plate of competing events filling up their lives—let alone a heavy load of classes and other school activities demanding their time and attention. Therefore, it is important to get the word out early in the school year to students about opportunities for becoming a peer buddy, rather than simply waiting and hoping that students will just sign up. In the following section, we describe strategies for doing just that. The particular strategies you decide to use, however, should be determined in light of the goals, time constraints, and available resources in your own school.

Inclusive Classrooms

A logical place to begin your recruiting efforts is within those general education classes, such as natural science, algebra, and American government, in which students with disabilities already are enrolled. General education students in these classes, of course, already are familiar with the course content of the class and some may have begun developing relationships with their special education peers. If you are a general or special education teacher, you could (a) approach one or more students discreetly about serving as a peer buddy or (b) make a brief announcement when a special education student is out of the classroom to see if a classmate shows interest in volunteering to work with the student. Without fail, one or more students will express an interest in becoming a peer buddy. If you are a school counselor, administrator, or pre-service teacher, you still will have opportunities to visit classrooms and identify potential recruits. Of course, permission to approach classmates should always first be sought from the student needing assistance or wishing to increase interactions with classmates.

"During first period, I make sure that the special education student is sitting near bright, understanding students who, on their own or with private prompting from me, act as peer buddies to the student."

Ms. Carroll
General Education Teacher

Teachers learn from each other. Below are strategies teachers report having used to identify peer buddies from within or outside their classrooms (Hughes & Carter, 2000):

- Begin by asking students with disabilities if there are particular peers in their general education classes with whom they would like to work or interact. Approach these peers and inquire whether they would be interested in being a peer buddy.
- Carefully observe your students throughout the class period. With whom do students with disabilities seem to interact? What naturally developing relationships are occurring between these students and their general education peers?
- Asking for volunteers is another effective approach. At the beginning of the school year, share with your class that a need exists for students interested in partnering with their classmates with disabilities to spend time with or provide ongoing support.
- In some classrooms, it may be difficult to identify a single peer who is always available to provide support. In such classrooms, consider identifying a small group of peers (three to five) who could rotate as a student's peer buddy over the course of a semester. As an added benefit, the student with a disability gains opportunities to spend time getting to know multiple classmates.
- Asking all students in a class to work with their classmate with a disability at some point during the school year is another strategy used by teachers. Although this approach enables students to interact with every one of their classmates at least once, it may have the drawback of limiting students' opportunities to develop ongoing relationships with any one student.
- Peer buddies can be recruited from outside of your classroom by posting an announcement on a bulletin board or asking other teachers to identify potential peers. You may also know of students who are enrolled in your classes during other periods who may make great peer buddies.
- Do not be surprised if the initiative to assist a classmate comes from a general education student him- or herself. Be observant of students who express an interest in or already have begun helping a classmate become part of a class or participate more in classroom activities.
- Selecting a peer buddy does not always have to be a formal process. A teacher may just pair two students together for a single assignment during a class period based on similar interests, proximity, or needs.

Related Classes

You also can present information about your newly developed peer buddy program during times when disability-related issues are addressed in health, government, science, or literature classes. For example, a teacher in a civics class may be teaching a unit on twentieth-century legislation. Volunteer to serve as a guest speaker and lead a discussion on legal issues related to the education of students with disabilities. Your conversation can lead naturally to a discussion of how students can be involved actively in improving the educational experiences of special education students in their own school. If your school has service–learning or community service credits or experiences required for graduation, this is a good chance to let students know that they can work toward these requirements by enrolling in the peer buddy program.

Teachers also report spreading the word about a peer buddy program by visiting classes that all students are required to take at some point before graduation, such as American history, physical education, or English. That way teachers can be assured that, over time, they have reached all students in a school. Classroom teachers often allow such brief announcements at the beginning or end of their class when it is not disruptive to the class period. Of course, it is difficult for one teacher to get around to all classrooms in a school. Currently enrolled peer buddies can help you (a) during a free period, (b) as part of their peer buddy responsibilities, or (c) as a member of the class where they are making the announcement.

Assemblies

Most schools have assemblies that are designed to provide the student body with information about activities and programs available within the school. Such assemblies are a great way to get the word out to a large number of students in a short amount of time. Make your presentation brief, clear, and entertaining—providing students with general information about the program, eligibility requirements, activities and benefits, and point of contact for additional information. Plan to have a few peer buddies present with you—students are more likely to sign up for a program when they see that their peers already are involved.

Student Organizations

Some student clubs are organized around or regularly address issues related to goals of peer buddy programs, such as building school communities. Setting up a time to speak at club meetings will allow you (or peer buddy volunteers) to reach students who already have expressed some interest in the goals that you are trying to accomplish. In addition, students in a service club may already be seeking opportunities to participate in service–learning activities. You can present how students could participate in such activities alongside their classmates with disabilities. For example, members of a health science club may be interested in learning about issues relating to medical treatment of disabilities. Other possible clubs include Future Teachers of America, National Honor Society, or Key Club.

Teachers

Many teachers within a school likely have a good idea of students in their classes who would be competent peer buddies. Sharing information about the peer buddy program at a faculty meeting and posting information in the faculty lounge are effective ways to let other teachers know about peer buddy opportunities for students (see Chapter 3). Interested teachers can "talk up" the program to students, stressing potential benefits that students are likely to experience. Identifying key teachers who are especially well-known or popular among students and getting these teachers on board may help to get your recruiting off the ground. For example, the enthusiasm and recommendation of a popular coach, teacher, educational assistant, or staff person can go a long way in fueling interest in the program among students.

"The peer buddy who was working with students in my class had been in the same class last year. This helped because she was familiar with the activities we do in class. This allowed the students to keep up in class and to get immediate 1:1 help on a consistent basis when I couldn't give it to them."

Ms. Martinez
General Education Teacher

Administrators

Not only is it important to have a building principal involved in developing a new peer buddy program, also remember that the principal interacts or comes in contact with most of the students in a school sometime throughout the typical day. For example, principals often interact with student officers or club leaders who are delivering announcements over the loudspeaker system from the central office. Therefore, the principal is an obvious person to consult for recommendations about students who can contribute to the school climate as peer buddies as well as benefit themselves from participation. Also, the principal is no doubt keenly aware of students who are less "successful" in a traditional sense in school but who have unique strengths to offer the program. For example, some principals we know have selected students who were close to dropping out of school but who had exceptional warmth and empathy for others. These students have ended up being invaluable sources of support in peer buddy relationships while finding for themselves a reason for staying in school.

"I feel that administrators should be very closely involved in supervision and follow-up. They should also play a big role in the screening process. There are many students who could benefit from participating in this type of program. It's not always the student who is already 'good,' but also the student who needs to be exposed to what it's like to have to live with a disability. Oftentimes, administrators can assist with suggesting such students."

Mr. Bowman
Principal

School Counselors

As with principals, school counselors typically are familiar with the strengths and interests of students whom they encounter each day. Moreover, counselors are likely to know of students who are considering pursuing careers in teaching or human services or have a special gift for working collaboratively with others. Tap into the resources of the school counselor. Of course, check with school counselors to see that a description of the peer buddy course is included in your school's schedule of classes during course registration. Encourage them to "talk up" the program to students when they are registering for fall or spring semester classes. A poster about the peer buddy program on the wall in the school counselors' office during registration will be visible to virtually the entire student body.

"The peer buddy course is truly a learning experience for all students. The special education students develop other friendships outside of the classroom. As for general education students, they too develop friendships while also earning elective credit."

Ms. Rankin
Guidance Counselor

"When my guidance counselor introduced me to the idea of becoming a peer buddy, I was a little unsure of what to expect. At first, I thought it would just be something to put on my college resume. When I came to the class, the students didn't really respond to me well. It discouraged me a bit, but I told myself to be persistent. When the students finally opened up, the class became fun. I started looking forward to being with them. It made me feel good to help others and I feel honored to have been in this program. The students mean a lot to me and I hope they consider me a friend as well!"

Lakesha Bryant
Peer Buddy

As an **administrator**, you set the tone in your school. Whether the school's atmosphere is one of tolerance, acceptance, caring, and belonging has much to do with how you interact with others and what patterns you establish for how teachers, students, staff, and parents treat each other (Osterman, 2003). It is important to express and model values of mutual respect and tolerance for one another, as well as to encourage adults and students to do so too. It is also important for you to see firsthand what is going on in classrooms by spending much of your time—perhaps a third—in classrooms observing student and teacher interactions and modeling an attitude of acceptance of diversity and a culture of tolerance of individual differences (Eisner, 2002). Your actions and attitudes can foster communication in school that leads to creating a community dedicated to promoting the common good of all involved.

General Advertising

You may decide to advertise your peer buddy program using the same avenues by which other school activities are advertised—through posters, brochures, articles in the student newspaper, videos, and school announcements. Involve the school's art, photography, audiovisual, and creative writing classes or clubs in designing and producing your promotional materials. Some schools have had audiovisual classes produce videotapes as recruitment tools that are shown on the schools' closed-circuit television displays in each classroom. Of course, all media presentations should highlight the benefits of your peer buddy program and provide testimonies of students who have participated in the past. Nothing is likely to be more effective in recruiting students than watching their peers in action.

Current Peer Buddies

You do not have to look far for the most effective recruiting resource you have: currently enrolled peer buddies. These students have unique insight into effective strategies for getting their peers involved since, as students, they know best what motivates other students. Moreover, their firsthand accounts of benefits and enjoyment they have experienced as peer buddies is a more convincing advertisement than any sales pitch delivered by a teacher. Peer buddies visiting classes or setting up a recruiting table outside the school cafeteria can go a long way toward recruiting additional peers. Involving a few well-known students such as athletes or student leaders can bring almost instant status to a program's recruiting efforts. In one of the schools we know of, when members of the football and baseball teams became peer buddies, enrollment in the program immediately shot up.

"I learned a lot about different people and different aspects of disabilities. I really liked just sitting in the lunchroom and hanging out with everybody. That was my favorite part. All of my friends said, 'Man, that's so cool! I wonder how I could do that.' But it was too late because all of my friends were graduating and they could no longer do it."

Joseph Owens
Peer Buddy

Strategies for Screening Students

Importance of Developing Screening Procedures

Developing and using sensitive screening procedures before peer buddies are actually enrolled in a program are critical to the program's success. First, a screening mechanism provides both teachers and potential peer buddies with requisite information before a commitment is made to enroll a peer buddy in the course. A screening process (a) aids teachers in determining whether a particular student would be an effective peer buddy and (b) helps students decide if the program really is right for them. Second, if the number of students wanting to enroll as peer buddies exceeds the number a program can accommodate, a screening tool can assist school staff in selecting which students should be involved during a particular semester. Because there should be no more peer buddies at any one time in a program than teachers feel they can work with, it may be necessary to pick which of several interested students can enroll. Additional students can be put on a waiting list for enrolling during another semester.

"One of the reasons I want to become a peer buddy is to understand how to deal with children and adults with disabilities and to be sensitive to them. I also want to learn how not to feel uncomfortable around them. Plus, my mom has a disability."

Ling Ling Chan
Peer Buddy

What Makes a Great Peer Buddy?—Screening Criteria

What characterizes a "good" peer buddy? To develop a screening procedure, you will need to articulate what qualities you are looking for in a student. An objective set of criteria is difficult to enumerate. Certainly patience, enthusiasm, flexibility, caring, responsibility, and consistency are important qualities to look for in a peer buddy.

Open-mindedness and an attitude of acceptance and tolerance of individual differences also are fundamental peer buddy characteristics. Consistent attendance is mandatory, because both teachers and special education classmates will rely on peer buddies to be present to promote inclusion in general education settings. A student who does not show up consistently during a class period will both inconvenience the teacher and disappoint the students in a class. Moreover, students who take initiative and require minimal supervision should be sought as you will need to delegate some of your duties, such as providing individual assistance to or modifying assignments with designated students. Finally, you will need to identify students who are willing to commit the time that will be involved without backing out during the semester.

As you gain experience with your own peer buddy program, you will begin to identify specific criteria for the role of a peer buddy in your school, which likely will differ from those of a neighboring school or school district. Peer buddy roles vary from school to school or district to district, requiring additional skills. Also, we have found that although an obvious choice for a peer buddy might be a high-achieving student, a student does not have to be a straight-A student to be a successful peer buddy. Students with disabilities and those struggling with their own school programs sometimes have the most to offer in the role of a peer buddy (e.g., Tournaki & Criscitiello, 2003).

"Shaping" a Peer Buddy

You can teach a student to be a "good" peer buddy. Hughes et al. (2002, 2004) found that some peer buddies, even when they were in proximity of special education classmates, virtually ignored these students. However, when a teacher or other adult provided a simple verbal directive to interact with their classmates, social interactions increased dramatically across many different activities and settings. It could be that peer buddies, even those who have participated in a peer buddy orientation training, are not clear about the expectations of their role unless specifically instructed when in a classroom or other school setting. Shaping—rewarding successive approximations of the target behavior (e.g., Alberto & Troutman, 2003)—can be used with anyone, even peer buddies.

Peer Buddy Screening Procedures

Although you will want to develop your own peer buddy screening procedures, it is helpful to know what other schools are using. Several school districts with which we are familiar have developed screening procedures for identifying potentially successful peer buddies. These procedures include (a) school counselor referrals, (b) teacher recommendations, and (c) written applications, which we describe below.

School Counselor Referrals.   School counselors are in a prime position to identify and screen students appropriate for participation in a peer buddy program. As they work with students to iron out course schedules, school counselors can spot students who express an interest in a peer buddy program and refer these students to the teacher who is coordinating the program. Counselors also can weed out students who might not have yet developed the skills needed for enrollment in a peer buddy course—such as consistency and responsibility—but who could begin to develop these skills through a less formal commitment to interacting with students with disabilities. Counselors also must consider students' programs of study when referring students to a peer buddy program. Students do need to complete their course requirements for graduation in addition to enrolling in an elective course such as the peer buddy program. Of course, students can be reminded of graduation requirements for service–learning or community service experiences that the peer buddy program may fulfill.

"As a senior, I needed to fill a period in my class schedule. My counselor told me to consider the peer buddy program. She tried to explain to me what the program was like and how it would help me in the career path I had chosen. I was nervous at first, because I didn't know what to expect or how to act around people with disabilities. As I went to the class regularly, I felt more and more comfortable working with the special education students. The program helped me learn how to work with them, and it made me realize how fortunate I am. I love coming to class and I am going to miss it next year!"

Tim Hill
Peer Buddy

When students volunteer on their own initiative to become a peer buddy or respond enthusiastically to your mention of the program, it is probably a good indicator that they are motivated to participate. When students are pushed into the program by teachers or school counselors, however, the results may not be as positive. We can recall several situations when students were signed up for a peer buddy course because of unsuccessful experiences in other classes or because it was the only class available during a certain class period. A reluctant student rarely makes an effective peer buddy and, more often than not, the peer buddy experience will be less than optimal if a student feels pressured to participate. However, it is true that an initially resistant student can be taught to be a "good" peer buddy (see box on page 60). As a **school counselor**, you will play an important role in gauging students' true level of interest in the program and their potential for improving their skills.

Teacher Recommendations.   Classroom teachers are likely to have a clear idea from observing in their classes about which students will contribute to and benefit most from a service–learning peer buddy program. Requiring a written recommendation from a teacher who knows a peer buddy candidate well involves teachers in the process of screening participants and provides helpful information to the person responsible for coordinating the program. A written recommendation does not need to be extensive, but should focus on reasons why a teacher would or would not recommend a student as a peer buddy. We have provided an example of a teacher recommendation form in Figure 4.1 that can be modified based on the expectations of your school's peer buddy program.

Written Applications.   We also recommend that each student complete a brief written application that includes (a) previous experiences with people with disabilities, (b) reasons why a student wants to be a peer buddy, (c) clubs or activities in which a student is involved that special education students could participate in as well, and (d) a student's class schedule. This information can be helpful in gauging students' motivation for involvement and the amount of support a particular student might need, as well as assisting with matching the student with a particular special education peer or group of peers. Moreover, students' responses to application questions can provide a baseline against which to evaluate students' personal growth as a result of their involvement in the peer buddy program. We have provided one example of a peer buddy written application and class schedule in Figure 4.2 that easily can be adapted.

FIGURE 4.1   Peer Buddy Teacher Recommendation

Peer Buddy Teacher Recommendation

We are identifying students to serve as peer buddies during the upcoming semester to increase the inclusion of students with disabilities in general education. We would appreciate your input on whether the following student would make an effective peer buddy. Keep in mind that we are looking for students who are dependable, flexible, enthusiastic, friendly, and work well with others.

The following student has expressed an interest in enrolling in the peer buddy program:

_____

How long have you known this student? _____

In what capacity?_____

We would like to know whether you would recommend this student to be involved in the program.

☐ I recommend the student without reservation for the following reasons:

_____

_____

_____

☐ I recommend the student, but I do have the following reservations:

_____

_____

_____

☐ I do not recommend the student because of the following concerns about this student's ability to be an effective peer buddy:

_____

_____

_____

Additional comments: _____

_____

Teacher's signature _____ Date _____

Return this form to _____ in Room _____.
Thank you for your assistance! If you have any questions, please feel free to contact me for any additional information.

FIGURE 4.2 **Peer Buddy Application**

Peer Buddy Application Form

Please complete the following questions:

Name: _____   Homeroom: _____

Grade: _____   Lunch period: _____

Are you available during lunch or after school? _____

Guidance counselor: _____

Please list a teacher who can be contacted as a reference:

Teacher's name: _____   Class taught: _____

1. Have you had any experience working with people with disabilities? If yes, please describe.

2. What are some of the reasons you are interested in interacting with your classmates with disabilities?

3. Please list any questions, concerns, or comments you may have regarding the peer buddy program.

(continued)

FIGURE 4.2 Continued

Peer Buddy Class Schedule

Name: _____   Date: _____

Fall Semester

Clubs and activities: _____   Meeting times: _____

_____   _____

_____   _____

Please include the course, teacher, and room number (if known).

	Monday	Tuesday	Wednesday	Thursday	Friday
1					
2					
3					
4					
5					
6					

Spring Semester

Clubs and activities: _____   Meeting times: _____

_____   _____

_____   _____

Please include the course, teacher, and room number (if known).

	Monday	Tuesday	Wednesday	Thursday	Friday
1					
2					
3					
4					
5					
6					

"Becoming a peer buddy was not a very hard decision for me. It's my senior year and I had almost all of the classes that I needed to graduate. I had a class period I needed to fill—why not be a peer buddy? At first I was nervous about the possibility of being responsible for helping another student the entire class period. Once I got into the actual class, I was relieved and excited to find that all I really had to do was be their friend and help them out every now and then. By working in this class as a peer buddy, I have learned more about people living with disabilities than any book could ever teach me this school year. The special education students have become some of my favorite people at school. They have truly found a place in my heart and I'll never forget them."

Joy McWilliams
Peer Buddy

Interviewing Students. Some teachers also choose to incorporate a brief interview into the screening process—allowing both the teacher and student to gain information about whether the student and program would be a good match. Although an interview need not be formal or lengthy, teachers should (a) discuss the time commitment associated with the peer buddy program, (b) explain their expectations for student involvement, and (c) allow students to ask any questions. It is also a good idea to ask students why they want to become a peer buddy and whether they have had previous experiences with people with disabilities that they would like to share.

Providing Opportunities for Prospective Students to Observe Classes. Ideally, interested students should have an opportunity to observe students with disabilities in their classrooms or during other school activities. For example, a student could participate in an English class during which another peer buddy is assisting a student with a visual impairment. Or a prospective peer buddy could join a student with an emotional disorder at lunch. Such opportunities allow students the chance to learn firsthand about the role of a peer buddy and give teachers who are present in the environment an opportunity to determine if a student is likely to be well-suited to the program.

"The peer buddy program has high visibility in our school. You have students like Anita Hamlin participating. Everyone knows Anita, and many students see her with special education students in the cafeteria. This draws attention to the program. We even have students volunteer to take the class without credit after seeing their friends with students with disabilities around school."

Mr. Chambers
Principal

Strategies for Matching Students

In some peer buddy programs with which we are familiar, peer buddies rotate their interactions among a group or groups of special education students. In other programs, peer buddies are matched on a more permanent basis with a particular student or students. In either case, consideration must be given to the process of matching peer buddies with their special education partners. It is critical that partnerships are mutually desired by all students involved. General education students represent only one part of the interaction equation. Be sure to solicit the preferences of both general and special education student participants when planning which students will work and interact together. Remember that the ultimate goal is building a caring community among *all* students.

Matching Students

A variety of strategies exist for matching general education peer buddies with their special education partners. For example, peer buddies may identify special education students with whom they would like to work (or vice versa), or the teacher may match students on the basis of their strengths, needs, and common interests. We already have presented several strategies for matching students within a single classroom on page 55.

When coordinating a peer buddy program across an entire school, the following tips may be helpful. First, if a peer buddy will be accompanying a single special education student to general education class, a student who already has taken or currently is enrolled in the class may find it easier to develop accommodations for the partner. Second, pairing students with shared interests or experiences is a good idea. After all, we often develop friendships with people with whom we share something in common. Third, some students may already know each other from riding the same school bus or living in the same neighborhood. Pairing these students together is an obvious choice if their prior experiences have been positive.

"This is Kelly's first year in high school and she has a vibrancy and easy-going happiness that she's never had before. It's not due to one thing, I suspect, but several that all have to do with her feeling accepted and acknowledged by the peer buddies and the teachers."

Ms. Goodall
Parent

Avoiding Stigma

Great care should be taken to design peer buddy experiences that avoid making students uncomfortable. Only those special education students who wish to interact with a peer buddy should be matched with one. Some students, particularly those with mild disabilities, may not feel comfortable with having a peer buddy during the school day. Other students may prefer only to work with a peer buddy during certain class periods. Still others may appreciate interacting with a variety of peer buddies throughout the entire school day. The peer buddy program should be explained as clearly as possible to special education students, and their preferences should be sought carefully and always respected. Parents' input regarding participation in the program also should be sought.

Summary

Peer buddy programs really do benefit everyone—students, administrators, general education teachers, special education teachers, educational assistants, and parents. A peer buddy program is a model for fostering a caring and compassionate school community that practices tolerance and fosters acceptance of individual differences. Motivating and recruiting students to participate in the program benefits not only the students themselves but everyone in the school environment. Thoughtfully planning and implementing a peer buddy recruitment, screening, and matching process that takes into consideration the characteristics and needs of an individual school environment is critical to the success of any peer buddy program.

CASE STUDY BOX: *Revisiting Recruitment at Roosevelt High*

Because Ms. Williams's first attempt at recruiting peer buddies at Roosevelt High seemed like such a disaster, she decided to meet with Mr. Haymaker, the school counselor, and several general education teachers to brainstorm peer buddy recruitment strategies. As a group, they decided that a sensible first step in the recruitment process would be to "cast a wide net" and widely publicize the program though a variety of means, such as posters in the hall and announcements over the loudspeaker system. That way, there would be a range of students from which to choose as they started up the first semester of the new program. Next, the group agreed that a critical step was to articulate the qualities they expected in a peer buddy. They reasoned that "if you don't know what you want, then don't be surprised with what you get!" Peer buddy qualities such as responsibility, friendliness, caring, and honesty quickly found places on the group's list. At the same time, they did not want to overlook students who might contribute to and benefit from the peer buddy experience, but who did not necessarily possess all of the qualities of the "perfect" peer buddy. The group felt that some students might not yet have had the opportunity to demonstrate their responsibility, compassion, or "hidden" talents—such as a sense of humor or the ability to draw out classmates who were shy or reserved. Therefore, the group committed to holding a brief interview with each student who expressed an interest in the peer buddy program. Such a conversation, they felt, would enable them also to apply their "teacher instincts" to the process of selecting peer buddies and picking that student who just seemed to have "it."

Ms. Williams and Mr. Haymaker decided to supplement their recruitment efforts by approaching other teachers with both a description of the program and the qualities that they were looking for in student participants. They asked the teachers to keep the program in mind over the next few weeks and to think about students who might benefit from participation in the program. Soon, these teachers began sharing the names of potential peer buddies, which were added to those identified from the schoolwide recruitment efforts, and the selection process had begun. Screening procedures consisted of interviewing students, having them complete written applications, and giving them a chance to observe some special education students in class. Based on this process, ten students were chosen as peer buddies to begin the new program. More peer buddies from the pool of students identified in the recruitment process would be added later once the new program got off the ground. Ms. Williams, Mr. Haymaker, and the rest of the group were thrilled with the new peer buddies they had selected and couldn't wait to get them started.

Learning Activities

- List five recruitment strategies discussed in this chapter that make the most sense within your particular school, classroom, or practicum site. What additional strategies would be effective within your school? Prioritize the strategies you plan to use in starting up a peer buddy program.
- List characteristics that you and others in your school agree would make a great peer buddy. What qualities differentiate between an effective peer buddy and a less effective peer buddy? Make a list of skills a peer buddy needs from Day 1 and another list of skills that could be taught "on the job."
- Outline a plan for recruiting, screening, and matching peer buddies in your school using strategies suggested in this chapter. Share your plan with teachers, administrators, and other staff and revise your plan as needed according to their feedback. Alternately, you can start the planning process by brainstorming a plan with others.

- Brainstorm with others how you can involve the widest range of students in a peer buddy program. For example, have you noticed that mainly young women rather that young men sign up to be peer buddies? Or do most of your recruits tend to be from a certain club or activity? Develop strategies for expanding your recruitment efforts to reach additional students, including students who rarely get involved in extracurricular or service–learning projects.

References

Alberto, P. A., & Troutman, A. C. (2003). *Applied behavior analysis for teachers* (6th ed.). Upper Saddle River, NJ: Prentice-Hall.

Carter, E. W., Hughes, C., Copeland, S. R., & Breen, C. (2001). Differences between high school students who do and do not volunteer to participate in peer interaction programs. *Journal of the Association for Persons with Severe Handicaps, 26*, 229–239.

Eisner, E. W. (2002). The kind of schools we need. *Phi Delta Kappan, 83*, 576–583.

Hughes, C., & Carter, E. W. (2000). *The transition handbook: Strategies high school teachers use that work!* Baltimore: Paul H. Brookes.

Hughes, C., Carter, E. W., Hughes, T., Bradford, E., & Copeland, S. R. (2002). Effects of instructional versus non-instructional roles on the social interactions of high school students. *Education and Training in Mental Retardation and Developmental Disabilities, 37*, 262–272.

Hughes, C., Copeland, S. R., Guth, C., Rung, L. L., Hwang, B., Kleeb, G., & Strong, M. (2001). General education students' perspectives on their involvement in a high school peer buddy program. *Education and Training in Mental Retardation and Developmental Disabilities, 36*, 343–356.

Hughes, C., Fowler, S. E., Copeland, S. R., Agran, M., Wehmeyer, M. L., & Church-Pupke, P. P. (2004). Supporting high school students to engage in recreational activities with peers. *Behavior Modification, 28*, 3–27.

Osterman, K. F. (2003). Preventing school violence. *Phi Delta Kappan, 84*, 622–627.

Tournaki, N., & Criscitiello, E. (2003). Using peer tutoring as a successful part of behavior management. *TEACHING Exceptional Children, 36*(2), 22–29.

5 Developing Procedures and Communicating Expectations

In this chapter, you will learn about . . .

- Developing procedures for day-to-day peer buddy program implementation.
- Establishing and communicating program expectations.
- Conducting orientation for new peer buddies.
- Compiling peer buddy student and staff handbooks.

Why? . . .

Developing clear procedures and communicating expectations to program participants can help ensure that students and school staff get the most out of a peer buddy program. In this chapter, we provide teacher-tested guidelines for the day-to-day operation of a service–learning peer buddy program to help get you off to a successful start. Conducting an orientation session can help prepare general education students for their participation in a service–learning program, to interact appropriately with their peers and to provide support effectively. This chapter provides strategies for (a) developing procedures that keep a program running smoothly, (b) communicating expectations to program participants, (c) conducting orientation for new peer buddies, and (d) creating peer buddy handbooks.

CASE STUDY BOX: Off to a Slow Start

Ms. Wylie, a seventh-grade school counselor at Shenandoah Middle School, had long been convinced that a peer buddy program could make a substantial and positive impact on her school community. As evidenced by the school's mission statement and school improvement plan, faculty and staff already had committed themselves to the goals of schoolwide inclusion, academic excellence, citizenship, and compassion. It seemed like a peer buddy program could go a long way toward supporting these schoolwide goals, which is why Ms. Wylie had been instrumental in getting a program up and running at Shenandoah.

However, although the Shenandoah peer buddy program was already in its third year, Ms. Wylie sensed that the program was not having the resounding impact she had envisioned. Sure, several peer buddies had enrolled in the program each semester and interacted with their schoolmates with disabilities across the school campus. But, as she watched and spoke with the peer buddies, she realized that they were often uncomfortable with their new roles. Unsure of their responsibilities within the program, many peer buddies shared that they were not always clear about teachers' expectations for them. Moreover, several students said they felt unprepared when interacting with students communicated with few words or who

(continued)

sometimes had behavioral outbursts. Ms. Wylie was certain that all students could benefit more from the program than they presently were.

At the same time, Ms. Wylie's conversations with participating general and special education teachers revealed that they too were encountering occasional challenges. For example, some teachers were unclear who was responsible for supervising and supporting peer buddies and their classmates with disabilities, especially when interactions occurred outside of the classroom. Moreover, some teachers felt that peer buddies could be doing a better job of supporting their classmates. It seemed that some teachers were spending an excessive amount of time trying to keep peer buddies focused on their responsibilities.

Ms. Wylie wanted to make certain that the program truly was a beneficial experience for everyone involved. Perhaps staff had jumped too quickly into the program without thinking through many of the issues that might arise. Determined that the program could be a real success if these issues were addressed, Ms. Wylie set out to determine exactly what support teachers and students would need for the program to be successful. But where should she begin?

With the support of school staff in hand (Chapter 3) and a cohort of peer buddies signed up (Chapter 4), you are almost ready to get your program under way. But as Ms. Wylie realized, to have a truly successful peer buddy program, school staff must develop and implement procedures that keep a program running effectively—whether a program involves only a few students or an entire school. Service–learning experiences, such as those gained through a peer buddy program, require careful planning prior to getting underway. Making certain that clear procedures have been developed and communicated to students, teachers, and other school staff maximizes benefits experienced by everyone. This chapter provides an overview of procedures that contribute to meaningful peer buddy experiences for all participants.

Developing Program Implementation Procedures

In Chapter 4, we discussed strategies for recruiting peer buddy participants. Before actually starting up your program, however, program procedures must be developed so that teachers, educational assistants, administrators, counselors, and students are clear about their roles and responsibilities (Hughes et al., 1999). In the following section, we discuss issues that must be addressed for (a) teachers and educational assistants, (b) administrators, (c) school counselors, and (d) peer buddies prior to getting a service–learning peer buddy program established.

Teachers and Educational Assistants

Several program-related issues must be addressed among special education teachers, general education teachers, and educational assistants. These issues are discussed in greater detail in Chapter 7, Implementing Peer Buddy Programs Inside and Outside of the Classroom.

Agreeing upon Expectations for Peer Buddies.   As a group, teachers and educational assistants in a school must meet to discuss and come to consensus regarding roles, responsibilities, and expectations for peer buddies in their particular school. Expectations and roles will vary from school to school, which is why staff should strive to develop their own expectations. For example, in some schools, peer buddies will be

FIGURE 5.1   Peer Buddy Expectation Checklist

Peer Buddy Expectation Checklist

☐ **What is the focus of peer buddies' interactions with their classmates with disabilities?**
Peer buddies at Hacienda High will (a) provide academic support to students with disabilities in content area classes, (b) interact socially during physical education classes and lunch, (c) accompany students to community-based job training experiences, and (d) work together on community service projects.

☐ **Where will students' interactions take place?**
Students will interact with each other (a) in general education, special education, and career exploration classrooms according to class schedules of students with disabilities; (b) during transition times between classes when moving from class to class; (c) in the cafeteria during lunch and in the gymnasium during physical education classes; and (d) in extracurricular activities and club settings. In classroom settings, teachers must identify how students will work together in ways that blend with the classroom routine and do not interrupt other classmates.

☐ **How will students be assigned to or matched with each other?**
In assigning peer buddies to special education students, the following guidelines should be followed: (a) Avoid placing too many students with disabilities and peer buddies in a single classroom, (b) match students with disabilities with peer buddies prior to enrolling them in a general education class, and (c) pair students who have shared interests or good relationships. Classroom teachers can choose to pair peer buddies with a single student or rotate students throughout the semester.

---

expected to accompany their special education classmates to work–study jobs. In other schools, peer buddies will focus more on adapting academic assignments and teaching study skills. Teachers in one school used the checklist in Figure 5.1 to help staff articulate and agree upon their expectations for peer buddies.

> "I like having one or two peer buddies per class. Two special education students can work well with one peer buddy in a class. I do not assign more than two students to a buddy in my classes."
>
> *Mr. Jensen*
> *General Education Teacher*

Maintaining Communication.   When peer buddy programs are implemented school-wide, peer buddies and their classmates with disabilities may be scattered across multiple school settings throughout the school day. As a result, it is important that general and special education teachers discuss how they will maintain communication and share information with each other. Similarly, a contact person should be established for peer buddies in case students need to ask questions or report challenges. This point of contact could be the classroom teacher, club sponsor, lunchroom monitor, special educator, job coach, educational assistant, or school counselor. A communication system also must be established for reporting emergencies, such as seizures or accidents (see p. 87).

Supervising Peer Buddies.   Most peer buddies will need occasional support, guidance, and information throughout their involvement in the program (see Chapter 6, Supporting Peer Buddy Participants). Therefore, it is important to determine which staff members will be responsible for the day-to-day supervision of peer buddies. For example, in a geography class, peer buddies could be told to go to the general education teacher for academic-related questions but to ask the special education teacher when they have questions about the social behavior of the student with whom they are working. Supervisory roles will differ across schools and even within school settings. In all settings, however, these roles must be established and communicated to program participants prior to program startup.

Defining Educational Assistant Roles.   For some students with disabilities, the assistance provided by peer buddies may be sufficient for these students to be successful in the general education classroom. Other students, particularly those with more severe disabilities, may require additional support from an educational assistant. In these situations, teachers should establish clear procedures to guide educational assistants in supervising students with disabilities and their peer buddies. Peer buddies should be informed with respect to the "chain of command" and who their immediate supervisor is. Boundaries should be established between the responsibilities of the peer buddy and those of the educational assistant.

"Teachers need to be mindful of what tasks they want the peer buddies to do. They need to remember that peer buddies are not educational assistants and should not be given certain responsibilities."

Mr. Solomon
Special Education Teacher

Administrators

Administrators should be kept abreast of any procedures established for the peer buddy program. Although administrators typically are not involved in the day-to-day operations of a peer buddy program, they are responsible for making sure that all students are benefiting from their educational experiences. Therefore, it is important to keep administrators aware of the activities in which students and teachers are engaged. For example, peer buddies may need permission from administrators to walk students from class to class or travel off-campus to a community-based job training site with students with disabilities. Teachers also should determine the type and frequency of communication that an administrator desires and which administrator in a school should serve as the contact for needed materials, resources, and questions.

School Counselors

School counselors ultimately are responsible for overseeing students' programs of study and ensuring that students have requisite academic credits to graduate or to be eligible for a particular post-school program, such as a vocational–technical school. As students sign up to be peer buddies, school counselors must check to see that they are receiving appropriate credit—such as ½ social studies elective credit—as well as that students are fulfilling their other course requirements. If a school has service–learning credits or community service requirements, counselors must make sure students are receiving appropriate credit for their peer buddy experiences.

Peer Buddies

Clear, reasonable procedures for students to follow are critical to a successful experience for peer buddies. We recommend articulating up front your expectations with regard to attendance, course assignments, completion of reflective journals, and grading standards. A course syllabus is beneficial for detailing these procedures so that peer buddies can refer to them as needed during a semester.

Attendance. For students with disabilities to fully access the general curriculum, most will require ongoing, regular support. If students receive only sporadic assistance in their chemistry, history, or geometry classes, they may quickly fall behind. Special education students will naturally count on their peer buddies to (a) assist them with assignments, (b) help them participate in class activities, (c) take notes during a lecture, (d) clarify unclear directions, and (e) introduce them to others in the class. Therefore, it is critical that you develop a clear attendance policy and communicate it to the students. Stress to all peer buddies the importance of their regular, punctual attendance both for the special education students and the classroom teachers. Posting a sign-in sheet (see Figure 5.2 for an example) in a designated area and incorporating it into the peer buddies' daily routines will ensure an accurate attendance record. For peer buddies who are assisting students with disabilities in community settings or multiple general education classrooms, a portable sign-in sheet can be taken by the peer buddy to different settings and initialed by the appropriate staff in charge.

FIGURE 5.2   Peer Buddy Sign-In Sheet

Peer Buddy Sign-In Sheet

Student's Name	Period	Location	Date	Time In	Time Out	Teacher's Initials

Assignments.   In addition to regular attendance, many teachers require class assignments to encourage peer buddies to become familiar with the special education field and reflect on current issues related to people with disabilities. Although assignments should be aligned with your expectations for and the roles of peer buddies, we list in Table 5.1 example assignments that teachers in the Metropolitan Nashville Peer Buddy Program have used in their schools. Shorter assignments can be scheduled weekly, while more in-depth projects can be due at the end of the semester. For students who are able to enroll in the program more than once, consider how assignments can be made more in-depth over multiple semesters. With all assignments, establish consequences for quality and timeliness and have a clear makeup policy for late or inadequate work.

TABLE 5.1   Sample Assignments and Activities

Have peer buddies . . .

- Write an essay on what they have learned as a result of their participation in the program.
- Compose an editorial letter to the school or local newspaper about an important issue in special education.
- Assist their peers in developing a resume and applying for a job.
- Teach their peer self-determination skills such as advocating for themselves, setting goals, evaluating their academic progress, or making good choices.
- Assist their classmates with severe disabilities in developing their portfolios to meet state alternative assessment requirements.
- Write about the pros and cons of a current disability issue, such as full inclusion, community participation, supported employment, or recent legislation (e.g., ADA, IDEA).
- Complete a list of required or recommended readings developed by the teacher.
- Assist their classmates with disabilities in preparing for an IEP or person-centered planning meeting.
- Interview a teacher, administrator, job coach, service provider, or other person who works with people with disabilities about his or her experiences.
- Develop an information sheet describing careers related to supporting people with disabilities.
- Write a report about a particular type of disability.
- Complete a case study (using a pseudonym) on a classmate with whom they have been working.
- Write an essay on the benefits of the peer buddy program for students in their school.
- Complete a report on their experiences as a peer buddy.
- Modify an instructional unit for a classmate with disabilities.
- Work with other students to establish a peer support network or "circle of friends" for a classmate with disabilities.
- Develop and implement a plan for recruiting additional peer buddies for the next semester.
- Contribute an article to a peer buddy newsletter to be shared with students in programs at other schools.
- Critique a popular film that depicts individual with disabilities.
- Interview students with disabilities about their experiences at their high school.
- Work with students in an audiovisual class to develop a videotape for recruiting peer buddies.
- Develop a website with information and photographs describing the peer buddy program.

Reflective Journals.   We recommend having peer buddies complete daily or weekly reflective journals to record and think about the activities in which they have engaged and interactions they have shared. Although several approaches can be taken to help students reflect on their peer buddy experiences, such as year-end projects or portfolios, several reasons exist for incorporating reflective journals into the peer buddy experience. First, having a journal provides peer buddies with structured reflection opportunities, a requisite component of service–learning experiences (Eyler, 2002). Such writing prompts students to think about, process, and learn from their experiences, as well as improve their skills as a peer buddy. Second, journaling reinforces the view that all students have much that they can learn from each other. Third, students' entries provide teachers with insight into both the successes and challenges that peer buddies are experiencing. For example, students' entries can offer insight into concerns that the peer buddies may not be comfortable expressing verbally and allow you to give students written feedback regarding those concerns. Checking student journals weekly may enable you to identify problems that are emerging even before a peer buddy may realize it. Finally, the information that students relay through their journals can provide teachers with valuable ideas and recommendations for improving their program. Remember, journals are the personal thoughts and feelings of students. Establish ahead of time who will have access to students' journals and be certain to ask permission from students to read or share material in their journals.

There are multiple ways for peer buddies to complete reflective journals. Students can be asked to respond to specific questions posed by the teacher, report on the activities they participate in with their classmates with disabilities, or be allowed to write about whatever aspect of their peer buddy experiences they would like. Use either the structured journal format in Figure 5.3 or the written prompts listed in Table 5.2 to stimulate students' reflections.

"I think the journals helped out a lot. Keeping a journal each day, I wrote about who I worked with and what I did. So, in a way, it kind of made me buddy up with somebody different each day, so I wouldn't always be writing about the same person. The journals helped me out a lot."

Joshua Redding
Peer Buddy

Grading.   A grading system should be established based on your expectations for participating students. Because virtually all of the peer buddies' time will be spent interacting with their classmates with disabilities, teachers typically place the greatest grading emphasis on the areas of regular attendance, positive attitude, and active participation. Credit also can be incorporated for completing journal entries and/or written assignments. Although a grading system should be individualized based on your school's program, Figure 5.4 depicts one possible grading scheme based on awarding points to peer buddies on a weekly basis. Of course, you also need to establish who will assign grades to peer buddies in your school. In some schools, this is either a designated special education teacher or the general education classroom teacher. In other schools, a grade is assigned jointly by a participating general and special education teacher.

FIGURE 5.3   Sample Peer Buddy Journal

Peer Buddy Reflection Journal

Peer buddy: _____ Week of: _____

Monday

With whom did you interact today? _____

Activity: _____ Location: _____

Reflections: _____

_____

_____

_____

_____

_____

_____

Tuesday

With whom did you interact today? _____

Activity: _____ Location: _____

Reflections: _____

_____

_____

_____

_____

_____

_____

Wednesday

With whom did you interact today? _____

Activity: _____ Location: _____

Reflections: _____

_____

_____

_____

_____

_____

_____

FIGURE 5.3 Continued

Thursday

With whom did you interact today? _____

Activity: _____ Location: _____

Reflections: _____

_____

_____

_____

_____

_____

_____

Friday

With whom did you interact today? _____

Activity: _____ Location: _____

Reflections: _____

_____

_____

_____

_____

_____

_____

Overall, how would you rate your week?   1   2   3   4   5

                                                        Not too good   So-so   Great!

List any changes (both positive and negative) that you have noticed in your partner(s) over the past week:

_____

_____

Is there anything about the program that you would like to change? _____

_____

_____

Benefits experienced by your partner(s): _____

_____

_____

Benefits experienced by you: _____

_____

_____

Do you have any questions, comments, or concerns about your experiences this week? _____

_____

_____

_____

TABLE 5.2   Reflection Prompts for Peer Buddy Journal

- What were your first impressions of the peer buddy program? How have your initial impressions changed (if at all) over the course of the semester?
- What are the greatest challenges that you are encountering as a peer buddy?
- What did you do with your partner this past week?
- What did you most enjoy about your interactions this week?
- Talk about a peer buddy experience that you found especially interesting or challenging.
- What did you learn from your interactions this week?
- What types of service activities would you like to be involved in after completing this program?
- Describe in some detail a typical day as a peer buddy.
- Are there aspects of this experience that have been particularly stressful? Enjoyable?
- Have your peer buddy experiences influenced your plans for a future career? If so, how?
- How do you think your partner is benefiting from having a peer buddy?
- How are you benefiting from your experience as a peer buddy?
- What needs within your school do you feel that you fill as a result of being a peer buddy?
- Does your involvement in the peer buddy program cause you to look at the future differently than you otherwise would have?
- How do you think your presence impacts the lives of the students with disabilities that you are interacting with?
- How do your interactions with students with disabilities impact your own life?
- What has been the highlight of your peer buddy experience? What has been the low point?
- Describe your relationship with the student that you are working with.
- What has been the most "eye-opening" experience as part of the peer buddy program?
- What is the most effective strategy that you use as a peer buddy? The least effective?
- How would you describe your peer buddy experience to a friend?
- What do you think you can do to make a difference in the lives of students at your school?
- How has the experience influenced your views on human diversity?
- In what ways have your experiences challenged or strengthened your personal values?

"I use a variety of measures when I grade peer buddies assigned to me as their supervisor. The first thing I look for is attitude. I want a peer buddy who is friendly and positive and takes initiative with special education students. Attendance is also very important as are written assignments and journals. All of these go into students' 6-weeks and semester grades."

Mr. Bramlett
Special Education Teacher

When informal peer buddy activities are implemented within a single classroom, it may not be necessary for **teachers** to incorporate additional assignments or reflective journaling into peer buddies' weekly responsibilities. In some classes, it may not be practical to expect peer buddies to assist their peers with disabilities and complete their own work in a class when additional demands are placed on them. However, clear procedures still should be established for peer buddies. For example, it still is necessary to stress the importance of regular class attendance and active participation. In addition, you may choose to provide extra credit in your class for the support that peer buddies provide.

FIGURE 5.4 Sample Grading System

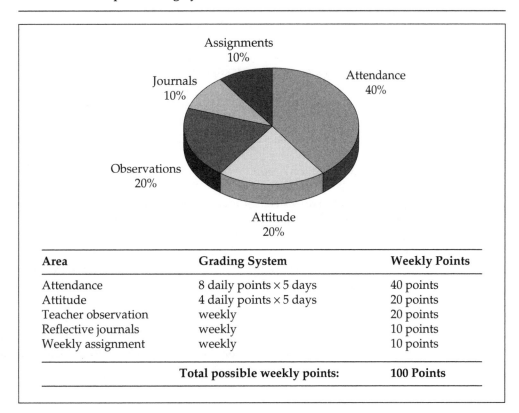

Area	Grading System	Weekly Points
Attendance	8 daily points × 5 days	40 points
Attitude	4 daily points × 5 days	20 points
Teacher observation	weekly	20 points
Reflective journals	weekly	10 points
Weekly assignment	weekly	10 points
Total possible weekly points:		**100 Points**

Communicating Expectations to Peer Buddies through Orientation Sessions

It is not unusual for peer buddies initially to feel some anxiety or hesitation about beginning their new role. Students often enroll in the peer buddy program unsure of exactly what to expect. Perhaps they have heard positive statements about the program from a friend, teacher, or school counselor, but they are not certain of what they will be doing day by day. Once you have developed clear procedures for the peer buddies enrolled in your school's program, it is critical that you communicate your expectations to them. Peer buddies will benefit from guidance and structure from a teacher, especially initially, to help them learn how to assist their classmates with disabilities in accessing social and academic activities and feel more comfortable when interacting with their special education peers. An orientation session for peer buddies is an effective way to achieve these goals.

"I was scared about being a peer buddy at first. I realize now that it was a great decision. It has helped me to understand that teenagers in special education are just like me in many ways. I really enjoy helping them learn and helping them be proud of their work. Working with the students has opened my eyes. I realize that being in special education shouldn't make anyone an outcast."

Charisse Johnston
Peer Buddy

Is a Peer Buddy Orientation Necessary?

With all the demands made on your time and resources, you may be tempted to skip an initial orientation training and send peer buddies throughout the school campus with their special education schoolmates. We strongly recommend that you not overlook the numerous benefits of a peer buddy orientation session. First, conducting orientation sessions is a systematic way to communicate to students what is expected of them as a peer buddy. Teachers often report that the best investment they made toward a successful peer buddy program was the time spent up front providing peer buddies with an initial orientation to the program. This initial training can get peer buddies off to a great start and help circumvent potential problems that peer buddies would be likely to otherwise face. Second, orientation sessions ensure that peer buddies have information needed to help them feel as comfortable as possible in their new roles, such as how to communicate with someone who uses a communication board to speak or what to do when a student refuses to comply with a request to clean up after eating. Third, orientation sessions allow teachers to set an overall tone for the program. An orientation session allows you to convey to students both the fun and responsibility of the program. Moreover, it makes it possible for you to acquaint peer buddies with disability-related issues and specific information related to the students with whom they will be interacting.

> "In retrospect, I should have taken more time for these important things. My expectations should have been clear from the very beginning and I should have done a better job of giving ongoing feedback to the students."
>
> *Ms. Mathis*
> *Special Education Teacher*

> "Initially, of course, I was timid and unaware of how to react to students with disabilities. But, we gradually became comfortable with each other. The peer buddy program has enriched my senior year and I encourage anyone who enjoys working with others to join the program. It definitely opened my mind and I feel like a better person because of it."
>
> *Paul Changas*
> *Peer Buddy*

Conducting an Orientation Session

If possible, orientation sessions should be offered during the first week of the semester, when peer buddies are just entering the program. Sessions do not need to be lengthy or exhaustive. Rather, they constitute the first step of what should be an ongoing flow of support from teachers to students. If expectations are not clear from the outset, everyone involved in the program is likely to become frustrated down the road. Some teachers devote a full class period to orientation activities for the first few days of the semester, completing all of the training before peer buddies ever start interacting with their classmates with disabilities. Other teachers who cannot allot an entire class period to training spread shorter orientation sessions over the first several weeks of the semester. For example, a teacher might meet with students once each week for 20 to 30 minutes over lunch, at a club meeting, or after school to address students' responsibilities and concerns. Such an arrangement allows students to ask questions as they become more familiar with their daily routines and responsibilities. A helpful supplement to an orientation program is ongoing opportunities to watch other peer buddies interacting with students, if possible. Regardless of the format used, teachers emphasize that the investment in time is returned many times over as peer buddies take more and more responsibility throughout the semester.

It may not be feasible to set aside time for training peer buddies during a general education classroom. However, **teachers** should not put off the orientation session altogether. Consider other approaches to orienting students, such as meeting with students before or after school, during study hall periods, or over a couple of pizzas during lunch. Guidance counselors or other teachers could also arrange to work with peer buddies outside of the classroom for several days.

As a **counselor**, you may already have considerable experience working with programs in which a primary goal is for students to work together in some capacity, such as in peer counseling, classwide tutoring, or other service–learning programs. Perhaps you have even conducted student orientations for these programs. If so, you may be able to provide valuable assistance to teachers by helping them design and implement peer buddy orientation sessions.

"Minimal time was required for training peer buddies after the initial few weeks. The peer buddies were very self-motivated and initiated activities with students."

Mr. Bowins
Special Education Teacher

"For new peer buddies who are just coming in, they need to have a couple of days where they talk to other peer buddies so they can learn about what to expect. Or, they could talk to teachers about the specific student they will be working with so they will know what to expect if, on certain days, their partner doesn't feel like doing anything."

Sammy Stokes
Peer Buddy

In this section we discuss topics that teachers have found beneficial to address within orientation sessions. A sample peer buddy orientation session schedule is found in Figure 5.5. Of course, your orientation session should be designed to reflect the topics and issues that are most relevant to the circumstances at your particular school. As you prepare for the training, develop handouts to distribute to peer buddies or to include in a peer buddy student handbook (see p. 88–90).

Program Procedures and Expectations.   Explain to peer buddies the procedures that have been established for the program and their responsibilities in the areas of attendance, assignments, journals, and other aspects of the program. Encourage students to

FIGURE 5.5   **Peer Buddy Orientation Schedule and Checklist**

Session One
- ☐ Provide an overview of the purpose of the peer buddy program.
- ☐ Allow students to observe other peer buddies interacting with students.
- ☐ Have peer buddies meet and get acquainted with the student(s) with whom they will be interacting.

Session Two
- ☐ Discuss the following topics with peer buddies:
    - ☐ Expectations for attendance, grading, assignments, and reflective journals.
    - ☐ Peer buddy roles.
    - ☐ People-first language and other disability awareness issues.
    - ☐ Student information and confidentiality.
    - ☐ Effective instructional strategies.
    - ☐ Interaction activities.
    - ☐ Suggestions for activities.
    - ☐ Addressing challenging behavior.
    - ☐ Emergency procedures.

Session Three
- ☐ Finish addressing any topics from Session Two that have not yet been covered.
- ☐ Review any forms that peer buddies will be required to complete throughout the semester.
- ☐ Brainstorm with the peer buddies strategies for increasing the social and academic participation of the students with disabilities with whom they will be interacting.
- ☐ Ask peer buddies if they have additional questions or concerns.

---

ask questions and make certain that they clearly understand your expectations and those of other participating teachers and staff.

Peer Buddy Roles.   Familiarize peer buddies with the roles that you will expect them to assume as they interact with their classmates with disabilities in various school settings. For example, peer buddies often are initially uncertain of whether their relationships should be more instructionally or socially oriented. Because the roles assigned to peer buddies are likely to influence their interactions and the nature of the relationships that may develop with their classmates (Hughes, Carter, Hughes, Bradford, & Copeland, 2002), careful consideration should be given to how these roles are assigned to students (see box on p. 83).

"I figured out my role by speaking with the teacher. She said, 'Don't try to be like the teacher. Because if you try to be a teacher, they'll treat you like a teacher. Just be their friend!'"

Benjamin Moore
Peer Buddy

"Be honest with students about what you're doing so that you don't seem fake. You've got to be true about yourself. You've got to build up a kind of bond so they know you're not there just be to like, well, I'm getting a grade for this. . . . So you know that they know that you're there for them, that you're doing this to help yourself out *and* them."

Brandi Sweeny
Peer Buddy

"I think an important component of the program is friendship. I think if you can relate to the students on a friendly level then they're more willing to be open with you or, you know, let them help you or let you help them or whatever."

Donna Davis
Peer Buddy

"You don't need to make students feel as if they're any different from anybody else. You need to talk to them about all the stuff they like to do. You just need to interact with them like you're talking to one of your other friends so they can feel important like other people."

Reggie Williams
Peer Buddy

"Most of the peer buddies maintained close interaction with their special education classmates and treated them as real friends."

Ms. McNelley
Special Education Teacher

Friendship versus Instructional Relationships

General education peer buddies may assume a variety of roles when interacting with their classmates with disabilities. For example, peer buddies may describe themselves as a friend, tutor, advocate, or instructor in relation to their peers with disabilities. Researchers suggest that there are potential benefits and drawbacks related to different peer buddy roles that should carefully be considered (e.g., Copeland et al., in press; Snell & Janney, 2000; Staub, Schwartz, Gallucci, & Peck, 1994; Van der Klift & Kunc, 1994).

Several challenges may arise from continuously placing peer buddies in the role of instructor. For example, some teachers have expressed concern that instructional roles may impede the development of friendships between general and special education students. It is argued that such roles may perpetuate stereotypes of students with disabilities and reinforce notions that these students should always be the recipients of help. Such a view also runs counter to a goal of service–learning: the reciprocity of benefits inherent in a service–learning relationship. On the other hand, assuming an instructional role may contribute to raised expectations toward peers with disabilities. When peer buddies provide instructional assistance to their classmates with disabilities, they may become more aware of their peers' capabilities.

(continued)

Peer buddy participants have reported that serving in a more egalitarian role promotes friendships with their special education classmates (Hughes et al., 2001). Indeed, friendships are more likely to occur when students view their interactions as reinforcing, reciprocal, and enjoyable. Further, reciprocal relationships help foster a climate of caring and compassion among students, a goal of service–learning peer buddy programs. Peer buddy roles should be adjusted as needed to meet students' needs, the context of the environment, and the goals of a school's peer buddy program.

"The students can really blow you away at times. Like one student just sits there and does his own little thing. Then we found out that he could read! It really shocked me when we found that out!"

Marcella Rochford
Peer Buddy

"As a peer buddy, I try to act as a role model and develop relationships with special education students. This class is a challenge and a good way to learn more about students with special needs. It is also a good way for students to help their peers with the problems that they have. Peer buddies often help their classmates improve their learning, too. This year, I have learned how to communicate with the students and to sit down with them as they read their work. Being a peer buddy is a great challenge and opportunity that most high school students need."

Andrea Dunaway
Peer Buddy

Disability and Diversity Awareness.   Often, students enter the program with far more questions than answers about issues related to disability and special education. Providing students with a general overview of issues such as person-first language, barriers to inclusion, and legislative developments can satisfy students' curiosity about people with disabilities and dispel existing stereotypes and negative images. Strategies for addressing disability issues can include showing a short disability awareness video, discussing myths and facts regarding disability, discussing similarities between people with and without disabilities, providing students with accurate information to read, or conducting a thoughtful disability simulation (Blaser, 2003; Hughes & Carter, 2000; Levison & St. Onge, 2001; National Information Center for Children and Youth with Disabilities, 2003). Some of this information also can be disseminated to students in a peer buddy handbook (pp. 88–90).

"I really did not understand people with disabilities. I felt sorry for them. I did not know what they were thinking or feeling. I never had much contact with people with disabilities. I was afraid of becoming friends with them. Now I know that every person has his or her limits and abilities. I now know that this is like becoming friends with anyone else."

Beth Hopkins
Peer Buddy

"Regardless if they have a disability or not, most people are alike. They have an individuality about themselves and they also have common links."

Lauren Kormick
Peer Buddy

Student Information and Confidentiality.   Provide peer buddies with basic information about the student(s) with whom they will be working throughout the semester. For example, it is beneficial if peer buddies are familiar with students' educational goals, modes of communication, strengths, interests, and dislikes. Some information will be specific to a student, such as issues related to his or her particular disability, and should only be shared with the peer buddies with whom the student will be interacting. Other information will be more generic and related to special education students in general.

Peer buddies must understand and remain committed to ensuring the confidentiality of the students with whom they are interacting. Although the peer buddies will benefit from knowing certain information about their classmates with disabilities, this information should remain private and not be shared with anyone without the consent of their classmate. Some teachers ask peer buddies to sign a confidentiality pledge promising not to share personal information about their partner.

"I think it would be very, very helpful to basically sit down with the peer buddies, like myself, and explain to them what the story is behind each student, what their habits are, what to expect, and stuff like that. Because I still don't know about the students. I have no idea what's wrong with them, why Bob can't talk or why John curls up and can't move his arms. It kind of frustrates me because I want to know and haven't been told."

Tammy Gentry
Peer Buddy

"I had to learn everything from my special education partner. I didn't know anything about his condition and some days he would tell me, 'Well, I'm tired and I don't feel like doing this because I'm on new medication and my medicine makes me feel this, makes me do that.'"

Carlos Soto
Peer Buddy

Instructional Strategies.   A common goal of peer buddy programs is to promote the general education access of students with disabilities. To this end, peer buddies should receive guidance on how to provide academic support to their classmates with disabilities in general education classrooms. Familiarizing peer buddies with basic instructional strategies will equip them to provide academic support more effectively. Among the topics that should be discussed during orientation sessions are (a) goal-setting strategies, (b) tips for motivating students, (c) positive reinforcement techniques, (d) ideas for modifying assignments, (e) providing instructional assistance through modeling and prompting, and (f) methods for easy data collection (see Chapter 6, Supporting Peer Buddy Participants).

"Katrina's vocabulary has increased since interacting with the peer buddies. Her communication is more age-appropriate. She's definitely more self-confident and poised."

Ms. Chadwick
Parent

Interaction Strategies.   Peer buddy programs are an effective vehicle for fostering friendships and building relationships among students. You can help these relationships get off on the right foot by providing peer buddies with some initial direction regarding how to interact socially with their classmates with disabilities. For example, you should reinforce the importance of engaging in age-appropriate interactions and activities. Peer buddies should be encouraged to interact with students as they would with their own friends, rather than as with a young child. Remember, you may be the primary model for how to interact with students with disabilities whom peer buddies see. Moreover, peer buddies should be taught effective strategies for communicating with and teaching social interaction skills to their classmates with disabilities (see Chapter 6, Supporting Peer Buddy Participants). As they interact, peer buddies will become role models for their special education peers. In addition, peer buddies will find it helpful, at least initially, if teachers provide a list of suggested activities to engage in with their special education classmates as the students get to know each other.

"My first week, Mr. Tarver asked the special education students to get up in front of the class and introduce themselves to me and I had to tell a little about me. That kind of opened them up a bit and let me know who they were and some of the things they like."

Carrie Holt
Peer Buddy

Suggestions for Activities.   Activities in which peer buddies and their special education peers engage will, of course, relate to the goals and emphasis of a particular school's program. Initially, peer buddies and their classmates with disabilities can be encouraged to get to know each other by finding out about each other's interests or eating lunch together. Daily activities, based on each school's own requirements, are likely to include (a) working on class assignments; (b) completing group projects in class; (c) finding information for a report in the library; (d) preparing a presentation for class; (e) participating in extracurricular events, such as a photography club, soccer game, or school play; (f) attending a student's off-campus work experience or community-based training site; (g) working on a community service or service–learning activity; or (g) enjoying free-time activities, such as playing games, looking at magazines, or talking about the weekend. A list of activities teachers report that peer buddies and special education peers often engage in are found in Table 5.3.

Addressing Challenging Behavior.   Provide peer buddies with recommendations for how to deal with any inappropriate behaviors that may arise during their interactions with their peers with disabilities, such as when their peer is having a difficult day and becomes uncooperative, displays overly affectionate behavior, engages in self-injuri-

---

TABLE 5.3 Frequent Activities of Peer Buddies and Classmates

- Teach classroom routines to their classmates (e.g., where to put homework, what to do when you first get to class, where to find materials).
- Read a test to a classmate and record his or her answers.
- Read or record selections from a textbook for a classmate, paraphrasing as needed.
- Help a student who uses an augmentative communication device explain to classmates how he or she uses the device to communicate.
- Help a classmate dress for physical education class.
- Model for a classmate how he or she can ask to join in an activity.
- Teach a classmate how to follow a picture schedule and locate his or her classes.
- Tutor a classmate in a specific skill, such as learning how to read a list of community words.
- Show a classmate how to "surf the Net" to find information for a classroom report.
- Take notes for a classmate during a teacher lecture and spend time discussing the notes and answering questions at the end of the period.
- Help a classmate fulfill his or her assigned role during cooperative learning activities.
- Get a classmate involved in conversations with other general education students during free time at the end of the class period.
- Work with a classmate to create a video report on an assigned topic.
- Plan and participate in a service activity within the school.

Source: Adapted from "The Peer Buddy Program is a win-win situation": Teachers' perspectives of a high school peer support program by Copeland, S. R., McCall, J., Williams, C. R., Guth, C., Carter, E. W., Presley, J. A., Fowler, S. E., & Hughes, C., *TEACHING Exceptional Children, 35*, 2002, 16–21. Copyright 2002 by The Council for Exceptional Children. Reprinted with permission.

ous behavior, or makes the peer buddy feel uncomfortable. The focus of this discussion should be what the peer buddy can do to prevent or alleviate challenging behavior and when it is appropriate for peer buddies to seek assistance from a teacher or educational assistant.

"At the beginning of the year, guidelines, instruction, and procedures were explained to the peer buddies during orientation. Additional training throughout the year was monitored by the educational assistants. About an hour or two training per week was required at first and then less later on."

Ms. Holland
Special Education Teacher

Emergency Procedures.   Peer buddies must know what to do in the case of emergencies. Schoolwide policies and procedures, such as locations of fire exits and routines for exiting school quickly, should be reviewed with students and posted. Procedures for addressing health concerns and responding to accidents or violence should be established and communicated to students, as well as how and when to consult the school nurse. Because some students may have medical conditions that require attention, such as frequent seizures or use of a catheter, procedures should be established and communicated to peer buddies regarding seeking assistance when needed.

"When I first started with the class, I did not know that Kareem, one of the students in our first period class, I did not know that he had seizures. When I actually saw him go into a seizure, I mean it scared me because I did not know what to do. I had no idea what he was doing. I know it was helpful for me to learn what to do in case something like that happened again, because a couple of weeks afterwards one of the students in my government class had a seizure in the class."

Meredith Taylor
Peer Buddy

Compiling Peer Buddy Handbooks

Peer Buddy Student Handbook

An orientation session provides students with an initial introduction to their roles as peer buddies. However, it is not possible to address everything that students will want to know as they participate in a peer buddy program. Throughout the semester, students are certain to have questions arise about their new roles and the students with whom they are interacting. Developing a peer buddy student handbook provides students with a valuable resource for addressing many of the ongoing questions they are likely to have. Peer buddies often report that their handbooks are one of the greatest assets available to them.

Peer buddy handbooks should be individualized to a program's goals. Moreover, the content of a handbook should expand and change along with the program. Teachers recommend keeping track of recurring questions that peer buddies ask and adding material to a handbook that addresses these questions. Topics that teachers agree are helpful to include in a peer buddy student handbook are discussed below. Table 5.4 provides resource ideas, including websites, newsletters, and additional printed materials, to include in a handbook. Because resources are constantly updated, we encourage you always to seek out current information to provide students.

"The teacher gave us this big handbook full of stuff about different things like some of the different problems that students have and you can read about it. So, it really helped me out."

Ebony Brewster
Peer Buddy

"I would have to say that the peer buddy book was most helpful. It gives you a lot of information on what to do with the kids, like how to find out information about them. That way, you have something to talk about. Like, if they are in a bad mood, you can find a way to cheer them up in no time at all."

Nicole Locke
Peer Buddy

TABLE 5.4 Resource Ideas for Peer Buddy Handbook

Topic	Resources
Disability information	*Websites:* ■ Family Village (www.familyvillage.wisc.edu) ■ National Dissemination Center for Children with Disabilities (www.nichcy.org). *Print:* ■ Batshaw, M. L. (2002). *Children with disabilities* (5th ed.). Baltimore: Paul H. Brookes. ■ U.S. Department of Justice (2002). *A guide to disability rights laws.* Washington, DC: Author.
Disability and diversity awareness	*Websites:* ■ Disability Studies for Teachers (www.disabilitystudiesforteachers.org) ■ Disability History Museum (www.disabilitymuseum.org) *Print:* ■ Getskow, V., & Konczal, D. (1996). *Kids with special needs: Information and activities to promote awareness and understanding.* Santa Barbara, CA: Learning Works. ■ Miller, N. B., & Simmons, C. C. (1999). *Everybody's different: Understanding and changing our reactions to disabilities.* Baltimore: Paul H. Brookes. ■ National Information Center for Children and Youth with Disabilities (2003). *Resources you can use: Disability awareness.* Washington, DC: Author.
Perspectives	*Websites:* ■ Disability World (www.disabilityworld.org) ■ Phi Delta Kappan Magazine (www.pdkintl.org) ■ Mouth Magazine (www.mouthmag.com) ■ Ragged Edge Magazine (www.ragged-edge-mag.com) *Print:* ■ Newspaper, magazine, and journal editorials ■ Podell, D. (Ed.) (1997). *Perspectives: Educating exceptional learners.* Boulder, CO: Coursewise. ■ Ryndak, D. L., & Fisher, D. (Eds.). (2001). *The foundations of inclusive education: A compendium of articles on effective strategies to achieve inclusive education.* Baltimore: TASH.
Activity ideas	*Websites:* ■ Corporation for National & Community Service (www.learnandserve.org) *Print:* ■ Hughes, C., & Carter, E. W. (2000). *The transition handbook: Strategies high school teachers use that work!* Baltimore: Paul H. Brookes. ■ Salend, S. J. (1999). Facilitating friendships among diverse students. *Intervention in School and Clinic, 35,* 9–15. ■ Wilcox, B., & Bellamy, G. T. (1987). *The activities catalog: An alternative curriculum for youth and adults with severe disabilities.* Baltimore: Paul H. Brookes.
Career information	*Websites:* ■ National Clearinghouse for Professions in Special Education (www.special-ed-careers.org) ■ National Resource Center for Paraprofessionals (www.nrcpara.org) *Print:* ■ Bureau of Labor Statistics (2002). *Occupational outlook handbook.* Indianapolis: Jist. ■ Crutchfield, M. (1997). Who's teaching our children with disabilities? *NICHCY News Digest, 27,* 1–24.

- *Disability information.* Peer buddies should have access to accurate information about disabilities. Include in your handbook information about types of disabilities, such as learning disabilities, mental retardation, emotional and behavioral disorders, and visual and hearing impairments. Teachers recommend including positive stories from magazines, newspapers, or books about people with various disabilities, such as Tom Cruise (learning disabilities) and Stevie Wonder (blindness).
- *Perspectives.* Introduce peer buddies to some of the issues influencing the lives of individuals with disabilities. Include stories, editorials, and position pieces that discuss special education legislation, accessibility, inclusion, civil rights, and other disability and educational issues.
- *Activity ideas.* Brainstorm activities peer buddies can participate in along with their classmates with disabilities at your school. Include creative ideas students can use to get to know their peers with disabilities.
- *Relevant forms.* Include copies of all forms or materials that peer buddies will need over the course of the semester.
- *Career information.* Often, peer buddies develop an interest in education or human services careers as a result of their peer buddy experiences. Include in the handbook information about careers in the areas of education (e.g., special education teacher, educational assistant, adapted PE teacher, job coach), related services (e.g., art or music therapist, speech-language pathologist, therapeutic recreation specialist, school psychologist), employment (e.g., job coach or vocational rehabilitation counselor), or other human services professions (e.g., interpreter, technology specialist, diagnostician).
- *Web resources.* The Internet is overflowing with up-to-date information about disability issues. Create a list of links to websites containing helpful information that may be of interest to peer buddies, such as disability organizations, resource centers, and newsletters or other publications.

Peer Buddy Staff Handbook

As procedures are developed for teachers, educational assistants, administrators, guidance counselors, and students, compile them into a peer buddy staff handbook containing program-related information for use by teachers, administrators, and educational assistants. Periodically revisit your procedures and adjust them as needed. As the program expands to other schools within your district, this handbook can be shared with others who want to establish a program in their own classroom or school.

> "I really cannot say that I felt prepared, but I did not feel scared about doing it. It is just like when you first get married or have a baby. You do not really feel prepared or know exactly what to expect. But when it is time to do it, you do it without any problems. You learn how to be a peer buddy by actually doing it! You learn what works and what does not work."
>
> *Fiona Hinkle*
> *Peer Buddy*

Summary

A successful service–learning peer buddy program begins with careful planning. The time invested in developing clear program procedures and establishing and communicating program expectations to participants will pay off handsomely as your program grows and develops. Planning and establishing procedures are important whether a program is being introduced in only one classroom by one teacher or across an entire school district by a group of administrators, teachers, and other school personnel. Taking the time to conduct orientation sessions with new peer buddies will ensure that they are well informed and equipped for new challenges they will face. Finally, compiling and distributing peer buddy handbooks to students and staff will provide an ongoing source of information and will encourage maintenance of program procedures. Ultimately, your efforts will pay off in providing a strong foundation for a peer buddy program that will promote inclusion; access to general education; and a sense of caring, acceptance, and tolerance for all students in your school.

CASE STUDY BOX: Jump Starting Our Program

It was clear to Ms. Wylie that the Shenandoah Middle School peer buddy program needed a kick start. It seemed everyone agreed on what they wanted—schoolwide inclusion and a caring and compassionate school community. However, the steps to get there were unclear. Ms. Wylie pushed her chair back from her desk and scratched her head. Maybe she had forgotten to outline the day-to-day procedures for running a peer buddy program. Just because she had an idea what a peer buddy program should look like didn't mean anyone else shared this same vision! Maybe it was time to meet with other staff at school and decide upon the procedures and expectations for a peer buddy program. For example, what were the roles of the teachers and principal in a peer buddy program, who should supervise the peer buddies, and how should the peer buddies be evaluated on how well they were doing their job? And, maybe it would be a good idea to get these procedures and expectations in writing so they could be communicated to participants in the program and staff at school. Finally, maybe she shouldn't just assume that the peer buddies would know what to do when they spent time with their peers. Maybe what they were telling her by their actions was that they needed some training and written information to help them out in their role as peer buddies. Had Ms. Wylie assumed too much of everyone else? Had she forgotten that everybody needed to be "on the same page" when it came to starting up a new program?

Ms. Wylie pulled up her chair, got out her notebook, and got to work. She outlined a list of activities to complete over the next few weeks:

1. Meet with teachers and staff and develop procedures for running the peer buddy program.
2. Agree upon the expectations for the peer buddies.
3. Define the roles of other participants in the peer buddy program, such as the principal and educational assistants.
4. Communicate expectations to students in a peer buddy orientation session.
5. Develop peer buddy program handbooks for students and staff.

It looked like Ms. Wylie had her work cut out for her for at least the next month. But she was convinced that it would be worth it. She knew the benefits that would be available to the entire school community when the program was running full force. Seeing general and special education students participating equally at Shenandoah Middle School and fostering a community of caring would be worth the work.

Learning Activities

- What are your expectations for a peer buddy program? What are the responsibilities of a peer buddy and in what activities should peer buddies participate with their special education peers? If you are not clear about these expectations, it is likely that no one else is either. List your expectations and share them with others in your school. Revise your list based on their input.

- List the roles you envision all participants in a peer buddy program should play. For example, what is the role of the school counselor in signing up peer buddies in a program and the role of a educational assistant in supervising peer buddies? Do others agree with the roles you have envisioned for them? Negotiate any differences that may arise.

- Devise a schedule and list of topics that should be included in a peer buddy orientation session. Seek input from peer buddies on the topics you have included and suggestions for additional topics. Keep a running list of topics that should be included in a peer buddy handbook to supplement your orientation sessions.

- Make a list of resources that you will need to manage an effective peer buddy program. Brainstorm strategies for obtaining these resources. Speak with faculty sponsors of other school programs to find out how they acquired needed resources.

- As you develop your peer buddy program, keep your own reflection journal to document the challenges and successes that you experience. You will likely find that the program is as much a learning experience for you as it is for participating students.

- Are students with disabilities always on the receiving end of service–learning activities at your school? Brainstorm and list ways in which students with disabilities can be involved actively in providing service to others. How can peer buddies assist their peers in becoming involved in more reciprocal relationships and service activities?

References

Blaser, A. (2003, September/October). Awareness days: Some alternatives to simulation exercises. *Ragged Edge Online, 24*(5). Retrieved on November 4, 2003 from http://www.raggededgemagazine.com/0903/index.htm

Copeland, S. R., Hughes, C., Carter, E. W., Guth, C., Presley, J., Williams, C. R., & Fowler, S. E. (2004). Increasing access to general education: Perspectives of participants in a high school peer support program. *Remedial and Special Education, 26,* 342–352.

Copeland, S. R., McCall, J., Williams, C. R., Guth, C., Carter, E. W., Presley, J. A., Fowler, S. E., & Hughes, C. (2002). "The Peer Buddy Program is a win-win situation": Teachers' perspectives of a high school peer support program. *TEACHING Exceptional Children, 35*(1), 16–21.

Eyler, J. (2002). Reflection: Linking service and learning—linking students and communities. *Journal of Social Issues, 58,* 517–534.

Hughes, C., & Carter, E. W. (2000). *The transition handbook: Strategies high school teachers use that work!* Baltimore: Paul H. Brookes.

Hughes, C., Carter, E. W., Hughes, T., Bradford, E., & Copeland, S. R. (2002). Effects of instructional versus non-instructional roles on the social interaction of high school students. *Education and Training in Mental Retardation and Developmental Disabilities, 37,* 146–162.

Hughes, C., Copeland, S. R., Guth, C., Rung, L. L., Hwang, B., Kleeb, G., & Strong, M. (2001). General education students' perspectives on their involvement in a high school peer buddy program. *Education and Training in Mental Retardation and Developmental Disabilities, 36,* 343–356.

Hughes, C., Guth, C., Hall, S., Presley, J., Dye, M., & Byers, C. (1999). "They are my best friends": Peer buddies promote inclusion in high school. *TEACHING Exceptional Children, 31*(5), 32–37.

Levison, L., & St. Onge, I. (2001). *Disability awareness in the classroom: A resource tool for teachers and students.* Springfield, IL: Charles C. Thomas.

National Information Center for Children and Youth with Disabilities. (2003). *Resources you can use: Disability awareness.* Washington, DC: Author.

Snell, M. E., & Janney, R. (2000). *Social relationships and peer support.* Baltimore: Paul H. Brookes.

Staub, D., Schwartz, I. S., Gallucci, C., & Peck, C. (1994). Four portraits of friendship at an inclusive school. *Journal of the Association for Persons with Severe Handicaps, 19,* 314–325.

Van der Klift, E., & Kunc, N. (1994). Beyond benevolence: Friendship and the politics of help. In J. S. Thousand, R. A. Villa, & A. I. Nevin (Eds.), *Creativity and collaborative learning: A practical guide to empowering students and teachers* (pp. 391–401). Baltimore: Paul H. Brookes.

"How Do I Keep It Going?": Administering a Peer Buddy Program

6 Supporting Peer Buddy Participants

In this chapter, you will learn about . . .

- Methods for supporting, monitoring, and communicating with peer buddies.
- Steps for setting up a peer buddy club.
- Ways to help peer buddies provide academic and social support to their classmates with disabilities.
- Strategies for communicating with and supporting participating school staff.
- Tips for recognizing the contributions of all peer buddy participants.

Why? . . .

Service–learning peer buddy programs are designed to provide students with opportunities to learn, grow, and develop relationships through their interactions with a range of peers in their school. To ensure that these opportunities are beneficial, school staff should provide ongoing support and encouragement to student participants throughout the school year. In this chapter, we present strategies to (a) ensure that peer buddies and their classmates with disabilities are provided sufficient support; (b) monitor, communicate with, and obtain ongoing feedback from participating peer buddies; (c) set up an ongoing peer buddy club, and (d) teach peer buddies skills to support the academic and social needs of their special education classmates. In addition, we provide suggestions for maintaining ongoing communication among all teachers, educational assistants, administrators, and counselors involved in a peer buddy program. Finally, we discuss ways in which school staff can recognize the contributions peer buddy participants are making to their school communities.

CASE STUDY BOX: *Peer Buddy Challenges*

Jose could not wait to become a peer buddy! In his American Government class during the previous semester, he occasionally had worked informally with Ruben, a classmate with disabilities, on several class projects and service–learning activities. The two students had developed a close friendship, which encouraged Jose to decide to begin assisting his classmates on a more formal, regular basis. Full of anticipation and enthusiasm, he enrolled the first chance he could in Cameron Middle School's peer buddy program.

The semester started off without a hitch. After a brief orientation to the program provided by Mr. Consacro, the special education teacher, Jose was paired with Lena, a student with autism in Mr. Kim's seventh-grade general education language arts class. It turned out that Jose and Lena had a lot in common—they lived in the same neighborhood and went to activities at the same community center. And they got along great as well. During each lan-

(continued)

CASE STUDY BOX *Continued*

guage arts class, Jose did his best to introduce Lena to other classmates and assist her in participating in class activities. Mr. Consacro quickly realized that Jose had a real knack for working with other people. Consequently, he began to focus his assistance on students who were enrolled in other general education classrooms who did not yet have peer buddy support.

As the semester progressed, however, the language arts course content became more and more challenging. Sentence structure, literary elements, clauses, characterization—all of these new concepts were being introduced so quickly. Lena struggled to keep up with the pace of the class, and Jose found that he was having a tough time figuring out how best to assist her. He enjoyed interacting with Lena, but Jose began to wonder if he really was much help to her any more. If he was having difficulty himself, how could he be expected to assist another student to keep up?

Jose thought about asking Mr. Kim for help, but he always seemed too busy with the twenty-five other students also enrolled in the class. And Mr. Consacro, assuming Jose and Lena were doing just fine, hardly ever stopped by the classroom any more. All Jose wanted was to figure out some new ideas for helping Lena. He knew that she could do well in the class if he just did things a little differently. Jose decided he would need to approach Mr. Consacro about meeting together to discuss some of the challenges Jose was experiencing.

Now that your program is in place, your attention should turn to helping students access the substantial learning and growth opportunities associated with service–learning peer buddy programs. The benefits available to students within peer buddy programs are indeed numerous, *but students will need your ongoing support to make the most out of the program.* Moreover, feedback and suggestions obtained from peer buddies and their special education classmates can serve to improve and strengthen your program. In addition, although the majority of your support will be directed toward student participants, it is critical that you maintain regular communication with all school personnel participating in the program. Teachers, educational assistants, counselors, administrators, and parents will all benefit from your support, and each can offer valuable recommendations for modifying or revising the program, as needed. Even if you are only one teacher or staff implementing a program with just a few students, it is critical to maintain communication with staff, students, and parents to maintain support of your program. This chapter describes strategies that can assist you in effectively supporting, communicating with, and recognizing the contributions of all peer buddy participants, including (a) peer buddies, (b) students with disabilities, (c) school staff, and (d) parents.

Addressing Peer Buddy Support Needs

Peer buddy programs are designed to provide meaningful service–learning experiences for students—experiences that are enhanced when school staff make thoughtful support and ongoing encouragement readily available to peer buddies. Adjusting to a new role takes time and most students do not become "master" peer buddies overnight. By providing support and guidance to peer buddies, teachers will improve students' abilities to involve actively their classmates with disabilities in the academic and social activities that comprise a typical school day. But exactly what type of support will your peer buddies need? The best way to monitor your peer buddies' support needs is to spend time regularly observing and communicating with them.

Observing Peer Buddies

Simply observing peer buddies can provide much insight. Regularly observe peer buddies to monitor their performance and needs as they interact with their classmates with disabilities in general education classrooms, extracurricular clubs, hallways, lunchrooms, community-based instruction sites, and other school activities. Before beginning your observations, develop a checklist of skills or behaviors that you feel are important for peer buddies to demonstrate. This list should include behaviors related to those peer buddy qualities you identified as important during recruitment (Chapter 4), such as consistent attendance or flexibility, and additional behaviors that are important within the setting in which peer buddies and their classmates are interacting, such as finding needed materials at a community job site. This checklist will help focus your observations and provide you with specific information and recommendations that subsequently can be shared with peer buddies. For example, we have developed a *Peer Buddy Observation Checklist* as a tool to identify peer buddies' needs for additional supervision, training, or feedback (see Figure 6.1). This form allows teachers to (a) record the date and context of an observation, (b) evaluate peer buddies' performance when interacting with their partners, (c) list effective strategies used by peer buddies, and (d) indicate recommendations, feedback, and additional comments. Of course, this form can be adapted easily to include peer buddy skills and behaviors that are most important to goals in your own program.

As you observe peer buddies at school, your observations should be directed toward answering several questions:

- *Are there areas in which a peer buddy would benefit from additional training, information, or support?* Peer buddies may need to learn additional skills to improve their interactions with as well as provide academic assistance to their classmates with disabilities. As a teacher or staff, you occasionally may need to: (a) model how peer buddies can deliver positive feedback to their classmates; (b) supply ideas for including classmates in school activities such as a career fair, club meeting, pep rally, or homecoming event; (c) offer strategies for communicating with classmates who use assistive technology; (d) suggest ways to interact with students with challenging behavior; or (e) provide a firm reminder to peer buddies to show up to class on time.

"It was sometimes disruptive when Joel, the peer buddy, was in the class, and I had to ask him to stay focused. It can be a problem if peer buddies want exclusively to socialize with other students in the class and forget about their responsibilities. I expect Joel to work with his special education classmates and to frequently check on how they are doing."

Ms. Randall
General Education Teacher

- *Are there responsibilities that a peer buddy is performing especially well?* Perhaps peer buddies are doing an outstanding job of adapting class activities, introducing their classmates to other students, or promoting their classmates' self-management or self-determination skills. You should note these strengths and communicate them to the peer buddies. Behaviors that are reinforced or rewarded frequently are more likely to maintain. In addition, effective strategies you observe being used by some peer buddies can later be shared with additional peer buddies working with other students.

FIGURE 6.1   Peer Buddy Observation Checklist

Peer Buddy Observation Checklist

Peer buddy: _____   Classmate(s): _____

Teacher: _____   Date: _____ Period: _____

Location: _____   Activity: _____

	Never	Seldom	Often	Always
1. Dependable and helpful	1	2	3	4
2. Shows a positive attitude	1	2	3	4
3. Starts on time	1	2	3	4
4. Uses time wisely	1	2	3	4
5. Initiates activities independently	1	2	3	4
6. Stays engaged in activity	1	2	3	4
7. Has good rapport with classmate	1	2	3	4
8. Uses reinforcement effectively	1	2	3	4
9. Seeks help if needed	1	2	3	4
10. Offers encouragement to classmates	1	2	3	4
11. _____	1	2	3	4
12. _____	1	2	3	4
13. _____	1	2	3	4

Effective strategies used: _____

_____

_____

Recommendations: _____

_____

_____

_____

_____

_____   _____
        Teacher signature   Peer buddy signature

■ *Are there ways that you might improve existing learning opportunities for peer buddy participants?* Opportunities for learning must be woven intentionally into service activities. If participants do not appear to be benefiting as a result of a peer buddy program, you will need to think about how their experiences might be redesigned to maximize student learning, such as assigning students to interview local celebrities about disability issues.

We recommend that a formal observation be conducted at least once per month with each peer buddy. The *Peer Buddy Observation Schedule* (Figure 6.2) helps teachers keep track of (a) the number, location, and date of observations completed for each peer buddy; (b) anecdotal observation notes; and (c) feedback provided to the student. As just one person, it may not be possible for you to observe every peer buddy as frequently as you would like—especially as your program expands to involve more participants. Collaborate with other teachers, educational assistants, and counselors who spend time with peer buddies in other school settings. Ask them to assist you in observing peer buddies and provide them with your peer buddy checklist (Figure 6.1) and observation schedule (Figure 6.2) to guide their feedback.

As a **teacher**, if you have just one or more peer buddies interacting with students with disabilities in your own classroom, you casually can observe peer buddies on a daily basis. If possible, periodically set aside time to carry out a more focused observation of peer buddies. Ask yourself: Are peer buddies interacting more with other students than with their classmates with disabilities? Do peer buddies appear comfortable with their responsibilities? If they are enrolled in your class, do peer buddies also have enough time to complete their own classwork? Adapt the checklist in Figure 6.1 to reflect the specific expectations you hold for peer buddies in your classroom.

Communicating with Peer Buddies

When you have had an opportunity to observe the peer buddies, arrange for a time to discuss your observations with them. We suggest that you use the information you gathered from completing the *Peer Buddy Observation Checklist* to provide the peer buddies with specific feedback and recommendations regarding their performance. Moreover, regular meetings with peer buddies allow you to (a) clarify your expectations, (b) inform students of any program-related changes, and (c) obtain students' feedback on their experiences in the program. Encourage peer buddies to share any challenges they are experiencing, particularly if they have indicated specific concerns in their reflective journal entries. Monitoring students' performance and providing them with corrective feedback will allow students to know how well they are doing when interacting with their peers, as well as minimize potential problems, such as tardiness or forgetting to praise a student. Do not fail to provide constructive criticism to a peer buddy when needed, such as when a peer buddy is short-tempered with a student or forgets to show up to meet with the student.

At the same time, remember that there is much that you can learn from your conversations with and observations of peer buddies. In addition to identifying and addressing peer buddies' need for support, find out what suggestions students have for improving their peer buddy experiences. Peers can provide excellent feedback regarding which aspects of a program are working well and which would benefit from

FIGURE 6.2 Peer Buddy Observation Schedule

Peer Buddy Observation Schedule

Peer buddy: _____   Semester: Fall   Spring   Teacher: _____

	Location	Date	Observation Notes	Feedback Provided to Peer Buddy
Month 1				
Month 2				
Month 3				
Month 4				
Month 5				

improvement (Hughes et al., 2001; Kamps et al., 1998). Be sure to respond to students' recommendations, either by implementing them or explaining to students why their suggested changes cannot be made.

"We need to know what kind of disabilities the students have so we know how to help if anything goes wrong. When I first started, I didn't know what to do. I didn't get much help at first—just needed some basic guidelines. I wish there was a talk-and-share time between the teachers and the peer buddies."

"Have peer buddies experience different kinds and levels of disabilities. Allow peer buddies to work with different disabilities—they would learn more. I would like to work with more students with problems with communication."

"I would allow underclassmen to participate so they could be peer buddies for two to three years. We should get more students involved earlier."

Overbrook High School Peer Buddies

Peer Buddy Clubs

As the semester progresses, peer buddies will benefit from periodically gathering together with other peer buddies to (a) share stories of their successes and challenges, (b) brainstorm creative ideas for increasing the social and academic participation of their classmates with disabilities, (c) advocate for their classmates, (d) offer recommendations for making the program a better learning experience, and (e) have fun getting to know each other. Indeed, many of the students are sharing common experiences and likely encountering similar challenges. Peer buddies, however, may have few opportunities to get together with those from other classes throughout the day to talk about their experiences. Establishing a peer buddy club creates a forum for students to meet regularly to support and learn from the experiences of other peer buddies. Moreover, it offers opportunities for teachers to provide additional support and training to peer buddies. In the following section and in Table 6.1, Steps for Starting a Peer Buddy Club, we describe strategies for establishing a peer buddy club (Breen, 1991; Haring & Breen, 1992).

Starting a Club. Speak with an administrator to gain his or her support and find out about existing procedures for establishing new school clubs. As a teacher or counselor, you will have to take the initial steps required to set up a new club. However, we recommend involving current peer buddies in as much of the early planning as possible. Decisions will need to be made about the purpose of the club, where and when to meet, and how to publicize the club. For example, meetings might be scheduled before or after school, during lunch, or during club meeting times existent in the school schedule.

Peer buddies can spread the word about the new club through many of the same avenues, such as posters or flyers, as described in Chapter 4, Recruiting Participants. Begin by inviting students who are enrolled formally (for course credit) or informally in the peer buddy program. In addition, consider inviting students who have expressed an interest in interacting with their classmates with disabilities, but are not able to participate in the peer buddy program due to class conflicts or other reasons.

Although a faculty member may need to facilitate the first few club meetings, responsibility for club activities should gradually be turned over to the students. A faculty member initially should introduce the purpose of the program to students,

TABLE 6.1   Steps for Starting a Peer Buddy Club

Before getting started . . .
1. Obtain approval from an administrator and ask about procedures for starting a new club.
2. Identify a faculty advisor (usually a teacher or counselor).
3. Gather a core group of peer buddies to begin planning.
4. Determine an initial meeting time and place.
5. Publicize the club through any of the following avenues: posters, flyers, school newspapers, school announcements, assemblies, and current peer buddies.

During the first meeting . . .
1. Discuss the purpose of the group.
2. Help students determine a name for the club.
3. Solicit students' input and be open to their suggestions.
4. Help students identify club leaders.

During future meetings . . .
1. Offer information and resources to peer buddies, as needed.
2. Begin to reduce your direct involvement by turning over leadership responsibilities to students.
3. Create occasional opportunities for participants to connect with peer buddies at other schools.
4. Enjoy watching the club grow!

Sources: Breen & Lovinger (1991); Haring & Breen (1992); Hughes et al. (1999).

supervise club activities, gather feedback from peer buddies about how the club is going, and make needed adjustments based on students' recommendations. Peer buddy participants progressively should take ownership of the club by leading meetings, planning activities, and problem solving.

Extending Clubs across Schools.   As a peer buddy program spreads to additional schools in a district, consider how to provide opportunities for peer buddies who attend different schools to gather together periodically. Because peer buddy programs typically are local efforts, student experiences will vary from school to school. By getting together, peer buddies can share creative strategies that have been effective at their respective schools. Moreover, teachers also will benefit from opportunities to engage in conversations with staff who are working with other peer buddy programs. For example, teachers at one school in the Metropolitan Nashville Peer Buddy program developed a useful tool for modifying grading in general education classrooms (see Chapter 7). Information about using the tool was shared with other teachers when participants in peer buddy programs across different schools gathered to connect and learn from each other.

"The schools that offer the peer buddy program should meet every couple of months to discuss how the students interact with one another and how to respond to them without hurting their feelings and to figure out new activities and trips to do with the students to help them learn more."

April Murphy
Peer Buddy

Additional Peer Buddy Support Strategies

Teachers have suggested additional strategies for providing regular support to peer buddies. These strategies can be adapted to the goals and logistics of your school's program.

- One school counselor schedules one class period every other week for peer buddies to meet for feedback sessions and additional training. She sends notes to their teachers asking permission to excuse them from class that day. By rotating class periods, the peer buddies only miss one period every twelve weeks in each of their courses.
- Even when students cannot be brought together physically due to scheduling or other logistical conflicts, there are still ways to make it possible for peer buddies to support and learn from each other. For example, students have designed and distributed peer buddy newsletters in which stories, strategies, resources, and information are shared with all peer buddies. Or, a peer buddy listserv or online message board could be developed that would allow peer buddies to exchange information, questions, strategies, and encouragement over the Internet.

"It would be a nice idea if there was a newsletter to send to all of the schools to keep teachers and peer buddies informed about what is working in other classrooms."

Mr. Rosswood
Special Education Teacher

- One teacher has a suggestion box where students can drop off feedback or recommendations for the peer buddy program—anonymously if they choose. Students may have legitimate concerns that they may not feel comfortable addressing face to face with a teacher or other school staff.

Helping Peer Buddies Assist Students with Disabilities

One goal of a service–learning peer buddy program is to promote the participation of students with disabilities in the mainstream of everyday school life and to help them gain access to the general education curriculum. Peer buddies can assist their classmates with disabilities in accomplishing this goal by helping them acquire academic and social interaction skills. However, peer buddies may be unsure of exactly how to assist their classmates to access the general curricula, develop meaningful social relationships, and participate in a variety of school activities. Teachers, educational assistants, counselors, administrators, and parents must provide peer buddies with the information and skills they need to provide academic and social support effectively to their special education classmates. In the following sections, we describe strategies for teaching peer buddies to address the social and academic needs of their classmates with disabilities.

"Although I follow the same routine, every day I see something new. I make sure that Savannah has done her journal. I help Jennifer with her math. And I talk to LaCrescia and Randall about what they did the day before. They have been the highlight of my peer buddy experience. When it is all over, I will miss all of the people I have met and appreciate all that I have learned."

Brandi Givens
Peer Buddy

Identifying Support Needs of Students with Disabilities

We have described how teachers can identify the support needs of peer buddies through periodic observations. Teachers also can identify the support needs of students with disabilities by observing these students' involvement across different school activities and carefully recording and evaluating their observations. A variety of informal and formal approaches to gathering observational information are available for use by teachers (Clark, Patton, & Moulton, 2000; Cohen & Spenciner, 2003; Hughes & Carter, 2000a, 2002). For example, you could observe how well a student is performing a sequence of tasks at a community job site, how a student responds when given a choice of how to spend free time, or whether a student interacts with others at lunch or in the gym. Consistent with the requirements of the 1997 Individuals with Disabilities Education Act Amendments (PL 105-17) for incorporating students' input into their educational programming, we recommend talking with students about their perceptions of their own needs for educational support. In addition, with respect to the peer buddy program, input should be sought from students with disabilities regarding their experiences interacting with their peer buddies, need for additional support, and recommendations for improving the program. After identifying students' support needs and preferences for how that support should be delivered, brainstorm with special education students ways that peer buddies could provide some of this support.

"The peer buddies help us with things like math and reading. Jaivonna helps me with my multiplication tables in 4th period, but she never tells me the answers. The peer buddies are friendly and have smiles on their faces when they look at us and help us with our work."

Theron Sinclair
Special Education Student

Helping Peer Buddies Provide Social Support

A problem that often is identified when teachers observe special education students is their limited social interaction skills. Social skills are important for everyone and in any place—at home with family members, shopping or spending leisure time in the community, traveling from city to city, and at school or work. Students with disabilities benefit from learning social skills that help them get along better with their classmates and teachers, develop lasting friendships, and gain access to activities in the general curricula. Peer buddies can learn to play an important role in helping their classmates with disabilities acquire these important skills. What are the benefits of involving peer buddies in teaching social skills (Hughes & Carter, 2000b)? First, students know better than anyone (even more than teachers) which social behaviors are acceptable among students at their school. Indeed, students are the ones who determine which clothing styles are fashionable, which topics of conversation are "cool," and which places are most trendy to "hang out." Second, when provided with training, peer buddies may be more successful than teachers at influencing their classmates' social behavior. The modeling and feedback provided by peers can have an especially powerful impact on students, particularly during adolescence when the influence of peers is most pronounced. Third, peer buddies have access to social situations and social cliques that adults are not privy to. For example, while it might be intrusive for a educational assistant to be present when a student with a disability is eating lunch and socializing with his friends, a peer buddy could provide subtle cues to the student about her social behavior. It just makes good sense to involve actively peer buddies in helping their classmates with disabilities fit in socially.

"Social interaction skills are a deficit for all of my students; these skills are the single most difficult set of skills for an adult to teach a teenager. Peer buddies are much more successful at teaching social skills. Often, they are not trying to work on social skills, but through the course of a regular conversation or interaction, it just seems to occur. My first peer buddy, Amy, worked with Melissa on reading skills everyday. Also during the school year, personal hygiene issues were often discussed between the two. I had absolutely nothing to do with these conversations. In a period of two months, we were seeing positive changes in Melissa's cleanliness and appearance. I had been working with Melissa for one year on these same issues, as had teachers for the past several years. We had no impact on her behavior, either singly or collectively. It was amazing to me what a peer was able to accomplish in such a short time and with very little effort. By the way, this interaction has had a long-term effect on Melissa. After two years, she has maintained the skills she learned from Amy with no prompting, such as keeping her hair washed and combed, brushing her teeth, and wearing clothes that match."

Ms. Bridges
Special Education Teacher

Peer-Delivered Social Interaction Strategies

Social skill instruction can help overcome some of the social barriers that students with disabilities experience in typical high schools. When provided with training and guidance, peer buddies can make excellent teachers of social interaction skills. In fact, the research literature is replete with examples of students successfully teaching a range of important social skills.

- Peers assisted classmates with severe disabilities in learning how to use communication books to increase their social interactions. The peers were taught by their teacher how to point to pictures in their classmates' communication book and to provide opportunities for their classmates to ask and respond to questions (Hunt, Alwell, & Goetz, 1991).
- Students with emotional and behavioral disorders were taught by their general education peers to express anger appropriately. Peers role-played scenarios with the students to teach them to respond appropriately to anger-producing situations (Presley & Hughes, 2000).
- Peer buddies taught their classmates with severe disabilities to use self-instruction to increase their social interactions with other students in the school. Peers taught their classmates to (a) state a problem ("I want to talk"), (b) state the appropriate response ("I need to look and talk"), (c) evaluate the response ("I did it! I talked."), and (d) reward themselves ("I did a good job"). Peer buddies also taught their classmates "cool" conversational openers that they could use to begin an interaction with others (Hughes, Killian, & Fischer, 1996).
- Peers assisted their classmates with mental retardation in learning how to respond to common social greetings used by students at their school (Nientimp & Cole, 1992).
- While participating in leisure activities, general education peers helped their classmates with autism improve their social skills. Peers modeled, prompted, and reinforced appropriate social skills in classrooms, during lunch, and at recess (Morrison, Kamps, Garcia, & Parker, 2001).
- With the assistance of a teacher, peers developed a social support network for a classmate with disabilities. The peers hung out with the student in between classes, reinforced the students' appropriate social behavior, and met weekly with other peers to plan activities that encouraged interaction (Haring & Breen, 1992)
- Peer buddies taught their classmates with disabilities how to use picture booklets to initiate and maintain conversations with their schoolmates (Hughes et al., 2000).

How can peer buddies teach social skills to their classmates with disabilities? The box on page 105 shows that there are many different social skills peer buddies can help their peers learn. It is helpful to know that general education students in these research studies quickly learned *how to teach* their classmates these important social skills. Peer buddies have been taught to use basic direct instruction techniques such as (a) modeling appropriate social behavior, (b) providing prompting and corrective feedback, (c) reinforcing correct performance, and (d) fading their assistance (e.g., Hughes, Hugo, & Blatt, 1996; Hughes et al., 2000) to teach new social skills to their peers.

Based on our own research, we have developed a simple guide that peer buddies can use when teaching a variety of important social skills to their classmates with disabilities. Using the *Social Skills Instruction Checklist* (Figure 6.3), peer buddies can walk themselves step-by-step through teaching social skills such as starting conversations with peers, responding to criticism, asking for help from a classmate, or complimenting a friend on a new outfit. Model to your peer buddies how to use the checklist, observe them in action with their classmates, and provide corrective feedback as needed as the peer buddies learn the new skill of teaching social interaction behaviors to others.

FIGURE 6.3   Social Skills Instruction Checklist

Social Skills Instruction Checklist

Follow these steps when teaching social skills to your classmates. As you complete each step, simply mark it off on the checklist. If you have any questions, ask your teacher.

☐ Spend time with the student and observe how he or she interacts with classmates and teachers.

☐ Find out from the teacher which skill he or she wants you to teach your classmate.

☐ Help the student set a social skills goal related to the skill identified by the teacher.

☐ Explain to the student why learning the skill will benefit him or her (give a rationale for learning the skill).

☐ Describe the skill you are going to teach.

☐ Demonstrate how to perform the skill (model the skill).

☐ Ask the student to perform the skill in the same way that you did (role-play the skill).

☐ Provide feedback to the student as he or she performs the skill (give corrective feedback if the student makes an error and provide praise when the student does it right).

☐ Provide opportunities for the student to use the skill in a variety of settings (practice).

☐ Praise the student every time you see him or her perform the skill correctly.

☐ Help the student evaluate progress toward meeting his or her goal.

☐ Remind students to use their new social skill whenever appropriate.

Source: Hughes et al. (2000, 2004).

"Throughout the year, I could see a change in how many of my students acted in social settings. I credit much of that change to the fact that the students had a peer buddy with them."

Mr. Renfro
Special Education Teacher

In addition to using the checklist, consider the following ways you can help peer buddies teach their classmates with disabilities new social skills:

- When explaining to peer buddies how to teach new social skills to their classmates, role-play the strategies that you are expecting peer buddies to use, such as modeling a behavior or verbally instructing a student. Peer buddies will feel more confident when they have practiced the strategy with you. In addition, by doing so you also will be showing them how to role-play the new skills with their classmates.

- Students with disabilities often learn social skills more quickly and use them in a greater variety of situations if they have more than one peer as a teacher (Hughes et al., 1996). Consider having a group of peer buddies each take turns teaching social interaction skills to a peer with disabilities. The students will learn to use their new skills with many people—not just with one peer who taught them the skill.

- Remember that peer buddies probably have not taught social skills to their classmates with disabilities before. You likely will need to remind them to use their new teaching strategies with their peers (Hughes, Carter, Hughes, Bradford, & Copeland, 2002). It may take several reminders from you before the peer buddies remember to and are comfortable with teaching their peers social skills.

- Some students may be hesitant to provide social feedback to their classmates with disabilities out of fear of hurting their feelings. Encourage peer buddies to respond to their classmates as they would to any of their other friends.

- Help peer buddies brainstorm ways that their classmates can become more actively involved in curricular and extracurricular activities at their school. Peer buddies are quite adept at coming up with creative strategies for promoting the social participation of their classmates. Moreover, they are acutely aware of the social expectations for different school activities and can help their peers learn social skills needed to fit in with others.

"One other person that I've really become friends with is Jacob. He was a challenge in my life that I will never forget. We have had our bad days, but we have become big friends. Jacob really started to put his trust in me after a while. Our friendship is great and it is overwhelming to see him put his trust in me. Overall, I think I have learned just as much as the students I am interacting with and this is a semester in my life I pray that I will never forget."

Jewel Agosti
Peer Buddy

"Ever since I became a peer buddy, I have enjoyed myself. The students are really nice and they are eager to learn. My favorite part of being a peer buddy was playing cards. Sometimes, my partners would win because they knew how to play their hands better than I did!"

Ramon Cruz
Peer Buddy

Helping Peer Buddies Provide Academic Support

The goal of promoting access to the general education curriculum for students with disabilities is consistent with both the Individuals with Disabilities Education Act Amendments of 1997 (PL 105-17) and the No Child Left Behind Act of 2001 (PL 107-110). Teachers are challenged to identify effective strategies for ensuring meaningful access for *all* students. Fortunately, peer buddies can play a valuable and practical role in promoting the full participation of their peers in general education classrooms. Peer buddies can help students learn a variety of academic skills—such as mathematics, language arts, or social studies skills—as well as academically related skills—such as classroom survival, problem solving, or organizational skills (Maheady, Harper, & Mallette, 2001).

You may wonder if your peer buddies will suffer academically themselves by taking time to help their special education classmates. Research suggests that both peer buddies and their classmates with disabilities benefit academically when peer buddies provide support to their classmates in general education settings (Cushing & Kennedy, 1997; Shukla, Kennedy, & Cushing, 1999). Academically strong students usually maintain their high grades when helping their special education peers. General education students who are having difficulty themselves in class may actually improve their own academic performance when assisting their classmates with disabilities. Why? First, when peer buddies are assisting their classmates with disabilities, they often get extra attention from the classroom teacher or educational assistant. Second, in order to provide assistance on classroom assignments, peer buddies must pay close attention themselves to classroom instruction. Taking responsibility for a classmate's learning has the added effect of helping peer buddies focus on their own learning. Third, many of the learning skills that peer buddies use to assist their classmates with disabilities actually help the peer buddies themselves with their own learning. For example, skills like self-monitoring, paraphrasing information, and clarifying instructions are beneficial learning strategies for *every* student.

"Being a peer buddy this year has been an unbelievable experience. I worked mainly with one particular partner. She had trouble with grammar skills, and I helped her with her workbook and assignments. She didn't always understand the first explanation I gave her, so that forced me to look more closely at my reasoning and choice of words."

Sondra Hines
Peer Buddy

"The peer buddy helps his partner to keep up in class. He provided immediate help to his partner, since I am not able to work individually with each student."

Ms. Peebles
General Education Teacher

"Our students benefit in so many ways from having peer buddies work with them. They receive so much more extra attention and the peer buddies are great role models."

Mr. Hodges
Special Education Teacher

"I liked being a peer buddy because it gave me a chance to work with others. This course helps you develop leadership and listening skills. I feel that my peer buddy experiences will help me in the future."

Jamario King
Peer Buddy

Peer-Delivered Academic Strategies

Peers can play an important role in helping their classmates with disabilities improve their academic and classroom performance. Here we overview several studies showing the effectiveness of peers as teachers of academic and academically related skills.

- Peers taught students with disabilities to self-monitor their performance of eleven important classroom survival skills, including arriving to class on time, bringing necessary materials, interacting appropriately with students and teachers, and recording class assignments in a planner (Gilberts, Agran, Hughes, & Wehmeyer, 2001).
- Peers promoted literacy and reading comprehension among seriously reading-delayed adolescents as part of Peer-Assisted Learning Strategies (PALS; Fuchs, Fuchs, & Kazdan, 1999).
- Peers were effective at teaching their classmates with severe disabilities to read sight words related to grocery shopping in the community. In fact, peers were almost as effective as teachers at helping their classmates learn new sight words (Miracle, Collins, Schuster, & Grisham-Brown, 2001).
- General education students helped three classmates with learning disabilities improve their spelling accuracy as part of a Classwide Peer Tutoring (CWPT) arrangement. Students were paired together daily to practice spelling words and awarded each other points for correct spelling (Sideridis et al., 1997).
- Students with learning disabilities and students who were at risk for academic failure increased their Spanish vocabulary as a result of participating in a reciprocal peer tutoring system (Wright, Cavanaugh, Sainato, & Heward, 1995).
- Peer tutors assisted their classmates with moderate disabilities in learning letter-writing skills in an English class. Specifically, peers provided verbal instructions and modeling to teach their classmates to write letters that included the date, greeting, body, and closing (Collins, Branson, Hall, & Rankin, 2001).

How can you help peer buddies learn to provide academic support to their classmates with disabilities? First, make certain that peer buddies receive guidance about the kinds of academic skills they are expected to teach their classmates. For example, provide clear directions and expectations as peer buddies assist their classmates in activities such as (a) designing a website in social studies class, (b) reviewing "order of operations" in an algebra class, or (c) completing a group project in health class. As they assist their classmates, peer buddies will find it helpful if they are provided a checklist—like the *Peer Buddy Checklist* in Figure 6.4—that shows clearly how they can support their peers' academic and classroom performance. Before peer buddies use the checklist with their classmates, teachers should explain each item. Teachers also can model for peer buddies how to monitor their own behavior using the checklist.

Second, for students with disabilities to fully access the general curriculum, classroom assignments, activities, and materials may need to be adapted (Janney & Snell, 2000). Although teachers should assume primary responsibility for curricular modifi-

FIGURE 6.4   Peer Buddy Checklist

Peer Buddy Checklist

Peer buddy: _____   Class: _____

Activity: _____

☐ Was I on time?

☐ Did I have a positive attitude?

☐ Did I let a teacher know in advance if I was going to be tardy or absent?

☐ Did I know which goals my classmate and I should be working on?

☐ Did I encourage my classmate by pointing out the things he or she was doing well?

☐ Did I make sure my classmate and I had all of the materials we needed for class?

☐ Did I give clear instructions to my classmate?

☐ Did I follow classroom expectations and rules?

☐ Did I ask for and listen to suggestions from the teacher?

☐ Did I ask for and listen to suggestions from my classmate?

☐ Did I respect the privacy of the classmate I was working with?

☐ _____

☐ _____

☐ _____

☐ _____

cations, peer buddies can be taught to use a variety of simple adaptations. Table 6.2 lists adaptations peer buddies have used to promote the academic participation of their classmates with disabilities. Model the use of these adaptations with actual examples, such as a written passage with important words already highlighted or an outline that has been used when taking notes during a lecture. Remember to provide peer buddies with support when needed as they assist their classmates. Suggest to peer buddies that if one type of adaptation does not work at first to "try another way" (Gold, 1980). Because students' needs and skills differ, an adaptation that works with one student may not work with another—that is why it is good for peer buddies to have a variety of adaptations available that they can use with their classmates.

Third, teach peer buddies strategies for helping their classmates with disabilities direct their own learning and take a more active role in their own education. Students with disabilities may benefit from learning self-management strategies that enable them to take more responsibility for their own academic performance. For example, general education students have taught peers with disabilities to prompt themselves to solve problems related to classroom task completion and sequencing their tasks (Hughes et al., 1996). Peer buddies also can assist their classmates in learning to self-monitor their performance of classroom behaviors associated with school success

---

TABLE 6.2 Example Classroom Adaptations

Materials
- Modify the assignment length.
- Break the assignment into smaller tasks.
- Provide an advance organizer of the activity or assignment.
- Highlight important words and concepts.
- Help the student use a tape recorder, computer, or calculator.
- Ask the teacher to provide an alternate assignment.
- Assist the student with using a personal organizer.
- Make sure the student has the right materials and is in the right place.

Learning environment
- Remove anything that may distract the student.
- Make sure the student has a clear view of the teacher and board.
- Help the student organize his or her materials.
- Help the student keep a clear desk.
- Show the student how to use a checklist to stay organized.

Instructional assistance
- Set realistic goals with the student.
- Assist with note taking.
- Give multiple, concrete examples.
- Relate the assignment to student's personal experiences.
- Provide clear, simple directions.
- Reword and paraphrase questions.
- Ask student to repeat directions back to you.
- Provide extra time to complete an activity.
- Model/demonstrate how to complete assignments.
- Praise the student often.
- Frequently review newly learned information.
- Help the student connect new information with previously learned information.
- Check frequently for student understanding.
- Teach test-taking strategies.
- Help the student evaluate his or her performance in relation to goals.

Sources: Janney & Snell (2000); Vaughn, Bos, & Schumm (2003); Williams (2001).

(Gilberts et al., 2001). Using the *Student Classroom Checklist* (Figure 6.5), peer buddies can model for their classmates how to keep track of whether they performed each of eleven important classroom behaviors. The form can easily be modified to reflect those behaviors most important within a specific classroom or adapted for use by students with more severe disabilities by simplifying the language or using pictures instead of words.

"Sometimes, it can be a challenge to think of similar alternative activities for special education students to work on when the other classroom activities are too difficult. Peer buddies can be very creative in adapting class activities for their classmates."

Ms. Stanfield
General Education Teacher

FIGURE 6.5 Student Classroom Checklist

Student Classroom Checklist

Student: _____ Peer buddy: _____

Teacher: _____ Class: _____ Date: _____

Today, my goal is _____ items checked "Yes."

☐ Yes ☐ No   Was I in the classroom when the bell rang?

☐ Yes ☐ No   Was I in my seat when the bell rang?

☐ Yes ☐ No   Did I bring all of the materials I needed to class?

☐ Yes ☐ No   Did I greet the teacher?

☐ Yes ☐ No   Did I greet other students?

☐ Yes ☐ No   Did I ask questions when appropriate?

☐ Yes ☐ No   Did I answer questions?

When addressed by the teacher:

☐ Yes ☐ No   Did I sit up straight?

☐ Yes ☐ No   Did I look at the teacher?

☐ Yes ☐ No   Did I acknowledge the teacher?

☐ Yes ☐ No   Did I record the class assignment in my planner?

Today's goal: _____

Number of items checked "Yes": _____

Did I meet my goal? ☐ Yes ☐ No

Tomorrow's goal is: _____

Source: Adapted from: Gilberts, G. H., Agran, M., Hughes, C., & Wehmeyer, M. (2001). The effects of peer-delivered self-monitoring strategies on the participation of students with severe disabilities in general education classrooms. *Journal of the Association for Persons with Severe Handicaps, 26,* 25-36. Reprinted with permission.

"Working with special education students has been an incredible experience this year. I have been able to see them grow and mature in ways I did not think were possible. When I first met the students, they hardly remembered my name. Now, they open up more and we have great friendships. Once a week, the educational assistants, peer buddies, and the teacher take turns cooking in the Home Economics classroom. It is a great activity because it gets everyone involved. Each person has a job to do and I think it makes the students feel special to know that they can do something themselves. This is just one of the many group activities we do in order to teach the students independent living skills."

Cara Gordon
Peer Buddy

As a **counselor**, you likely are familiar with various resources and strategies for promoting the social and academic skills of students. Share this information with teachers and peer buddies through casual conversations or by offering informal "in-services." In addition, offer to assist teachers with observing peer buddies and their classmates throughout the school day, particularly during times when teachers themselves are unavailable to observe students. Using the *Peer Buddy Observation Schedule* in Figure 6.2 to record what you see will help you to share your observations with teachers and will provide a permanent record.

As an **administrator**, your job is to ensure that students' schedules are arranged so that all students within your school have opportunities to interact with each other and develop friendships and a sense of community. Informally survey your school to make sure that every student has access to all school facilities, activities, and programs. Moreover, ensure that you are fostering a school climate in which students are encouraged to develop caring relationships with each other. Ask students, teachers, and other school staff for their input on the degree to which this goal is being met. Are there skills that peer buddies or their classmates with disabilities could learn in order to help create an inclusive school community?

Communicating with and Supporting School Staff

Although most of your effort will be focused on supporting peer buddies and their classmates, remember to maintain regular communication and exchange support with school staff who also are participating in the peer buddy program. Over the course of each semester, teachers, educational assistants, counselors, administrators, and parents may experience occasional challenges and frustrations. For example, a teacher may want to know how to address a peer buddy who "does too much" for his classmate with disabilities or who is frequently absent; a counselor may express frustration that she lacks the time to plan with teachers or is unsure of where to assign peer buddies; or an administrator may feel "out of the loop" of program activities. Therefore, it is essential that some mechanism be put in place by which staff can regularly communicate their frustrations and recommendations with each other. Below are strategies that can help ensure that the support needs of participating school staff are being addressed.

- Make sure that all participating teachers, counselors, and administrators have access to a peer buddy staff handbook (Chapter 5). As questions arise about program procedures, update the handbook with additional resources and information. Ask program participants to identify additional information or topics that they feel should be included in the handbook.
- Regularly check in with general education teachers in whose classrooms peer buddies are assisting students with disabilities. Respond to any questions or concerns that teachers raise and clarify your expectations for the students and their peer buddies.
- Establish agreed-upon communication avenues by which staff can contact each other if questions or concerns arise. For example, staff members might be encouraged to stop by your room, drop a note in your faculty box, or send you an email if they are having a problem. Occasionally meet as a group over lunch or coffee to address common concerns or to congratulate each other on program progress.

- Share with other teachers and staff the feedback that you are receiving from your observations of and conversations with peer buddies and their classmates with disabilities. Brainstorm solutions to any problems or concerns or plan to provide positive feedback for program successes.

- Decide if you want to require peer buddies or students with disabilities to have general education teachers initial their checklists (see Figures 6.4 and 6.5) before turning them in to you. Add a line to each form on which teachers can indicate whether they wish to be contacted by you regarding students' classroom performance.

Parent interest in school activities is a strong motivator for students. Parents of peer buddies can be supportive of a peer buddy program by asking their children about their experiences as a peer buddy. They also can model how they treat people with disabilities in the community with respect. These parents can encourage and provide opportunities for students to participate in afterschool or weekend activities with their special education peers. Parents of students with disabilities can advocate for peer buddy activities for their children both in and out of school. Remember to keep parents who are involved in the peer buddy experience informed about their youth's activities, responsibilities, and accomplishments.

Showing Appreciation to Peer Buddy Program Participants

It is important that students understand that their participation really does make a difference to their school community. Recognizing and celebrating students' contributions is an important aspect of service–learning activities (Points of Light Foundation, 2002). Why? First, recognition activities help students understand the impact they have had on their school community. Recognition fosters feelings of success and accomplishment among participants and reinforces their connection to what they have accomplished. Second, recognition activities offer a way for students to share their accomplishments with others. Parents, administrators, school staff, students, and other community members should all be given opportunities to learn about the contributions students have made to their school. Third, recognition activities bring added visibility to a peer buddy program and can help recruit a cadre of new student participants. Fourth, recognition activities can be celebratory and fun—they give participants a chance to socialize together and get to know each other better.

As an **administrator**, don't overlook the effort faculty members and counselors at your school have contributed toward making the peer buddy program a successful experience for all students. These individuals likely have given much of their own time in order to make the program a meaningful learning experience for students. Publicly recognize their contributions at faculty meetings, in school publications, and at student assemblies.

The number of formal and informal ways of providing recognition to peer buddy program participants is limited only by the creativity of your school staff. Brainstorm small and large ways to reward students with and without disabilities, school staff, and parents for their contributions to the school. Remember, recognition does not need to be elaborate, but it should be meaningful. Below are strategies school staff have used to recognize peer buddy program participants.

- Design and distribute a quarterly *Peer Buddy Newsletter* that highlights the activities and accomplishments of peer buddies and students with disabilities. Encourage students and teachers to submit positive stories about peer buddy events at their school.
- Encourage staff from the school or community newspaper to write an article about the peer buddy program and its participants.
- Devote some part of a school assembly to recognizing students for making an important contribution to the school's overall mission.
- Show your appreciation by awarding certificates of accomplishment to all peer buddy participants.
- Assist special education students in planning a pizza party to thank peer buddies for their participation.
- Plan an end-of-semester banquet for peer buddy participants, their families, and other school staff. Individually recognize students for specific accomplishments they have achieved over the past semester. Show a video or presentation of highlights and stories from the past semester.
- Recognize students by posting a short acknowledgment on the school's website or announcing accomplishments over the school's intercom or closed-circuit television system.
- If peer buddies and their classmates with disabilities have worked on a service–learning activity together, provide them with an opportunity to present publicly the project that they completed together.
- Allow peer buddies and their partners to plan an off-campus trip to celebrate their program involvement.
- The simplest way to show students, school staff, and parents that they are appreciated is to regularly tell them. A simple thank you, a brief note, or a quick email message are all effective ways to let others know much you appreciate their contribution to the school.
- Recognize students who are not enrolled in the credit course but still interact as peer buddies. Such experiences may eventually lead them to participate in the program.
- Hold an appreciation breakfast for counselors who assisted in spreading the word about the program, enrolling peer buddies, and helping teachers with the program.

Typically, recognition events are used to bring closure to service–learning activities. This should not be case with peer buddy programs. Recognition events and activities should occur throughout the lifetime of a peer buddy program. Even when students come to the end of their formal participation as a peer buddy, this should not signal that their relationships with their classmates must end.

Summary

A successful service-learning peer buddy program offers learning opportunities and provides support to all participants. To maximize these opportunities, thoughtful assistance and ongoing communication must be made available to students, teachers, counselors, administrators, and parents—whether a single classroom or an entire school or district is involved in the program. When participants are provided the support they need to effectively fulfill their roles, a peer buddy program will thrive. And when it does, be sure to let everyone know the important role that they played in making it happen by showing appreciation to program participants.

CASE STUDY BOX: *Jose Asks for Help*

To be honest, Mr. Consacro was a little surprised when Jose stopped by his classroom after school. At the beginning of the semester, Jose stood out as one of the most capable and personable peer buddies ever enrolled in the program. Mr. Consacro had no idea that Jose and Lena were having such difficulty in their language arts class. In fact, Mr. Consacro was a little ashamed that he had not been more accessible to Jose and Lena. With so many other students included in different general education classrooms, he had inadvertently let Jose and Lena slip through without his support.

Over the next few days, Mr. Consacro spent a few classes observing Jose and Lena, along with other peer buddies and their classmates, trying to figure out exactly what sort of support they needed. Quickly, Mr. Consacro realized that many of the peer buddies were experiencing similar challenges in other general education classes. Therefore, he arranged for all the peer buddies to meet together in an ongoing peer buddy club. It was time for them to learn additional strategies for helping their classmates with disabilities participate in the academic and social activities taking place within the general education classroom. Over pizza at the peer buddy meeting, Mr. Consacro shared simple strategies for adapting class activities, modeled creative ideas for explaining new concepts to classmates, and taught peer buddies how to assist their classmates in self-monitoring classroom behavior. In addition, Mr. Consacro provided students with opportunities to talk with each other about their experiences, the challenges that they were encountering, and strategies they had identified for overcoming those challenges. Jose found it incredibly helpful to receive encouragement and support from his peers as well as from Mr. Consacro. It also was good to know that they would be getting together again to meet and share experiences.

Within a few weeks, things had really turned around for Jose and Lena. Lena was showing improvement on her assignments and could see her grades beginning to rise. Jose found that the strategies Mr. Consacro taught him, such as breaking an assignment into smaller tasks, not only benefited Lena, but also helped him with his own work. From then on, Mr. Consacro made certain that he regularly observed each of the peer buddies and encouraged them to let him know about any challenges that they encountered between peer buddy club meetings.

Learning Activities

- What do you anticipate will be the biggest challenges that peer buddies encounter as a result of participating in the program? What challenges do you anticipate students with disabilities might encounter? Sit down with students to talk about their experiences in the program. How did their perceptions differ from yours? In what ways were they similar? Together with the students, list steps for addressing the most pressing challenges identified.
- Occasionally invite speakers to your peer buddy club meetings or to meetings with other school staff. Sometimes meeting people who have been involved in service–learning peer buddy programs in other schools or districts can be a "shot in the arm" for participants. List new ideas your speakers present and brainstorm with participants in your school how these ideas could be put into action.
- Make a list of academic and social goals that you are currently working on with your students. Which of these goals might peer buddies assist you in teaching or modeling for your students? Are there skills that are best taught by teachers? By peer buddies?

- How will you address problems that arise over the course of the peer buddy program? For example, a peer buddy continually may neglect her responsibilities, a teacher may decide that she no longer wants to enroll students with disabilities in her class, or an administrator may decide that peer buddy enrollment in your school should be limited. Are there actions that you could take ahead of time to prevent these situations from arising in the first place?
- List at least five new ways you can communicate with parents and staff about the peer buddy program in your school. Try to put each of these ideas into action during the current or upcoming semester.
- Ask other educators at your school about recognition activities that they have arranged for students. Which activities do they think have been most meaningful for students? Decide how you will recognize peer buddy participants for contributing to the school's mission.

References

Breen, C. G. (1991). Setting up and managing peer support networks. In C. G. Breen, C. H. Kennedy, & T. G. Haring (Eds.), *Social context research project: Methods for facilitating the inclusion of students with disabilities in integrated school and community contexts* (pp. 54–104). Santa Barbara: University of California.

Breen, C. G., & Lovinger L. (1991). PAL (Partners at Lunch) Club: Evaluation of a program to support social relationships. In C. G. Breen, C. H. Kennedy, & T. G. Haring (Eds.), *Social context research project: Methods for facilitating the inclusion of students with disabilities in integrated school and community contexts* (pp. 106–128). Santa Barbara: University of California.

Clark, G. M., Patton, J. R., & Moulton, R. (2000). *Informal assessments in transition planning.* Austin, TX: PRO-ED.

Cohen, L., G., & Spenciner, L. J. (2003). *Assessment of children and youth with special needs* (2nd ed.). Boston: Allyn and Bacon.

Collins, B. C., Branson, T. A., Hall, M., & Rankin, S. W. (2001). Teaching secondary students with moderate disabilities in an inclusive academic classroom setting. *Journal of Developmental and Physical Disabilities, 13,* 41–59.

Cushing, L. S., & Kennedy, C. H. (1997). Academic effects of providing peer support in general education classrooms on students without disabilities. *Journal of Applied Behavior Analysis, 30,* 139–152.

Fuchs, L. S., Fuchs, D., & Kazdan, S. (1999). Effects of Peer-Assisted Learning strategies on high school students with serious reading problems. *Remedial and Special Education, 20,* 309–318.

Gilberts, G. H., Agran, M., Hughes, C., & Wehmeyer, M. (2001). The effects of peer-delivered self-monitoring strategies on the participation of students with severe disabilities in general education classrooms. *Journal of the Association for Persons with Severe Handicaps, 26,* 25–36.

Gold, M. (1980). *Did I say that?* Champaign, IL: Research Press.

Haring, T. G., & Breen, C. G. (1992). A peer-mediated social network intervention to enhance the social integration of persons with moderate and severe disabilities. *Journal of Applied Behavior Analysis, 25,* 319–333.

Hughes, C., & Carter, E. W. (2000a). Strategies for identifying and promoting students' strengths. In *The transition handbook: Strategies high school teachers use that work!* (pp. 139–178). Baltimore: Paul H. Brookes.

Hughes, C., & Carter, E. W. (2000b). Strategies that promote social interaction. In *The transition handbook: Strategies high school teachers use that work!* (pp. 261–297). Baltimore: Paul H. Brookes.

Hughes, C., & Carter, E. W. (2002). Informal assessment procedures. In C. L. Sax & C. A. Thomas (Eds.), *Transition assessment: Wise practices for quality lives* (pp. 51–69). Baltimore: Paul H. Brookes.

Hughes, C., Carter, E. W., Hughes, T., Bradford, E., & Copeland, S. R. (2002). Effects of instructional versus non-instructional roles on the social interactions of high school students. *Education and Training in Mental Retardation and Developmental Disabilities, 37,* 262–272.

Hughes, C., Copeland, S. R., Guth, C., Rung, L. L., Hwang, B., Kleeb, G., & Strong, M. (2001). General education students' perspectives on their involvement in a high school peer buddy program. *Education and Training in Mental Retardation and Developmental Disabilities, 36,* 343–356.

Hughes, C., Fowler, S. E., Copeland, S. R., Agran, M., Wehmeyer, M. L, & Church-Pupke, P. P. (2004). Supporting high school students to engage in recreational activities with peers. *Behavior Modification, 28,* 3–27.

Hughes, C., Guth, C., Hall, S., Presley, J., Dye, M., & Byers, C. (1999). They are my best friends: Peer buddies promote inclusion in high school. *TEACHING Exceptional Children, 31*(5), 32–37.

Hughes, C., Hugo, K., & Blatt, J. (1996). Self-instructional intervention for teaching generalized problem-solving within a functional task sequence. *American Journal of Mental Retardation, 100,* 565–579.

Hughes, C., Killian, D. J., & Fischer, G. M. (1996). Validation and assessment of a conversational interaction intervention. *American Journal of Mental Retardation, 100,* 493–509.

Hughes, C., Rung, L. L., Wehmeyer, M., Agran, M., Copeland, S. R., & Hwang, B. (2000). Self-prompted communication book use to increase social interaction among high school students. *The Journal of the Association for Persons with Severe Handicaps, 25,* 153–166.

Hunt, P., Alwell, M., & Goetz, L. (1991). Establishing conversational exchanges with family and friends: Moving from training to meaningful communication. *The Journal of Special Education, 25,* 305–319.

Individuals with Disabilities Education Act Amendments of 1997, PL 105–17, 20 U. S. C. § 1400 *et seq.* (1997).

Janney, R., & Snell, M. E. (2000). *Modifying schoolwork.* Baltimore: Paul H. Brookes.

Kamps, D. M., Kravits, T., Gonzalez-Lopez, A., Kemmerer, K., Potucek, J., & Harrell, L. G. (1998). What do peers think? Social validity of peer-mediated programs. *Education and Treatment of Children, 21,* 107–134.

Maheady, L., Harper, G. F., & Mallette, B. (2001). Peer-mediated instruction and interventions and students with mild disabilities. *Remedial and Special Education, 22,* 4–14.

Miracle, S. A., Collins, B. A., Schuster, J. W., & Grisham-Brown, J. (2001). Peer- versus teacher-delivered instruction: Effects on acquisition and maintenance. *Education and Training in Mental Retardation and Developmental Disabilities, 36,* 373–385.

Morrison, L., Kamps, D., Garcia, J., & Parker, D. (2001). Peer mediation and monitoring strategies to improve initiations and social skills for students with autism. *Journal of Positive Behavior Interventions, 3,* 237–250.

Nientimp, E. G., & Cole, C. L. (1992). Teaching socially valid social interaction responses to students with severe disabilities in an integrated school setting. *Journal of School Psychology, 30,* 343–354.

No Child Left Behind Act of 2001, PL 107–110, 115 Stat. 1425 (2002).

Points of Light Foundation. (2002). *Recognition in service–learning.* Washington, DC: Author.

Presley, J. A., & Hughes, C. (2000). Peers as teachers of anger management to high school students with behavioral disorders. *Behavioral Disorders, 25,* 114–130.

Shukla, S., Kennedy, C., & Cushing, L. (1999). Intermediate school students with severe disabilities: Supporting their social participation in general education classrooms. *Journal of Positive Behavior Interventions, 1,* 130–140.

Sideridis, G. D., Utley, C., Greenwood, C. R., Delquadri, J., Dawson, H., Palmer, P., & Reddy, S. (1997). Classwide peer tutoring: Effects on the spelling performance and social interactions of students with mild disabilities and their typical peers in an integrated instructional setting. *Journal of Behavioral Education, 7,* 435–462.

Vaughn, S., Bos, C. S., & Schumm, J. S. (2003). *Teaching exceptional, diverse, and at-risk students in general education classrooms* (3rd ed.). Boston: Allyn and Bacon.

Williams, J. (2001). *Adaptations and accommodations for students with disabilities.* Washington, DC: National Information Center for Children and Youth with Disabilities.

Wright, J. E., Cavanaugh, R. A., Sainato, D. M., & Heward, W. L. (1995). Somos todos ayudantes y estudiantes: Evaluation of a classwide peer tutoring program in a modified Spanish class for secondary students identified as learning disabled or academically at-risk. *Education & Treatment of Children, 18,* 33–52.

Implementing Peer Buddy Programs Inside and Outside the Classroom

In this chapter, you will learn about . . .

- Teaming with other school personnel to promote inclusion in general education classrooms.
- Promoting inclusion during noninstructional times such as lunch, extracurricular activities, and after school.
- Extending peer buddy programs to community-based learning experiences.
- Transitioning students from special education to general education classrooms with the assistance of peer buddies.

Why? . . .

Recent legislative initiatives, such as the 1997 Amendments to the Individuals with Disabilities Education Act (IDEA) and the No Child Left Behind Act of 2001, emphasize the importance of providing all *students with opportunities to participate in the full range of curricular and extracurricular activities offered within school—both inside and outside the classroom. This participation is expected to extend off-campus as well, to include activities such as school sports events, community-based learning experiences, and recreational opportunities. Service–learning peer buddy programs, which pair general and special education students, are effective at promoting students' inclusion in a range of school and community settings and activities, both instructional and noninstructional. This chapter addresses issues, challenges, and new opportunities that may be encountered when implementing a peer buddy program across different settings. We also discuss strategies for adapting a program to the unique demands of different settings and tying a program into schoolwide inclusion efforts.*

CASE STUDY BOX: *A Time for Change?*

As a veteran teacher, Mr. Mason had long argued that his World History classes ran like a "well-oiled machine." Over many semesters teaching five sections of this required freshman-level course at Cedar Hill High School, Mr. Mason insisted that he carefully had worked out all of the kinks in his lectures, class activities, student assignments, and tests. But lately, Mr. Mason was beginning to encounter new challenges in his classroom. The instructional strategies and lesson plans that he had used year after year no longer seemed to be reaching all of his students. Over time, Mr. Mason noticed that his classroom was becoming increasingly, well, "diverse"—to use the new terminology he was hearing around school. Students now arrived in World History the first day of class with a wide range of backgrounds and preparation (or lack of!) for learning the course material. Some students had recently moved to the

(continued)

CASE STUDY BOX *Continued*

country and were still learning to speak English, some had considerable difficulty reading on grade level and lacked study skills, while others had little support or resources at home and often came to school tired, distracted, or hungry.

At the same time, Cedar Hill High School was taking steps to increase the inclusion of students with disabilities in general education classrooms. Mr. Mason was all for having special education students in his class, but he felt unprepared to address what he thought were their unique needs, behaviors, and challenges. Considering that he already had a classroom of students with "unique challenges" he hadn't faced in the past, how could he meet these students' needs as well of those of a whole new group of students with disabilities and get through the day without tearing out what hair he still had left on his head? Mr. Mason was beginning to think that maybe he would have to change some of his "tried-and-true" ways of teaching if he were to expect to accommodate the needs of all students in his classes.

Over a cup of coffee in the teachers' lounge, Mr. Mason struck up a conversation about his classes with a fellow history teacher, Ms. Terino. Although he hated to admit that he didn't have all the answers, he shared with Ms. Terino some of his frustrations with the wide range of needs he was facing among his students, particularly those with disabilities. He wondered how she was handling these challenges. Did she have any advice for him? With a knowing look, Ms. Terino assured Mr. Mason that she was wrestling with the same issues. But amazingly, Ms. Terino began rattling off some ideas to meet the needs of students in her class, including something that she called a "peer buddy" program. Ms. Terino said that she actually had some of her general education students helping out students with disabilities who were having difficulties, as well as other students in the class who needed help. She even shared how much the students said they enjoyed working together and how they were all benefiting, socially and academically.

Pairing students without disabilities and their classmates with disabilities—the idea certainly piqued Mr. Mason's interest. But, wasn't it his job to provide instruction and support in his classroom, not his students' ? After all, he was the teacher. Besides, Ms. Terino's idea sounded like it might take a lot of work to get off the ground. Was he really ready to change his teaching methods at this point in his career? With a hint of a smile but without a word, Ms. Terino listened carefully to Mr. Mason's hesitations about starting a peer buddy program in his class. As she left the teachers' lounge to return to class, however, she suggested that he stop by her classroom sometime to take a look for himself.

As we have emphasized throughout this book, promoting access to the general curriculum for *all* students is supported by educational legislation, including the 1997 IDEA Amendments, No Child Left Behind Act of 2001, and the 2002 President's Commission on Excellence in Special Education. But, exactly what is the general curriculum? Generally speaking, it comprises the full range of courses, activities, scope and sequence of lessons, and materials typically accessed by other students within a school (Nolet & McLaughlin, 2000). In addition to academic and career education classes, the general curriculum also refers to all of the other extracurricular, community-based, and noninstructional activities that comprise a typical school day. For example, students work together on the yearbook and school newspaper staff, shop for costumes and props for a school play, search for their friends when they sit down to eat in the school cafeteria, and pile into cars as they travel to a field trip or an "away" football game. An inclusive school community includes *all* students in the medley of activities that characterizes contemporary secondary school life.

Gaining access to the general education classroom is a part, but not the entire thrust, of the intent of legislation supporting inclusive education. Exemplary secondary school programs support the full range of student populations—including English language learners, students from culturally and ethnically diverse groups, and students with disabilities—in all aspects of school life. This book advocates peer buddy programs as cost-effective and beneficial means—coupled with additional school inclusion efforts—to involve *all* students in the entire spectrum of typical secondary school activities. In this chapter, we address issues that teachers, school counselors, administrators, and parents may encounter when implementing service–learning peer buddy programs in different settings and across a variety of activities. We propose variations peer buddy programs can take when applied in inclusive classrooms, during noninstructional school activities (e.g., lunch, extracurricular clubs, afterschool activities), and during community-based learning experiences. In addition, we discuss how peer buddy programs can help students make the transition from special to general education classrooms. Considerations discussed in this chapter for extending peer buddy interactions across settings are important whether a peer buddy program is being implemented on a single classroom or schoolwide scale.

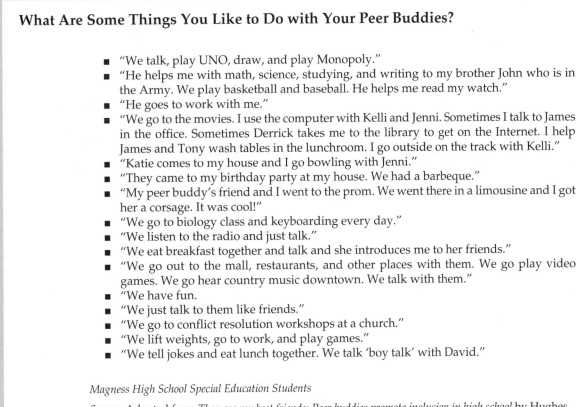

What Are Some Things You Like to Do with Your Peer Buddies?

- "We talk, play UNO, draw, and play Monopoly."
- "He helps me with math, science, studying, and writing to my brother John who is in the Army. We play basketball and baseball. He helps me read my watch."
- "He goes to work with me."
- "We go to the movies. I use the computer with Kelli and Jenni. Sometimes I talk to James in the office. Sometimes Derrick takes me to the library to get on the Internet. I help James and Tony wash tables in the lunchroom. I go outside on the track with Kelli."
- "Katie comes to my house and I go bowling with Jenni."
- "They came to my birthday party at my house. We had a barbeque."
- "My peer buddy's friend and I went to the prom. We went there in a limousine and I got her a corsage. It was cool!"
- "We go to biology class and keyboarding every day."
- "We listen to the radio and just talk."
- "We eat breakfast together and talk and she introduces me to her friends."
- "We go out to the mall, restaurants, and other places with them. We go play video games. We go hear country music downtown. We talk with them."
- "We have fun.
- "We just talk to them like friends."
- "We go to conflict resolution workshops at a church."
- "We lift weights, go to work, and play games."
- "We tell jokes and eat lunch together. We talk 'boy talk' with David."

Magness High School Special Education Students

Source: Adapted from *They are my best friends: Peer buddies promote inclusion in high school* by Hughes, C., Guth, C., Hall, S., Presley, J., Dye, M., & Byers, C., *TEACHING Exceptional Children*, 31(5), 1999, 32–37. Copyright 1999 by The Council for Exceptional Children. Reprinted with permission.

Including Students in General Education Classrooms

Including students with disabilities in general education classrooms can pose a challenge for middle and high school educators. Teachers must identify effective strategies for supporting students with disabilities and other students with academic needs in accessing challenging curricula, making progress on educational goals, and participating interactively in the social environment of the classroom. As we have discussed throughout this book, service–learning peer buddy programs can promote the goals of inclusive education and caring school communities in which students interact with and learn from each other. Strategies for maximizing the benefits of participation in general education classes include (a) creating a team approach to inclusion, (b) maximizing students' social outcomes, and (c) maximizing students' academic outcomes.

Taking a Team Approach to Inclusion

Effective inclusive practices begin with and are maintained by meaningful collaboration among all participants in a school's inclusion efforts (Snell & Janney, 2000). Promoting inclusive school environments and caring school communities requires a team effort involving students, parents, teachers, school counselors, and administrators. As we described in Chapter 3, the roles and responsibilities of all school staff in promoting inclusion in the general education class should be defined, supported, and carried out. "Dumping" a special education student into a general education teacher's class with no communication with or support from the special education teacher is unlikely to result in a successful experience for any member of a classroom environment—even if the student is accompanied by a peer buddy.

Before including a student from a special education class in the general education classroom environment, school personnel must determine who is responsible for critical inclusion tasks, including adapting materials, supervising peer buddies and their special education classmates, providing individualized instruction, monitoring student progress, modifying assignments, and assigning grades (e.g., Friend & Bursuck, 2002). Ongoing communication and collaboration must be maintained among general educators and special education teachers and educational assistants who are not present daily in the general education classroom. Together as a team, school staff need to determine how best to promote favorable social and academic outcomes for *all* students in general education classes.

> "The teachers benefit from the program. They have a peer buddy to help out and they don't have to put all of their extra time into trying to assist one student. So, now they have enough time to go around and work with all of the students in the classroom."
>
> *Edward Belsey*
> *Peer Buddy*

Maximizing Students' Social Outcomes

Research shows that peer interaction plays an important role in adolescents' intellectual development, learning, academic performance, social behavior, and self-esteem (Bukowski, Newcomb, & Hartup, 1996). Just because a special education student is physically included in a general education classroom, however, does not ensure that social interaction will occur between the student and her general education classmates. In fact, research shows that unless school personnel or others take deliberate steps to promote such interaction, it is not likely to occur (Carter, Hughes, Guth, & Copeland, in press). Luckily, there are strategies teachers can use to promote peer interaction in inclusive school settings (Carter & Hughes, 2005). These strategies involve teaching social skills to students with disabilities and arranging classroom environments to maximize opportunities for interaction.

Teaching Social Skills.   Some students with disabilities may not yet have learned the social skills needed to interact with their general education classmates. These students may be reluctant to start up a conversation with their classmates, have difficulty expressing themselves with others, or lack an effective way to communicate. Learning new social skills may increase these students' social interaction with their peers. Table 7.1 summarizes research showing that social skill instruction for students with disabilities includes teaching (a) self-management strategies, (b) leisure skills, (c) communication skills, and (d) social skills alone. For example, students can be taught to use communication picture books to start conversations with their classmates or they can learn to participate in leisure skills, such as card games, to prompt their interaction with peers. Teaching these new skills, however, need not be the sole responsibility of the teacher alone. Peer buddies can learn to assist in teaching these new skills to their classmates with disabilities (see Chapter 6).

"This year I have a student in my class who has severe autism. When Kim first came into my room, she appeared to have no interest in others and only initiated interactions when she wanted to eat or go to the restroom. Then Kim developed a friendship with her peer buddy Corie. Now she watches the door for Corie everyday. When they are together, Kim makes eye contact with her peer buddy frequently, laughs often, and even initiates conversation. We never saw her do these things before. Kim also has increased her vocal repertoire from 4 to 11 words. We have been truly amazed with the difference peer buddies have made in the lives of our students."

Ms. Richardson
Special Education Teacher

TABLE 7.1   Strategies for Teaching Social Skills

Strategy	How to Use	Example
Teaching self-management strategies	Students are taught to direct their own social behavior using strategies such as goal setting, self-prompting, self-monitoring, and self-evaluation.	A student is taught by peers to use self-instruction to initiate conversations with classmates (e.g., "Here comes Sarah . . . I'm going to ask her how her weekend was . . . I spoke with her . . . I did a great job!").
Teaching leisure skills	Students are taught to participate competently in typical leisure activities, providing a context for interacting with their peers.	A student is taught to play a computer game or engage in other recreational activities, such as looking through a school yearbook or playing a popular card game.
Teaching communication skills	Students are taught to use an augmentative and alternative communication (AAC) system, providing them with a effective way to interact with peers and teachers.	A student is taught to use her communication device to make "yes" or "no" choices while participating in a class activity with her peer.
Teaching social skills alone	Students are taught generic social skills such as initiating conversations, responding to peers, and discerning social cues.	A student is taught a variety of "cool" ways to start up conversations with peers, such as asking about the latest music video or popular movie.

Source: Carter & Hughes (2005).

Modifying Classroom Environments.   Unfortunately, the general education classroom environment, particularly in middle and high schools, may hinder rather than support peer interaction. For example, students may spend most of their trigonometry class period working independently at their desks or listening to a lecture or instructions delivered by their teacher. Such arrangements may offer students little opportunity to support, learn from, or interact with each other. By rearranging aspects of classroom instruction, teachers can create environments that foster interaction among students, build cooperative classroom communities, and promote academic success (Schnorr, 1997). Table 7.2 summarizes research suggesting that classroom environments can be arranged so that peer interaction is supported by (a) having peers provide social and academic support, (b) establishing cooperative student groups, (c) assigning friendship roles to peers, and (d) providing disability information and interaction strategies to classmates. For example, teachers can encourage peer buddies to interact with their classmates with disabilities in a friendship versus a teacher role, or students can be assigned to work together cooperatively on classroom projects to promote peer interaction.

> "John, a student who has muscular dystrophy, can hardly move. So when he gets upset or excited he has to talk it out. John has learned to adapt to his situation and express through words what others express through body language. Luke is just the opposite. Due to his autism, Luke cannot speak at all and has learned to use all body language and a lot of grunting to communicate his needs and feelings. By watching their behavior and adaptations, I have learned to better articulate my emotions verbally so I can get along better with them and others."
>
> *Ashley Schroeder*
> *Peer Buddy*

TABLE 7.2   Strategies for Arranging Classrooms to Promote Social Interaction

Strategy	How to Use	Example
Having peers provide academic and social support	Peer buddies work with their classmates with disabilities, assisting them with class assignments and introducing them to peers.	A student enrolled in an ecology class receives instructional and social support from a peer buddy.
Arranging cooperative student groupings	Students with disabilities work together with three or four of their classmates on a learning activity, and each student is responsible for helping teammates learn the content.	During a world history class, students are expected to work collaboratively to complete a presentation on ancient Greece.
Assigning friendship roles to peers	Peer buddies are instructed to interact with their classmates with disabilities in the same way that they would interact with any of their other classmates.	A teacher asks a peer buddy to interact with a student with a disability as a friend, rather than tutor.
Providing disability information and interaction strategies to classmate	Classmates are provided relevant information about disabilities and taught strategies for communicating with students with diverse abilities.	A special education teacher demonstrates how students can assist their classmate with a disability to participate in a group activity.

Source: Carter & Hughes (2005).

Maximizing Students' Academic Outcomes

In addition to confirming the social benefits students receive through membership in inclusive classrooms, research also is demonstrating the myriad ways students benefit academically when they access the general curriculum. For example, general education class participation for students with disabilities has been shown to relate to higher quality IEP goals and objectives, increased academic engagement, and increased instructional time (e.g., Hunt & Goetz, 1997; Katz & Mirenda, 2002). Moreover, academic benefits can be expected to accumulate for general education peers who assist their classmates with disabilities (e.g., Cushing & Kennedy, 1997). Academic assistance can be provided either by one peer buddy within a class or a group of peers in a cooperative learning arrangement in order to share mentoring responsibilities among students. If a peer buddy is enrolled in the class as well, consideration should be made by the teacher with respect to the peer completing his or her own assignments, as needed. To promote the academic success of students with disabilities in general education classrooms, we recommend considering the following issues.

Infusing IEP Goals. It is essential that educators consider how students' individualized educational goals will be infused into each of the general education classes in which students are enrolled. General and special education teachers should collaborate to determine which of the students' goals will be addressed within a particular class and how. For example, a student may be working on the goal of *writing complete sentences* in English, math, and biology classes; *using a calculator* in math and woodworking classes; and *bringing necessary materials* and *asking for help when needed* in all of her classes. Peer buddies should know which of these goals you would like them to assist the student in achieving.

In addition, it is essential that students' progress on educational goals within general education classes is monitored regularly (Salend & Garrick Duhaney, 2002). Collaborate with general education teachers to determine who will take responsibility for monitoring students' progress and how that progress will be assessed. For example, teachers in the Metropolitan Nashville Peer Buddy Program developed a modified grading scale to familiarize general education teachers with the educational goals of students with disabilities in their classrooms and assist teachers in assigning grades (see Figure 7.1 on p. 126). This form is designed to allow teachers to include (a) suggested modifications and adaptations, (b) a list of objectives the student should be working toward, and (c) recommendations for evaluating the student's progress on those objectives.

Introducing Appropriate Adaptations. Students' opportunities for learning can be increased by providing appropriate adaptations. Although some students with disabilities may work on the same activities and materials as the rest of the class, other students may work on similar activities, but with adapted materials (e.g., Wolfe & Hall, 2003). Teachers should take primary responsibility for ensuring that the curriculum is adapted properly. However, peer buddies can be taught to make relatively simple adaptations to ongoing class activities (see Table 6.2, Classroom Adaptations, on page 111 of Chapter 6).

Adjusting Roles of Special Educators. Many schools rely heavily on educational assistants or special education teachers as the dominant means to support students with disabilities within general education classrooms. These special educators often assume primary responsibility for helping students with disabilities learn course content and meet individualized educational goals. An overreliance on educational assistants and special education teachers, however, actually may have the unintended effect of hindering students' academic progress in general education classrooms (Giangreco & Doyle, 2002). For example, a one-on-one arrangement with an educational assistant

FIGURE 7.1   Modified Grading System

Modified Grading System for Students in General Education Classrooms

Student: _____ Grading period (circle one):   1   2   3   4   5   6

General education teacher: _____ Course title: _____

Suggested modifications/adaptations: _____

Objectives	Date													Average

Scoring: You may assign either a letter grade or a numerical grade

Suggested codes: I = 100   Meets objective independently
P = 90   Needs a prompt to meet objective
S = 80   Requires several prompts to meet objective
U = 70   Unable to meet objective

Directions: Each time you grade the class members on assigned work or tests, you may choose to grade this student on the above modified criteria, if appropriate. Place return this sheet to me at the end of the grading period. Thank you!

Source: From Hughes, C., & Carter, E.W. (2000). *The transition handbook: Strategies high school teachers use that work!* (p. 335). Baltimore: Paul H. Brookes Publishing Co.; Reprinted by permission.

may limit a student's interactions with the classroom teacher, lead the classroom teacher to defer primary responsibility for providing instruction to the educational assistant, or cause the student to become overly dependent for assistance on the educational assistant. On the other hand, peer buddy arrangements may allow students to access the general curriculum without encountering these challenges.

Peer buddies are not intended to take the place of adults in providing academic assistance in general education classrooms. Rather, special educators simply should adjust their roles in classrooms where peer buddies are providing support to their classmates with disabilities. After teaching peer buddies strategies for adapting assignments, interacting with their classmates with disabilities, and including their classmates in ongoing activities, special educators can shift to a more supportive role. For example, the special educator may check in periodically with students throughout the class period to see if any assistance is needed. When not providing help directly to peer buddies and their classmates, the special educator is free to work with other students who may need assistance or to assist the classroom teacher. In fact, such arrangements end up benefiting every student in the classroom academically by providing another adult, in addition to the classroom teacher, who is available to circulate around the classroom assisting students.

"The peer buddy program creates a lot of natural supports that make our job a lot easier."

Ms. Reeves
Special Education Teacher

"I feel there is a misconception that students with disabilities cannot learn. Sherman felt more confident with a peer buddy and turned this idea around for me. He received the typing award this year because he worked very hard."

Mr. Thompson
General Education Teacher

Including Students in Noninstructional School, Extracurricular, and Afterschool Activities

Much of the activity in a school takes place outside of the classroom—especially for secondary students. It often is during noninstructional times such as lunch, walking through the hallway between classes, at a track meet, or before and after school that students really get the opportunity to get to know each other, develop friendships, and enjoy each other's company. In fact, it is these times of the school day that students often look forward to most.

At the same time, it is during these unstructured times that students with disabilities often are most isolated from their classmates. Whether they are physically separated from their peers in school or lack the skills or supports needed to participate more fully, many students miss out on the social opportunities that abound in most schools. The 1997 IDEA Amendments stress the importance of ensuring that students with disabilities participate with their general education peers in both curricular *and* extracurricular activities to the maximum extent appropriate. Peer buddy program activities can promote the inclusion of special education students outside the classroom just as effectively as they can within the general education classroom environment. These activities include establishing a Lunch Bunch, promoting inclusion in extracurricular clubs and activities, and increasing participation in afterschool activities. A description of these activities and guidelines for their implementation follow.

Establishing a Lunch Bunch

The cafeteria is the social epicenter of most middle and high schools, a place where students are free from the constraints of classroom lectures and assignments. Students are free to relax with their friends, get a bite to eat, and talk about an upcoming school dance, football game, or holiday break. At the same time, cafeterias may be one of the more segregated settings for students with disabilities, particularly for those students whose disabilities are more severe (Hughes, Rodi, et al., 1999). It is not uncommon to see students sitting together at tables in the corner of the cafeteria with only other students with severe disabilities or eating with their teachers and educational assistants in the classroom. Starting a Lunch Bunch is an effective strategy for promoting inclusion in a cafeteria by bringing students together who otherwise might not join each other for lunch.

A Lunch Bunch is an informal, regular gathering of students with and without disabilities during which students eat, share conversation, get to know each other, and develop relationships. Although a Lunch Bunch eventually will take on a life of its own, school staff will need to take some initial efforts to serve as a catalyst for getting the group underway (Breen & Lovinger, 1991). We suggest first talking with peer buddies about their recommendations for getting a Lunch Bunch off the ground. In addition to encouraging peer buddies to invite their own friends to join the group, consider inviting (a) students who share a general education class with students with disabilities, (b) students who, because of class conflicts, are unable to enroll in the peer buddy program, and (c) other peers whom participating students with disabilities are interested in getting to know. You also can spread the word through such avenues as announcements by students over the intercom, reminders on closed circuit TV, or flyers (see Figure 7.2 and Chapter 4, Recruiting Peer Buddies).

FIGURE 7.2   Sample Lunch Bunch Flyer

The Lunch Bunch

. . . is looking for participants!

What: The Lunch Bunch is a group of students who meet together
                      weekly in the cafeteria to share lunch and good conversation.
When: We meet every Tuesday during the first lunch period.
Where: In the Courtyard on sunny days and in the North Cafeteria on
                      rainy days.
Why: To meet new people, develop friendships, enjoy good
                      conversation, and have fun!
Who: Anyone interested in making new friends.

For more information. . .
contact Ms. Hendrix or stop by The Lunch Bunch

At first, schedule the group to meet once or more each week, such as every Tuesday and Thursday. We found that providing pizza, snacks, and soda is a guaranteed way to draw a good-sized crowd to the first several Lunch Bunch gatherings. These group gatherings provide a comfortable context for students to get to know each other and have fun. Moreover, students who are in a hurry and don't have time to eat can feel comfortable just stopping by to say hello. As students begin to develop relationships with each other, expect to see students with disabilities being invited to other tables to join their general education peers for lunch. In fact, it may be beneficial to prompt students periodically to invite their peers with disabilities to eat with them on days that the Lunch Bunch does not meet.

"Yesterday was Lanika's birthday and we all sang happy birthday to her in the cafeteria. All of our friends know her too now."

Georgina Mills
Peer Buddy

Promoting Inclusion in Extracurricular Clubs and Activities

School clubs, programs, organizations, and athletic teams provide valuable experiences within which students can explore their interests, develop important skills, establish new friendships, and participate in experiences that will contribute to a smooth transition to life after high school. Moreover, participation in school activities may (a) foster among students a sense of belonging and connection with the wider school community, (b) reduce dropout rates, (c) promote academic achievement, (d) bring students into contact with diverse peer perspectives, and (e) allow students to develop new skills and pursue interests (e.g., Mahoney & Cairns, 1997; McNeal, 1995). Unfortunately, many students with disabilities miss out on opportunities to become involved in the array of extracurricular activities that are available within most schools (Simeonsson, Carlson, Huntington, McMillen, & Brent, 2001; Wagner, Cameto, & Newman, 2003). Often, students with disabilities are either not encouraged to participate in these activities or not provided adequate support to ensure that their experiences are successful.

Participation by students with disabilities in extracurricular activities that align with their interests—such as student council, thespian society, model United Nations, school literary magazine, or the senior prom committee—can be promoted when coupled with the support of peer buddies and thoughtful planning by school staff. For example, peer buddies can help their classmates rehearse lines for the school play, learn new moves for a chess club tournament, dress for lacrosse club practice, decorate a float for the homecoming parade, or provide a ride home from marching band practice.

"The special education students have made friends too. I'm sure they like knowing people when they walk in the hallway and say 'hi.' And at football and basketball games, they come and sit with us."

Jack Elliott
Peer Buddy

"I also think that students meet new people through their peer buddies. There was going to be a skating party down at the Sportsplex. Serena wanted to go and she didn't have a ride and so I was going to take her. So, the students get a chance to go out and do things with other students that they otherwise might not get to do."

Angelica Perez
Peer Buddy

How can staff support the involvement of students with disabilities and their peer buddies in extracurricular school activities? In the following box, we present steps that school staff should take when planning for and supporting the participation of students with disabilities in extracurricular activities. Each step prompts school staff to think about issues to address and opportunities to take advantage of to ensure that *all* students have access to the *full* range of extracurricular activities available within a school environment.

Promoting Extracurricular Activity Participation: Steps and Considerations

- *Identify potential activities:* Obtain a list of all clubs, programs, and other events available within your school. What activities are students interested in? Find out about students' likes, hobbies, and future goals for life after high school by speaking with them, their peer buddies, parents, and other teachers. Observe what activities a student chooses during free time. Brainstorm activities that students would enjoy, that offer opportunities to develop new friendships, and that provide occasions for additional skill development.
- *Determine activity requirements:* Are students required to have parent permission prior to participating? Are there fees or dues associated with the activity? Will students need certain supplies (e.g., an instrument for jazz band or a camera for photography club) or a uniform (e.g., formalwear for concert choir or a jersey for intramural soccer)?
- *Address logistical issues:* Where do activities take place—on-campus, off-campus, or both? Are these locations accessible? If not, determine what accommodations are needed to ensure that students have access to these activities. Is transportation provided to and from off-campus activities? If not, devise alternate means of getting a student to and from the activity via a ride from a peer buddy, parents, faculty sponsor, or city transportation.
- *Identify peer buddies:* Arranging for a peer buddy to interact with and support a student during extracurricular activities is a natural way to ensure a successful experience. Are there students already participating in activities who could assist their classmates with disabilities in participating in an activity? Or, is there a current peer buddy who shares similar interests and would be willing to become involved in a club or activity along with her classmate with disabilities? Consider employing some of the strategies described in Chapter 4 for recruiting peer buddies into an activity.
- *Determine support needs:* Almost every school-sponsored extracurricular activity has an adult sponsor. Determine what sort of adult supervision is provided for participating students. Is the faculty sponsor open to having a student with a disability and her peer buddy involved in the activity? Will the nature of the activity require that a educational assistant or special education teacher also be present?
- *Determine peer buddy responsibilities:* Determine exactly what type of support students with disabilities will need to participate in the activities. For example, students may

need assistance getting to and from club activities, learning typical routines, getting along with other participants, and completing certain activities. Which of these supports can best be provided by a peer buddy? Decide what information and training peer buddies will need in order to provide this support and periodically observe students to identify emerging needs (see Chapter 6, Supporting Peer Buddy Participants).

- *Collaborate with staff:* School staff should regularly collaborate with each other to ensure that extracurricular activities are beneficial experiences for all participants. Provide faculty sponsors with information that may be beneficial for meeting the needs of participating students. Discuss emergency procedures, especially when club activities occur off-campus.

- *Address potential challenges:* Students with disabilities may not have been encouraged to participate in certain extracurricular activities because of staff concerns about potential problems that could arise. For example, a student may (a) have a reputation for engaging in challenging behavior such as wandering off, having verbal outbursts, or interacting with peers inappropriately; (b) lack an effective communication system, making it difficult for her to communicate when she needs to use the restroom; or (c) not possess skills related to participating in the activity, such as safely crossing the street or chewing food sufficiently to avoid choking. Teachers should be proactive about addressing these challenges before they occur. Peer buddies should be (a) familiar with issues that may arise, (b) provided with necessary information about how to react during potentially difficult situations, and (c) informed about when to ask for assistance from school staff.

"My peer buddy is cool to play games with. When I'm down, I can talk to him. He's a cool person!"

Jacob Radnor
Special Education Student

"Each of the students has taught me different things that influence my daily life. Susannah's hunger for excitement and perfection helps me at my job in retail. Meg's love for crafts and art and Jessica and Dontay's love for music have caused me to stay in tune to the pleasures and simple things that we all enjoy. By working with these students, I have not only helped them learn life skills, but I have acquired brand new skills myself!"

Jessica Nesbit
Peer Buddy

"Participating in the Unified Basketball Olympics this year was an unforgettable experience. I learned that the Olympics brings out the best in everyone, whether or not they have a disability. The athletes had so much hope and determination. I didn't see one person with a frown on their face, even if they didn't come in first place. Since I have been involved in Unified Olympics and the peer buddy program, I have had a better outlook on life. The only regret I have is that it took me so long to get involved in the program."

Ronnie Shaw
Peer Buddy

As a **teacher**, consider sponsoring a school club or organization yourself. This is a great way to meet and get to know members of the student body outside of instructional settings. Pick an activity that interests you, such as computers, wrestling, or singing. As you extend an invitation to the student body to participate, make sure that students with disabilities and other students who may be only marginally included in the school community also are hearing about the club. Encourage peer buddies who have similar interests to join in partnership with special education students or students from culturally diverse groups.

Increasing Participation in Afterschool Activities

Spring dances, home football games, weekend movies, trips to the mall, basketball games at the community center—for most students, these are typical activities enjoyed with friends beyond the school day. Unfortunately, students with disabilities often have limited opportunities to participate with their peers in these everyday activities due to several factors (Amado, 1993; Nisbet & Hagner, 2000). First, students may not have developed friendships with peers with whom they can attend afterschool events. Second, many students with disabilities still do not attend their neighborhood school but may be bussed to a school in another area of town. These students are not spending their school day with peers who live in the same neighborhoods as they do and may not have the opportunity to get to know these peers outside of school. Third, many students with disabilities, particularly those with more severe disabilities, have limited transportation options. Therefore, these students may not be able to travel independently to afterschool activities.

A primary purpose of service–learning peer buddy programs is to expand students' opportunities to develop meaningful relationships with their classmates. Although peer buddy programs are effective interventions for accomplishing this goal during the school day, it is important also to consider how students' interactions with their peers can be promoted after the school day ends. Without intentional planning, relationships between students and their peer buddies may not carry over to community settings (Kishi & Meyer, 1994).

What can you do to promote interaction that extends beyond the instructional day? As a teacher, counselor, or administrator, your role in encouraging interaction will be indirect rather than direct. But, there are practical steps you can take to prompt and support these interactions.

Supporting Participation in Afterschool Activities: Steps and Considerations

- *Coordinate with parents.* Parents want their children to have close friendships with their peers (e.g., Blue-Banning, Turnbull, & Pereira, 2002). Because most adolescents rely on their parents for transportation, finances, and permission, parents can play an instrumental role in assisting students with disabilities and their peer buddies to get together outside of the school day. Keep parents of students with disabilities and their peer buddies informed about opportunities for students to get together. For example, send home a flyer each month describing upcoming afterschool events such as a school play, fundraising activity, community service project, or athletic event. With permission, a list of phone numbers of participating students can be shared so that parents can contact other parents to coordinate activities. In addition, obtain input from parents regarding students' activity interests and favorite peers.

- *Prompt peer buddies.* Peer buddies initially may not be aware of the benefits of extending interactions with their classmates with disabilities beyond the school day. Brainstorm with peer buddies ideas for arranging formal and informal ways to get together with their classmates. These get-togethers can be done either as a part of or outside the peer buddy program. For example, you can help peer buddies and their classmates with disabilities organize a weekend outing. Students could get together at a community center, church youth group, skate park, Unified Olympics event, or a pizza restaurant.
- *Prepare students with disabilities.* Encourage students to become involved in community activities. Students with disabilities will benefit from learning skills that increase their participation in the community. The more competent students are, the more likely they are to enjoy an activity and want to participate in it with a peer. For example, instruction might focus on teaching students to ride city transportation to a peer buddy's house, shop at a local record store, participate in popular leisure activities (e.g., video games, sports), or manage conflicts with teachers or peers.

 Many **parents** want their children with disabilities to become involved in community activities with their same-age peers, but they are not sure exactly how to accomplish this goal. Provide parents with information about leisure and recreational opportunities within the community and supports available to help students become involved. Then, think about how a student's peer buddies could also become involved. Ask for input from parents or other family members about students' interests and preferences.

"The peer buddy program has been great for Katrina! I wish it could be used more in her life to help her get involved in extracurricular activities at school and I wish that she could be involved more with peer buddies on the weekend and outside of school."

Ms. Breyers
Parent

"The students are fun to work with and I have gained five new friends from this experience. My most memorable time with my partners was during Unified Olympics. When Tony won his event, we were all very excited. I was proud of him for achieving his goal."

LaShondra Miles
Peer Buddy

Including Students in Community-Based Instruction

Special education students, particularly those with more severe disabilities, often spend one or more class periods per day receiving instruction in the community, learning to use public transportation or making purchases at a community business. Although community-based instruction has been advanced as an effective strategy for teaching students with disabilities various community living skills, some educators have expressed concerns that such activities can separate students with disabilities from their general education peers during the school day (e.g., Fisher & Sax, 1999; Wehmeyer, Sands, Knowlton, & Kozleski, 2002). Community-based instruction for students with disabilities, however, can be implemented alongside general education peers. In fact, peer buddies can participate in these experiences along with their class-mates with disabilities. Indeed, the general education curriculum also includes instructional activities in the community, such as field trips to museums, plays, or concerts as well as requirements for community service or service–learning projects within the community, in which both general and special education students can participate.

Students with disabilities should be included in the same community-based learning activities in which other students at their school participate. For example, as part of their classes, students may regularly (a) use the public library to conduct research, (b) visit an art museum for a unit on Impressionism, (c) travel to a senior citizen center as part of a service–learning project, or (d) visit local businesses to learn about different occupations. These experiences offer opportunities for students with disabilities to acquire beneficial community skills alongside their general education peers. On such trips, students with disabilities can be paired informally with a participating classmate, or a peer buddy can be paired with a student.

General and special education teachers should work together to implement joint community-based activities that involve all students (Billingsley & Albertson, 1999). Service–learning projects offer an excellent opportunity for students with and without disabilities to work together toward a common service goal. For example, all students can take pride in conducting a community needs survey or delivering Meals on Wheels to persons who are homebound (see Promoting Peer Interaction and Service–Learning box on p. 25).

Even when students with disabilities are participating in community-based instruction activities that extend beyond what typically takes place as part of the general education curriculum, peer buddies can accompany students off-campus. For example, students with disabilities may benefit from spending time in the community once or more per week learning skills such as shopping, using community transportation, and accessing recreational activities. Or, students frequently may participate in off-campus job training to build work experience and refine career interests (Wehman, 2001). Peer buddies can participate in all of these experiences, providing helpful support and assisting students with learning new skills.

In all cases of community-based instruction, several steps and issues must be considered, as shown in the following box.

Involving Students in Community-Based Instruction: Steps and Considerations

- *Obtain administrative support.* It is essential that you obtain support from your building administrators when planning community-based instructional activities. Explain how the activities you are planning relate to the curriculum and address students' educational needs. Be prepared to respond to administrators' concerns about issues related to liability, transportation, missed class time, and costs (see below).
- *Address liability issues.* Moving instruction out of the classroom and into the community raises liability issues that must be addressed. Inquire of your administrator about the school's procedures for community-based learning. For example, procedures may include obtaining parental permission, developing emergency procedures, compiling student identification information, and ensuring adequate student/teacher ratios. Ask your school's work-based learning coordinator for examples of how he or she addresses liability issues related to off-campus employment training.
- *Arrange transportation.* Costs associated with and limited options for transportation are some of the main barriers to implementing community-based learning. Determine the shortest transportation routes and least expensive options.

- *Scheduling activities.* When class periods last just 45 to 55 minutes, creative planning will be required to avoid having students miss other classes. If a school is not on a block schedule, students may have to miss other classes in order to participate. This problem can be avoided by scheduling community experiences before or after lunch.
- *Identifying peer buddies.* Start by trying to identify general education peers who are already going on the trip who can provide assistance to a student. If none can be identified, try to find another peer buddy who can join the student.
- *Providing instruction.* Community-based instruction is designed to provide opportunities for students to learn in meaningful, actual settings. Peers can be effective teachers of a variety of community skills, including recreational skills (e.g., Vandercook, 1991), life skills (e.g., Tekin-Iftar, 2003), and work skills (e.g., Dolyniuk et al., 2002). Prior to going off-campus, review with peer buddies all goals and procedures for the community-based activity and discuss how they can assist their classmates with disabilities in achieving instructional goals.
- *Address potential challenges.* Emergency situations may arise with little warning. Just as when preparing for extracurricular activities outside the classroom, procedures for responding to emergency situations must be established (see box, Promoting Extracurricular Activity Participation: Steps and Considerations on p. 130). When routines for dealing with emergencies are clear to all participants, there should be no cause for anxiety about involving students with disabilities in community-based activities.

"Last fall, my peer buddy Catrina helped me bowl when we went on our field trip to the bowling alley. Last school year, we went on a field trip and the peer buddies went with us. Peer buddies go on field trips with us because the teachers are busy with other students. The peer buddies hang out with us and keep us from getting lost or in trouble. The peer buddies show a lot of responsibility and I like working with them."

Jeremy Lowe
Special Education Student

Transitioning Students from Special to General Education Classrooms

Not only is inclusive education the letter of the law, but increasingly, teachers and administrators are recognizing the benefits of including *all* students in the general curriculum and creating a climate of acceptance and community in which *all* students participate. Despite efforts to promote inclusive education, however, many students with disabilities—particularly on the secondary level—remain in special education classrooms apart from their general education peers for the majority of their school day (U.S. Department of Education, 2002). Not only is access to the general curriculum severely limited for these students, they also are likely to have few opportunities to interact socially and build friendships with their general education peers.

To provide opportunities for peer interaction for students in less inclusive settings, teachers can arrange for peer buddies to interact with students with disabilities within the context of the special education classroom. This type of "reverse mainstreaming" approach, in which general education students join their peers with disabilities in special education classrooms, allows for peer interaction opportunities in situations where more inclusive in-school environments currently are not available for some students.

We recommend, however, that peer buddy programs not serve as a substitute for inclusive education or full participation in general education classrooms. For schools that are not consistently providing general education access for students with disabilities, peer buddy programs may serve as a vehicle that assists schools in moving toward fully inclusive services. Although peer buddy programs can comprise one piece of a school's efforts to promote general education access for students with disabilities, these programs should be coupled with other schoolwide efforts toward inclusion. For example, peer buddies can begin accompanying special education students into general education classes on a 1:1 basis. Academic performance of students can be monitored and the benefits versus risks of the program can be evaluated by administrators and teachers. Strategies for expanding participation in the peer buddy program, such as described in this book, could then be introduced gradually by school staff. Successful opportunities for inclusion documented through the peer buddy program could help fuel a systemic schoolwide restructuring process (e.g., Fisher, Sax, & Pumpian, 1999) aimed at inclusive experiences for *all* students within an accepting, tolerant, and compassionate school community.

Without the commitment and support of the administration, any efforts to move toward inclusive education are destined to fall short. As an **administrator**, you, no doubt, are fully aware of the legislative press toward bringing students with disabilities "to the table" within general education. The press toward full participation and accountability, of course, also includes students who are members of groups that have traditionally been underrepresented, such as English language learners, minority students, and students from high poverty backgrounds. As an administrator in your school, you "grease the wheels" of inclusion by modeling and promoting a welcoming community and a climate of acceptance. Your sanction of efforts to promote inclusion and your guidance to staff in adopting more inclusive practices is critical to the success of any inclusion project, including a peer buddy program.

Summary

In this chapter, we have discussed a variety of routes by which special education students can be supported to access the general education curriculum. These routes include (a) maximizing participation in the general education classroom; (b) involving students in noninstructional activities, such as lunch or afterschool events; (c) extending peer buddy programs to community-based learning experiences; and (d) transitioning students from special to general education classrooms with peer buddy assistance. Tips are provided for implementing peer buddy activities across a variety of settings, including the community. A team approach among school personnel, students, and parents is advocated as a means to promote schoolwide inclusion and a school climate of caring, acceptance, and tolerance.

CASE STUDY BOX: *A Time to Learn*

Life wasn't getting any easier for Mr. Mason in his World History classes. He made a few attempts to update his video library with clips from recent movie hits and opened class with a few jokes he downloaded from an Internet website. However, the blank stares or guffaws he received from a large number of his students as well as an increasingly high number of failing grades on his quizzes and tests convinced Mr. Mason that he was continuing to miss the boat with much of the class. In desperation, during his next planning period, Mr. Mason dropped by Ms. Terino's tenth-grade American History class. If she had some answers to handing the academic and cultural diversity of his classes, he was ready to learn!

Upon entering Ms. Terino's classroom, the first thing Mr. Mason noticed was how engaged all the students seemed to be. A small group of students over by the bulletin board was painting a mural depicting a scene from Sinclair Lewis's book, *The Jungle*. Mr. Mason immediately recognized one of the students, Ricky, who had been in his class for a short time the previous year. Mr. Mason had become frustrated with Ricky and sent him back to his special education class for the remainder of the year when he never seemed to pay attention or couldn't seem to learn anything in class. Yet, here was Ricky talking and making decisions with his peers about how to complete the mural, pitching in, and enthusiastically working with his group.

Another group of students at the computer center was searching for information about the U.S. industrial revolution on the Internet for a research report. Anatole, an English language learner, was working alongside a classmate who periodically helped her with English translations. In return, Anatole was explaining to her group how the industrial revolution had affected her home country in Eastern Europe. Additional clusters of students around the room worked on other projects related to the industrial revolution and were similarly animated, attentive, and engaged with each other and their projects. What was most remarkable to Mr. Mason was that not one student was staring off into space, falling asleep, being disruptive, or even acting disinterested. The entire class appeared productively engaged even while they interacted socially with each other. In the midst of all the activity, Ms. Terino appeared calm and friendly as she moved about the room, chatting first with one group and then another, checking on their progress on their projects. She didn't appear frustrated, worn out, or even close to tearing out her hair. In fact, just like the students, she really seemed to be enjoying herself! The secret, Ms. Terino revealed, after the bell rang and the students left for their next class, was what she called her "peer buddies"—students in the class who were members of each of the groups and who helped out students who were having difficulties with the work. That way Ms. Terino didn't have to be everywhere at once addressing each and every problem a student might be having. Instead, she was freed up to be able to supervise the class as a whole.

After a few more days of observation during his planning period, Mr. Mason was convinced. Peer buddies were the way to go! He already had some ideas of students in each of his classes who he just knew would be real "buddies" to their classmates. And Ms. Terino said that if he needed more peer buddies that Mr. Raoul, the senior counselor, had some students on a list just waiting to enroll in the peer buddy program.

Mr. Mason couldn't wait to get started. Actually, to tell the truth, even he had to admit that he was getting a little tired of the same old lecture notes in World History year after year. Maybe it was time for a change, and time for him to turn some of the teaching over to his students. And maybe the old, veteran teacher could do a little learning himself! And, you know what? It looked like it was going to be a lot of fun.

Learning Activities

- If you are a "lone" special education teacher in a school trying to start up a peer buddy program on your own and transition students from the special to the general education class, think about who might be likely to collaborate with or at least support you in your efforts. It may be one of your student's parents who could advocate for increased participation of her child in a general education class, or it may be the teacher down the hall who has a child with disabilities of his own. Engage these individuals casually in conversation and begin to get an idea if they would advocate for your efforts in pairing peer buddies with students with disabilities in the general education class. Then, start putting your plan into action using the ideas you have learned in this book.

- Find out where students in your school go for field trips, such as a local history museum, newspaper office, or medical center. Are students with disabilities, English language learners, or students in career education classes invited to attend these events? Suggest to the administration that these students could be paired with peer buddies in order to participate in such valuable instructional activities in the community.

- Visit your school cafeteria when students are eating. Where do special education students tend to sit? Are they eating as a separate group or interspersed throughout the cafeteria eating at tables with their general education friends? If they are not, it might be time to start a Lunch Bunch in your school. Follow the suggestions on p. 128 of this chapter for making lunchtime an inclusive experience for students with disabilities.

- Check the resources in the Appendix of this book for ideas about starting up joint service–learning projects involving both general and special education students. Find out what type of permission students will need to travel to the community and complete their projects. What sort of transportation is available in your community? Could your school provide a bus or van? Survey the community for possible projects that students could become involved in, such as redecorating a community center, reading to children in a day care, or walking dogs at a Humane Society.

References

Amado, A. N. (1993). *Friendships and community connections between people with and without developmental disabilities.* Baltimore: Paul H. Brookes.

Billingsley, F. F., & Albertson, L. R. (1999). Finding a future for functional skills. *Journal of the Association for Persons with Severe Handicaps, 24,* 298–302.

Blue-Banning, M., Turnbull, A., P. & Pereira, L. (2002). Hispanic youth/young adults with disabilities: Parents' visions for the future. *Research & Practice for Persons with Severe Disabilities, 27,* 204–219.

Breen, C. G., & Lovinger, L. (1991). PAL (Partners at Lunch) club: Evaluation of a program to support social relationships in a junior high school. In C. G. Breen, C. H. Kennedy, & T. G. Haring (Eds.), *Social context research project: Methods for facilitating the inclusion of students with disabilities in integrated school and community contexts* (pp. 106–128). Santa Barbara: University of California.

Bukowski, W. M., Newcomb, A. F., & Hartup, W. W. (Eds.). (1996). *The company they keep: Friendship in childhood and adolescence.* New York: Cambridge University Press.

Carter, E. W., & Hughes, C. (2005). *Social interaction interventions in secondary school settings: Effective practices.* Manuscript in preparation.

Carter, E. W., Hughes, C., Guth, C., & Copeland, S. R. (in press). Factors influencing social interaction among high school students. *American Journal on Retardation.*

Cushing, L. S., & Kennedy, C. H. (1997). Academic effects on students without disabilities who serve as peer supports for students with disabilities in general education classrooms. *Journal of Applied Behavior Analysis, 30,* 139–152.

Dolynuik, C. A., Kamens, M. W., Corman, H., Dinardo, P. O., Totaro, R. M., & Rockoff, J. C. (2002). Students with developmental disabilities go to college: Description of a collaborative transition project on a regular college campus. *Focus on Autism and Other Developmental Disabilities, 17,* 236–241.

Fisher, D., & Sax, C. (1999). Noticing differences between secondary and postsecondary education: Extending Agran, Snow, and Swaner's discussion. *Journal of the Association for Persons with Severe Handicaps, 24,* 303–305.

Fisher, D., Sax, C., & Pumpian, I. (1999). *Inclusive high schools: Learning from contemporary classrooms.* Baltimore: Paul H. Brookes.

Friend, M., & Bursuck, W. D. (2002). *Including student with special needs: A practical guide for classroom teachers* (3rd ed.). Boston: Allyn and Bacon.

Giangreco, M. F., & Doyle, M. B. (2002). Students with disabilities and paraprofessional supports: Benefits, balance, and band-aids. *Focus on Exceptional Children, 34(7),* 1–12.

Hughes, C., & Carter, E. W. (2000). *The transition handbook: Strategies high school teachers use that work!* (p. 335). Baltimore: Paul H. Brookes.

Hughes, C., Guth, C., Hall, S., Presley, J., Dye, M., & Byers, C. (1999). "They are my best friends": Peer buddies promote inclusion in high school. *TEACHING Exceptional Children, 31(5),* 32–37.

Hughes, C., Rodi, M. S., & Lorden, S. W., Pitkin, S. E., Derer, K. R., Hwang, B., & Cai, X. (1999). Social interactions of high school students with mental retardation and their general education peers. *American Journal on Mental Retardation, 104,* 533–544.

Hunt, P., & Goetz, L. (1997). Research on inclusive educational programs, practices, and outcomes for students with severe disabilities. *The Journal of Special Education, 31,* 3–29.

Individuals with Disabilities Education Act Amendments of 1997, PL 105-17, 20 U. S. C. § 1400 *et seq.* (1997).

Katz, J., & Mirenda, P. (2002). Including students with developmental disabilities in general education classrooms: Educational benefits. *International Journal of Special Education, 17* (2), 14–25.

Kishi, G. S., & Meyer, L. H. (1994). What children report and remember: A six-year follow-up of the effects of social contact between peers with and without disabilities. *Journal of the Association for Persons with Severe Handicaps, 19,* 277–289.

Mahoney, J. L., & Cairns, R. B. (1997). Do extracurricular activities protect against early school dropout? *Developmental Psychology, 33,* 241–253.

McNeal, R. B. (1995). Extracurricular activities and high school dropouts. *Sociology of Education, 68,* 62–80.

Nisbet, J., & Hagner, D. (Eds.). (2000). *Part of the community: Strategies for including everyone.* Baltimore: Paul H. Brookes.

No Child Left Behind Act of 2001, PL 107–110, 115 Stat. 1425 (2002).

Nolet, V., & McLaughlin, M. J. (2000). *Accessing the general curriculum: Including students with disabilities in standards-based reform.* Thousand Oaks, CA: Corwin.

Salend, S. J., & Garrick Duhaney, L. M. (2002). Grading students in inclusive settings. *TEACHING Exceptional Children, 34*(3), 8–15.

Schnorr, R. F. (1997). From enrollment to membership: "Belonging" in middle and high schools. *Journal of the Association for Persons with Severe Handicaps, 22,* 1–15.

Simeonsson, R. J., Carlson, D., Huntington, G. S., McMillen, J. S., & Brent, J. L. (2001). Students with disabilities: A national survey of participation in school activities. *Disability and Rehabilitation, 23,* 49–63.

Snell, M. E., & Janney, R. (2000). *Collaborative teaming.* Baltimore: Paul H. Brookes.

Tekin-Iftar, E. (2003). Effectiveness of peer delivered simultaneous prompting on teaching community signs to students with developmental disabilities. *Education and Training in Developmental Disabilities, 38,* 77–94.

U. S. Department of Education. (2002). *Twenty-fourth annual report to Congress on the implementation of the Individuals with Disabilities Education Act.* Washington, DC: Author.

Vandercook, T. (1991). Leisure instruction outcomes: Criterion performance, positive interactions, and acceptance by typical high school peers. *The Journal of Special Education, 25,* 320–339.

Wagner, M., Cameto, R., & Newman, L. (2003). *Youth with disabilities: A changing population: A report of findings from the National Longitudinal Transition Study (NLTS) and the National Longitudinal Transition Study-2 (NLTS2).* Menlo Park, CA: SRI International.

Wehman, P. (2001). *Life beyond the classroom: Transition strategies for young people with disabilities* (3rd ed.). Baltimore: Paul H. Brookes.

Wehmeyer, M. L., Sands, D. J., Knowlton, H. E., & Kozleski, E. B. (2002). *Providing access to the general curriculum: Teaching students with mental retardation.* Baltimore: Paul H. Brookes.

Wolfe, P. S., & Hall, T. E. (2003). Making inclusion a reality for students with severe disabilities. *TEACHING Exceptional Children, 35*(4), 56–60.

CHAPTER
8

Evaluating, Sustaining, and Expanding a Peer Buddy Program

In this chapter, you will learn about . . .

- Strategies for evaluating the impact of a peer buddy program on participants.
- Recommendations for incorporating participant feedback into program modifications.
- Suggestions for partnering with parents and establishing and maintaining an advisory board.
- Ideas for extending the program to other classrooms and schools.

Why? . . .

Obtaining ongoing feedback from participants is critical to ensuring both the short- and long-term success of your service–learning peer buddy program. In this chapter, we provide information you need to evaluate the impact your school's peer buddy program is having on program participants and translate participant feedback into programmatic changes. An advisory board is suggested as a means for obtaining ongoing input from participants and for partnering with parents. We also discuss ideas for expanding the program to additional schools.

CASE STUDY BOX: *The Wheel Squeaks Again*

Ms. Marantz was one of those "squeaky wheels" who rapidly gains a reputation in a school. Her reputation for advocating for her daughter Katie, a student receiving special education services, was already well established at Beech Street Elementary School and Randolph Park Middle School, where Katie previously had been a student. Katie had been identified with severe disabilities even before she went to school, and Ms. Marantz realized that Katie did need extra help and was slower at picking up new skills than her classmates in general education. But Ms. Marantz could never agree to having Katie spend her entire day in a self-contained class for special education students. She knew too well how much Katie learned from spending time with her friends in the neighborhood and how her friends benefited too from knowing Katie. Just watching Katie and her friends go swimming and how everyone pitched in helping Katie lower herself into the water from her wheelchair and how Katie brightened up everyone's day as they splashed around in the pool was enough to convince anyone of the values of inclusion education, Ms. Marantz contended.

Of course, both Beech Street and Randolph Park had had peer buddy programs where special education students were accompanied to general education classes, such as math and reading, by their peers. Ms. Marantz, of course, was one of the first parents to sign her child up for the peer buddy program in both schools. And that wasn't the end of it. When Katie had said that she would like to play the drums in the band at Beech Street and wanted a peer to go with her, Ms. Marantz made it clear to the staff that a peer buddy who was also learning to play the drums would accompany Katie to band class. And when Katie got in middle school and wanted to join the afterschool Chess Club at Randolph Park, Ms. Marantz made sure with the Chess Club sponsor that peer buddies in the club would help out Katie when she needed it. The peer buddies were all too happy to do so, and Katie became one of the most popular partners to play in the club. At Ms. Marantz's urging in response to Katie's expressed desire, peer buddies also assisted Katie in Spanish, biology, and art classes during her last year at Randolph Park Middle School. Having peer buddies in her life really made Katie's school days an enriching experience!

You can imagine, then, how anxious Ms. Marantz became when Katie was ready to enter her freshman year at Hudson Heights High School, and they both learned at freshman orientation that there was no peer buddy program at school! What was worse was when the freshman counselor said that most of the students with severe disabilities at Hudson Heights spent the majority of their day in special education, rarely attending general education classes with their peers. Katie, however, had been looking forward to all the new classes she could take in high school with the support and assistance of her peer buddies, such as keyboarding and drama.

Ms. Marantz knew that she couldn't take this lying down. She had spoken up before, and she knew she could do it again. It was time to establish her "squeaky wheel" reputation at yet another school. Tomorrow, Ms. Marantz would be heading over to Hudson Heights High School to visit with the school administration, teachers, and counselors to begin to convince them of the benefits of starting a peer buddy program this fall. And Katie, of course, would be one of the first students signed up.

After much dedication and diligence, your service–learning peer buddy program is underway. You have worked hard over the past semesters to lay a strong foundation, garner support among school staff, and recruit and orient participants to the program. Peer buddies and their classmates with disabilities are working together and getting to know each other in general education classrooms, during lunch, between classes, during extracurricular and other school activities, and even in the community. But, is the program really successful? Are you meeting the goals that you and your colleagues at school initially set out to accomplish? What can you do to ensure that a successful program thrives and expands? In this chapter, we provide you with strategies for answering these and other questions related to evaluating, modifying, sustaining, and expanding a peer buddy program.

Evaluating Peer Buddy Programs and Incorporating Participant Feedback

There are several reasons why you should invest time in evaluating your peer buddy program (Payne, 2000). First, it is important to find out and document the peer buddy program's impact on the school community. Is it truly improving the quality of education that students are receiving? Do students, teachers, counselors, administrators, and parents conclude that the program is producing outcomes that they think are important and satisfying? Are students really increasing their access to the general curriculum, developing meaningful relationships, acquiring citizenship skills, and contributing to a caring school community? Are all students and school staff who wish to participate involved in the program? Talking with participants and observing peer buddy activities can provide teachers with evidence of the program's impact, which can then be used in program modifications.

Second, identifying positive outcomes resulting from a peer buddy program provides valuable information that can be used to promote the program to others. Perhaps you know of a neighboring school in your district where school administrators and teachers are not aware of the potential benefits of a peer buddy program. They may be reluctant to invest their time and energy in a program in which they do not readily see an immediate benefit. As a person who knows firsthand the benefits of a peer buddy program, it is critical for you to identify and promote the potential rewards available to administrators (e.g., fulfilling legislative mandates to increase access to general education), teachers (e.g., opportunities to provide individualized instruction), and students (e.g., enhanced sense of self-worth, development of new friendships) to encourage widespread interest and ownership in a program (Copeland et al., 2004)

> "It would be a good idea for teachers to visit a classroom where there are peer buddies and to talk to teachers who have experienced success with the peer buddy program. They should also talk to teachers who have had special education students in their classes. This will help them gain acceptance of these students. We could also have workshops in the summer that cover this aspect of education."
>
> *Ms. Clark*
> *General Education Teacher*

Third, the evaluation process can lead to recommendations for improving the program. As you take stock of all that has been accomplished over the previous semesters, you will certainly identify aspects of the program that can be enhanced. Program participants are sure to have ideas about how to improve a struggling program or expand a successful one. Even when a program is running smoothly, it is beneficial to keep an eye on the next level to which you wish to take your peer buddy program, for example, by expanding to include a service–learning program in the community soup kitchen or students with autism who previously had not participated in the program.

The impact of peer buddy programs can be assessed using a broad approach to evaluation that includes informal and formal observations, interviews, questionnaires, and assessments of students' educational programs and performance. In addition, we recommend an approach to evaluation that involves gathering input from multiple program participants and stakeholders, such as family members. When multiple perspectives are sought out and considered, a more comprehensive picture of a peer buddy program is possible. In the following sections, we describe a variety of strategies for gathering feedback about peer buddy program experiences from (a) students with disabilities; (b) peer buddies; (c) teachers, administrators, and counselors; and (d) parents.

Assessing Program Impact on Students with Disabilities

When designing inclusive instruction and practices, it is critical to consider the point of view of participating students with disabilities. Too often, the input and perspectives of students with disabilities are not allowed to inform educational decision making (Grigal, Neubert, Moon, & Graham, 2003). Yet, these students have much that they can offer with regard to feedback on and recommendations for improving peer buddy programs. *Do students with disabilities find having a peer buddy to be helpful, satisfying, detrimental, or intrusive? Do students feel that they are learning more, making new friends, and taking part in important school and community activities?* Feedback from students with disabilities who are interacting with peer buddies can help teachers identify optimal support strategies and curricular areas and settings in which peer buddies may be most helpful and appropriate.

"I like to go downtown with April to hear music. Kimberly likes to play baseball with the peer buddies. We all like to eat lunch in the cafeteria with the peer buddies. Sometimes we also go out to eat with them at the mall. They're nice."

Rosalynn Young
Special Education Student

School staff can take several approaches to allow students with disabilities to share their experiences in a peer buddy program. We suggest that you use a combination of methods in order to obtain a complete picture of a student's experiences. If students have significant cognitive or communicative disabilities, you may need to adjust the means by which you try to obtain student input.

First, periodically sit down with students and inquire about their interactions with their peer buddies. A casual conversation can go a long way toward identifying peer buddy arrangements that are working and those that lack a good fit. For example, students might share their (a) preferences for which peer buddy they would like to work with during an upcoming semester, (b) suggestions for courses in which they would like a peer buddy to assist them, or (c) perceptions of whether it was helpful to have a peer buddy. If students are able to respond in writing, they also can be provided with a brief written survey on which to reply to different questions about the program. For example, we have provided in Figure 8.1 on page 144 an example of a short questionnaire on which students can respond to various questions about a peer buddy program. For students who have difficulty reading or writing, these questions can be adapted as needed and asked orally as students' answers are written down.

Why Do You Like to Spend Time with Your Peer Buddies?

- "Because they are my best friends"
- "Because it's fun!"
- "Because I like having friends."
- "They are my best friends and they are nice to me."
- "He is a good friend—a good pal."
- "Kelli is my friend. I'm going to miss her next year."
- "I like having someone in biology class who knows the material and can explain things I don't understand."
- "Because she introduces me to her friends and now I have a lot of friends."
- "I like him. He's fun and makes me laugh."

Greenwood High School Special Education Students

Source: Reprinted from "They are my best friends:" Peer buddies promote inclusion in high school by Hughes, C., Guth, C., Hall, S., Presley, J., Dye, M., & Byers, C., *TEACHING Exceptional Children*, *31*(5), 1999, 32–37. Copyright 1999 by The Council for Exceptional Children. Reprinted with permission.

Second, regularly observe students as they interact with their peer buddies in classrooms, hallways, cafeterias, gymnasiums, during other school activities, and during afterschool or community events. Observations are especially important with students with more severe disabilities who may have difficulty communicating feedback on their experiences in a peer buddy program. Watching students spend time inter-

FIGURE 8.1   Student Questionnaire

Name: _____   Grade: _____

Supervising teacher: _____   Date: _____

Respond to each of the following questions by writing a short paragraph explaining your feelings.

1. Give examples of some of the things you do with your peer buddies.

   _____
   _____
   _____
   _____
   _____
   _____

2. What have you learned from your experiences in the peer buddy program?

   _____
   _____
   _____
   _____
   _____
   _____

3. Do you feel the peer buddy program is beneficial to you? Tell how.

   _____
   _____
   _____
   _____
   _____
   _____

4. Do you feel that peer buddies benefit from being in the program? Tell how.

   _____
   _____
   _____
   _____
   _____
   _____

FIGURE 8.1 Continued

5. What do you like most about the peer buddy program?

_____

_____

_____

_____

_____

_____

_____

6. How would you make the peer buddy program better?

_____

_____

_____

_____

_____

_____

_____

7. Would you recommend that we continue having the peer buddy program? Why or why not?

_____

_____

_____

_____

_____

_____

_____

8. Do you spend time with your peer buddies outside of school? If so, tell what you do.

_____

_____

_____

_____

_____

_____

acting with each other can provide information about (a) the quality of relationships that students are developing with their peers, (b) the extent to which peer buddies are assisting their classmates with disabilities in accessing the general education curriculum, and (c) whether students are becoming equal participants in the school community. It may be that students with disabilities are attending classes with their general education peers but they have few interactions with or are completing different activities than their general education classmates. Directly observing students with disabilities whenever possible throughout the day can reveal much about the quality of a student's inclusion activities.

"I'll never forget the day Tami got her college athletic scholarship. All the students she invited to the signing ceremony were all the special education students. And when Tami came into the room, the students thought the princess had arrived!"

Mr. Longmire
Principal

Third, provide opportunities for students to share their experiences in the peer buddy program using a multimedia format. Students with disabilities and their classmates can work together to complete a culminating project that showcases the activities they participated in, the relationships they developed, and the lessons they learned. For example, students could develop a video or Power Point demonstration, record their impressions into a cassette tape recorder, develop a photographic portfolio of their activities, or create a "storybook" of their experiences with illustrative drawings.

Fourth, closely examine students' educational programs for evidence of academic performance improvement. Peer buddy programs are designed, in part, to promote positive educational outcomes for all students. When you look at students' class schedules, are students with disabilities participating in the full spectrum of activities that comprise a typical school day? Do their schedules resemble those of their schoolmates without disabilities? Are they enrolled in more general education classes than before they participated in the peer buddy program? Are they actively participating in those classes? Are students demonstrating progress on their individualized education program (IEP) goals? Are students' social circles expanding? The answers to these questions can confirm the benefits of a peer buddy program or suggest areas for additional program improvement. Remember: You are only one person. Seek the help of others in answering some of these questions. You can't be expected to be in all places at all times to observe or interview students. Other staff such as school counselors or fellow teachers can be recruited to assist you. Remember that parents or other family members know a student from other perspectives as well and can provide information that will add to a more comprehensive picture of the student.

"Most special education students did not participate in school social activities before we had a peer buddy program because of self-conscious feelings. Some students were afraid to leave the classroom or their teachers. Peer buddies provided them with a natural and age-appropriate way to participate in high school activities. Now these students are eager to accompany peer buddies to activities. Several of them attended the Senior Prom with their peer buddies."

Ms. Paschall
Special Education Teacher

Assessing Program Impact on Peer Buddies

As with special education students, it is important to assess the impact of a peer buddy program on general education participants. Peer buddy programs are designed as service–learning experiences that challenge and extend *all* students academically, socially, and personally. It is important to understand how well this goal is being met and, if not, to identify strategies for improving a program. In addition, peer buddies can provide input from their own experiences and perspectives regarding aspects of the program that they find to be beneficial and those that they feel hinder their interactions with their classmates. Moreover, the views of peer buddies can identify barriers to general education participation faced by students with disabilities that are not readily apparent to teachers, counselors, and administrators. Peer buddies' input as participants in a program is critical to ongoing evaluation and continual improvement of the program.

Dear Mr. Cisneros,

I just wanted to express a few opinions I had of this class. If I could only use one word to describe the course I have taken this year, that one word would be . . . REMARKABLE. The teachers, students, assistants, and of course all the peer buddies seem to work together as a team with one goal in mind: to learn and grow. I can honestly say I have learned so much about the special education students this year. I have found that I will probably never in my life have the type of friendships again as the ones I have had with these students. They have made an impression on me, and I will always have this year as a memory. I want to thank you for giving me the opportunity to be a part of your class and for all your wonderful words of encouragement. You and your students have made this school my school, and I will always look back with fond memories.

Thank you,

Cameron Ferron

Peer Buddy

There are several direct and indirect ways to assess whether the peer buddy program is accomplishing the intended goals for participants. (See Chapter 6 for additional description of assessment strategies.) First, have frequent conversations with peer buddies about their experiences in the program. Asking students to share what is working well, personal lessons they are learning, challenges they have encountered, and benefits they have experienced will inform you about their day-to-day encounters in the program. These informal conversations allow students to relay often poignant stories that provide individual snapshots of the program's impact. Conversations can take place more formally with small groups of peer buddies. For example, in some schools, teachers provide opportunities for peer buddies to get together during the school day to share pizza and reflect as a group on the successes and challenges that they have experienced participating in the program (see Peer Buddy Clubs in Chapter 6). Staff should look for patterns in students' comments and incorporate this feedback into appropriate changes in a program.

"You become more open-minded to other people—not only people with disabilities, but also people from other cultures. During class, you become more open-minded totally because you're not afraid of a person with a disability. I know with me, I know if I see someone walking down the street with a disability, it doesn't bother me, not like it did before I started this class."

Ron Jarvis
Peer Buddy

Second, questionnaires may be an efficient way to gather feedback from multiple peer buddies, particularly when your program has expanded across an entire school. We have provided an example peer buddy questionnaire in Figure 8.2 that can be modified easily to address areas you believe are most relevant to your particular program. By posing the same questions to students (a) before they enroll in a peer buddy program and (b) after they have participated for a length of time, you can assess changes in students' responses over time. For example, you could develop a list of questions to assess changes in students' attitudes or knowledge about disability issues as a result of being a peer buddy (see box on page 155). Also, be sure to ask students about their recommendations for improving their peer buddy experiences. Our involvement in schools has shown us that peer buddies—who have actually "lived" the program—have many creative recommendations for improving a peer buddy program.

"I think the teachers should explain a little background on each of the students they will be interacting with so the peer buddies can understand who they are, what to expect, and why they do the things that they do."

Valencia Sanders
Peer Buddy

Third, students' assignments, class projects, and reflective journals provide additional insight into what peer buddies are gaining from their experiences (see Chapter 5, Sample Assignments and Activities). Some schools plan a culminating assignment at the end of the semester in which students self-evaluate and reflect on their peer buddy experiences (Longwill & Kleinert, 1998). Remember, of course, that you should not wait until the end of the semester to discover there is a problem or that you missed an opportunity to adjust a program before it is too late. It is important to read through students' journals (with their permission, of course) and other written projects periodically to keep informed about peer buddies' reactions to the program.

"I found the journal to be helpful, because you can look back and see how you have changed during the time between when you first entered the program and now."

Meghan Parrish
Peer Buddy

FIGURE 8.2 Peer Buddy Questionnaire

Peer Buddy Questionnaire

Name: _____   Grade: _____

Supervising teacher: _____   Date: _____

Respond to each of the following questions by writing a short paragraph explaining your feelings.

1. Describe your responsibilities as part of the program. Give examples of some of the activities you participated in with your classmates with disabilities.

   _____
   _____
   _____
   _____
   _____

2. What have you learned from your experiences in the peer buddy program?

   _____
   _____
   _____
   _____
   _____

3. Do you feel the peer buddy program is beneficial to you? In what ways?

   _____
   _____
   _____
   _____
   _____

4. Do you feel that the peer buddy program is beneficial for students with disabilities? In what ways?

   _____
   _____
   _____
   _____
   _____

5. How are students with disabilities different from you? How are they similar to you?

   _____
   _____
   _____
   _____
   _____

(continued)

FIGURE 8.2 Continued

6. Do you feel comfortable hanging out with your classmates with disabilities? Why or why not?

_____

_____

_____

_____

_____

_____

_____

7. What did you like most about being a peer buddy?

_____

_____

_____

_____

_____

_____

8. Would you change or improve anything about the peer buddy program? If so, explain.

_____

_____

_____

_____

_____

_____

9. Would you recommend that your friends consider becoming involved in the program? Why or why not?

_____

_____

_____

_____

_____

_____

10. How do you think your experiences will influence your future career decisions?

_____

_____

_____

_____

_____

_____

Assessing Program Impact on Teachers, Administrators, and Counselors

It is critical that teachers and other school staff have a voice in planning, conducting, and improving a service–learning peer buddy program. Make it a point to regularly obtain feedback from participating staff about how well a program is meeting its intended goals. If teachers, administrators, or counselors do not feel a peer buddy program is beneficial for students and works well within the context of classroom routines, it is not going to be implemented as intended. It is essential in a school that *all* participants in a peer buddy program have input into and feel ownership of the program if the program is going to succeed. What are the benefits and challenges of a program as perceived by different participants? What recommendations do different school staff have for improving or expanding the program? If staff are not "on the same page" with respect to expected goals and outcomes of a program, it is unlikely that they can work together cooperatively to improve, expand, or sustain a program. Even when programs are going well, it is informative to get feedback from school staff regarding factors they believe are contributing to the success of a program. Their perceptions and recommendations subsequently can be shared with staff who are not experiencing similar successes either within the school or in other schools. Teachers and other staff also are likely to have insight into how a program is benefiting students—information that is important regarding what motivates students to participate in a peer buddy program.

"I recommend enrolling no more than one or two students with disabilities accompanied by a peer buddy in a single general education class. This maintains natural proportions of students with and without disabilities and ensures that students who need supports receive them."

Mr. Aguilar
General Education Teacher

Because teachers, administrators, and counselors have multiple demands on their time, remember to be considerate when you approach staff for feedback on the program. Below are approaches you can take to make the gathering of recommendations from participating teachers and other school staff more enjoyable.

- Hold a luncheon once during each semester and invite all teachers who are participating in the program to share a meal and conversation about what is and is not working well. Use some of the following questions to prompt discussion: *Is the program having the impact that you anticipated? Do you have the training and resources you need to make the program successful? If you could improve one thing about the program, what would it be? Can you share any recommendations you have for improving various aspects of the program (e.g., selecting peer buddies, peer buddy orientations, scheduling)? What feature of this program has been most valuable to you and your students?*
- Ask an administrator for permission to meet with participating teachers and other school staff during an in-service day or in lieu of a departmental faculty meeting. Be sure to have bagels, muffins, or other snacks available.
- Periodically send out brief email messages to teachers asking if anyone has any questions or is encountering specific challenges. Encourage other teachers to respond with their own advice or recommendations at a time when it is convenient for them.

■ Develop a brief questionnaire, such as the example in Figure 8.3, which can be distributed to school staff in the middle or at the end of the semester. As questionnaires are completed, they can be entered in a lottery for a small prize, such as a movie pass or computer supplies.

Congratulations! You now have had a peer buddy program up and running in your classroom for a semester or more. You and your colleagues at school also, no doubt, have developed a good sense of the goals you would like the program to accomplish. At the same time, you likely have had some challenges in meeting these goals. If other **teachers** in your school also are working with peer buddies in their classes, chances are that they are asking similar questions and facing similar challenges. Share your experiences with other teachers and ask for their feedback about how they are addressing these challenges successfully.

Assessing Program Impact on Parents

The importance of obtaining feedback from and partnering with parents when implementing a peer buddy program cannot be overemphasized. Through their conversations at home with their children and observations of interactions outside of the school day, parents gain useful insight regarding the impact of the program. For example, students may share concerns with their parents that they are uncomfortable sharing with their teachers. Moreover, parents both of peer buddies and of students with disabilities will know whether their children are contacting each other after school, talking together on the telephone, or spending time together on the weekend. Parents also have a unique vantage point from which to provide advice for improving or recommendations for extending the program beyond the school day. Therefore, we recommend that you try to obtain feedback on the program from the parents of peer buddies *and* students with disabilities.

As a **parent**, it is important that you speak up and let your perspective be known at school. Teachers have limited access to what goes on with students outside of the school day. The insight you have into your own child's goals, dreams, fears, and personal experiences is invaluable to designing inclusive educational experiences that reflect your child's individual circumstances. What does your child like to do during his spare time? Who are his friends? What transportation options does he have for going out in the community? What supports does he need? Remember, the 1997 IDEA Amendments emphasize and support the need for parental input into the educational process.

It is also important to regard parents as valuable partners in the peer buddy program. Their support is particularly critical in extending the program beyond the school day. When seeking input from parents, provide them with opportunities to share stories or anecdotes about their child's participation in the peer buddy program. Ask parents about any changes in their children's attitudes toward school, interests in classes, and relationships with peers. Listen closely and respond to parents' concerns and recommendations. For example, some parents we have known have held barbeques or trips to a skating rink that all peer buddies and students with disabilities in a class attended. If you are unsure of exactly how to involve parents, just ask them about the best way to support their participation.

FIGURE 8.3   School Staff Questionnaire

School Staff Questionnaire

Name: _____   Date: _____

Position: _____

Respond to each of the following questions by writing a short paragraph explaining your feelings.

1. Describe some of the activities that peer buddies do with their classmates with disabilities in your school.

   _____
   _____
   _____
   _____
   _____

2. How would you describe the peer buddies' relationships with their classmates?

   _____
   _____
   _____
   _____
   _____

3. Do you feel the peer buddy program is beneficial to your school? In what ways?

   _____
   _____
   _____
   _____
   _____

4. Do you feel that the peer buddy program is beneficial for students with disabilities? In what ways?

   _____
   _____
   _____
   _____
   _____

5. Do you feel that the peer buddy program is beneficial for peer buddies? In what ways?

   _____
   _____
   _____
   _____
   _____

FIGURE 4.3 Continued

6. Do you have any recommendations for how peer buddies and students with disabilities work together in your school?

_____

_____

_____

_____

_____

_____

_____

7. Describe any additional supports or resources that you feel would assist you.

_____

_____

_____

_____

_____

_____

8. Would you change or improve anything about the peer buddy program? If so, explain.

_____

_____

_____

_____

_____

_____

Additional comments:

_____

_____

_____

_____

_____

_____

_____

_____

_____

_____

_____

Strategies for Evaluating the Effects of Peer Buddy Programs

In addition to the forms provided in this chapter, several other approaches exist for assessing the impact of peer buddy programs on participants. Below, we describe examples of tools that can be modified to assess outcomes of your program. Possible approaches include using questionnaires, interviews, or direct observation.

- Attitude questionnaires can be given to students to determine how their perceptions of people with disabilities, knowledge about disability issues, and/or willingness to interact with their special education classmates change as a result of participating in a peer buddy program. Questionnaires can be given to students prior to and after becoming a peer buddy to allow you to make comparisons. Examples: Burns, Storey, & Certo (1999); Carter, Hughes, Copeland, & Breen (2001).

- Open-ended questionnaires can be given to students and teachers addressing areas such as (a) attitudes toward students with disabilities or inclusion, (b) perceptions of program benefits, (c) descriptions of activities that peer buddies and students with disabilities participate in together, (d) perceptions of the contributions peer buddy programs make toward students' education, and (e) suggestions for improving the program. Examples: Copeland et al. (2002); Helmstetter, Peck, & Giangreco (1994); Hughes et al. (2001).

- Conversations can be conducted one on one with high school students about their experiences interacting with their classmates with disabilities over the past school semester. You can ask some of the following questions: *What have you gotten out of this experience? What did you like most and least? How has this experience affected other areas of your life? Are there some aspects of this experience that have been difficult for you? For other students? Do you have any recommendations for additional activities students could participate in with their classmates with disabilities?* Examples: Kamps et al. (1998); Peck, Donaldson, & Pezzoli (1990).

- Interviews also can be conducted efficiently with small groups of students to gather their input on the following issues: (a) barriers to inclusion experienced by students with disabilities, (b) recommendations for increasing the social and academic participation of their peers, and (c) ideas for helping students with disabilities participate in school activities. Examples: Copeland et al. (2004); Fisher (1999); York & Tundidor (1995).

- Directly observing students with disabilities and their peer buddies as they interact allows you to see firsthand the impact that peer buddy programs have on participants. Consider focusing your observations on the types of support behaviors students exchange, students' active engagement in class activities, or the degree to which students provide and receive various social interaction behaviors, such as assistance, instruction, criticism, joking, social greetings, and compliments. Examples: Mu, Siegel, & Allinder (2000); Shukla et al. (1998, 1999).

Working with Advisory Boards to Sustain Programs

One purpose of assessing program impact on and obtaining feedback from participants is to use their responses to inform and shape peer buddy program goals and procedures for upcoming semesters. Input from participants may indicate programmatic changes that should occur as well as examples of program successes. Exactly how do you interpret the feedback that you receive? What if you find differences of opinion regarding outcomes? An advisory board can help you weigh participant responses and answer these questions, as follows.

As your peer buddy program grows, we recommend that you establish an advisory board composed of various participants and stakeholders who can provide support, feedback, and advice. There are several benefits of advisory boards. First, regularly bringing together a group of committed people multiplies both the intangible and material resources available to your program. The more perspectives that you can bring together, the more likely that you will be able to find an innovative solution to any challenges that may arise. Having a range of participants including students, parents, teachers, counselors, and administrators also can help you interpret feedback—including conflicting perspectives—that you received when assessing program impact. In addition, you can be assured that all voices are being heard when making programmatic decisions. Second, advisory boards build interest and encourage others to participate in your program. An advisory board gives principals, counselors, parents, and community members a practical way to contribute actively to the success of the program. Because advisory boards allow each participant a voice, they bring everyone to the table and promote a sense of ownership of and responsibility toward a program. Third, the support of an advisory board can contribute to the sustainability of your program. Advisory board members can serve as a sounding board for new ideas or assist in tackling challenging issues that come up throughout the semester. Fourth, advisory boards can ensure that an eye is kept on the "big picture." Advisory board members can make sure that a program stays focused on and is successful in meeting the goals for which it was developed.

Your advisory board should be composed of representatives of all participants and stakeholders. Who has a stake in the success of peer buddy programs? Throughout this book, we have described a number of different people who play a role in the success of a peer buddy program, including peer buddies, students with disabilities, special and general education teachers, administrators, counselors, parents, and community members. Consider inviting people to participate who have a sincere interest in the program, have time available to attend meetings, and are willing to contribute suggestions and promote the program. For logistical reasons, we suggest that you consider limiting the advisory board to no more than seven to ten people. Doing so ensures success with the task of setting an acceptable meeting time, length does not become too difficult, and meetings remain manageable. Try to make sure that multiple perspectives are represented and have a voice in program implementation. Also, remember that advisory board members are volunteering their time when they attend meetings. Reward them with some delicious snacks or other tokens of appreciation.

Excerpt from an Advisory Board Meeting's Minutes: Feedback from Participants

MS. ROSE, SPECIAL EDUCATION TEACHER: We need to talk to the school counselors and ask that they not just stick students in the peer buddy program. They need to let the students visit the classes first and see if it is something they really want to do. Counselors are still having students assigned to a class without meeting the teachers first. The screening procedures for peer buddies are not always being followed. Also, we sometimes have too many peer buddies signed up for one class and not enough for another.

MR. ANDERSON, SPECIAL EDUCATION TEACHER: I agree. Scheduling can be a problem. I know ten football players who would be good peer buddies, but their schedules are so tight, they can't work it in.

MS. DONNELLY, GENERAL EDUCATION TEACHER: I liked having special education students in my class this semester. I think the general education students appreciated the teacher's job more. I also think they appreciated their own skills more. It was time-consuming though, having students on many different levels. It would have been good to have a peer buddy in the class who had already taken the course and knew the different units we were going to cover.

MR. HOLLINS, PARENT: Shariff loved being in his keyboarding class this semester. His peer buddy Richard went with him every day and helped him out. Richard had been in the class last semester so he knew what to do. Shariff will use his computer skills on the job next year.

We suggest that an advisory board should meet at least once per semester to provide ongoing insight and recommendations. If a peer buddy program is new in your school, it will be beneficial initially to meet more often. Developing a written agenda prior to each meeting can guide and focus advisory board members so that meetings remain productive and efficient. We have provided an example advisory board agenda in Table 8.1, which can be adapted to reflect particular issues to be addressed by the advisory board of your peer buddy program. A sample invitation for an advisory board meeting is found in Figure 8.4.

Advisory boards can play an important role in setting goals and providing future direction for a peer buddy program. Most peer buddy programs will evolve over time in response to changing goals and expectations, new school priorities, emerging research, and program successes and challenges. To assist the advisory board in providing program guidance, it may be helpful to have members look backward at past successes and challenges and look forward toward future plans. In Table 8.2 on page 159, we provide a list of questions that can be used to prompt members to reflect on program progress and future directions.

As with all feedback gathered as part of the peer buddy program, plans should be developed for addressing issues and implementing solutions discussed during advisory board meetings. It may be helpful to designate a person to be responsible for ensuring that each recommendation is followed.

TABLE 8.1 Sample Advisory Board Agenda

- Introduce everyone present at the meeting.
- Provide an overview of the purpose of the advisory board.
- Briefly review how topics discussed at previous meetings have been addressed.
- Make arrangements for different people to facilitate the meeting, take notes, and keep track of time.
- Make any announcements about events related to the peer buddy program, such as upcoming trips or recognition activities.
- Present topics for discussion (see examples below). Try to limit discussion to two to four issues during a single advisory board meeting:
  - Program goals
  - Course credit issues
  - Publicizing the program
  - Increasing school and community support
  - Recruiting peer buddies
  - Orientation and training activities
  - Strategies for promoting additional inclusion
  - Student support needs
  - Teacher training needs
  - Outcomes for students and the school community
  - Strategies for expanding the program within or across schools
  - Other concerns of participants
- Summarize the group's discussion.
- Determine date and location of next meeting.
- Adjourn.
- Show your appreciation to advisory board members by sending a thank-you note after the meeting.

FIGURE 8.4   Sample Advisory Board Invitation

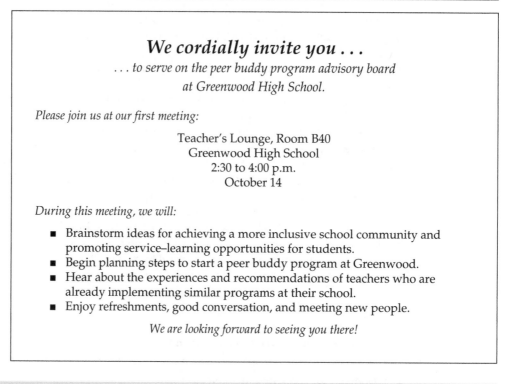

We cordially invite you . . .
*. . . to serve on the peer buddy program advisory board
at Greenwood High School.*

Please join us at our first meeting:

Teacher's Lounge, Room B40
Greenwood High School
2:30 to 4:00 p.m.
October 14

During this meeting, we will:

■ Brainstorm ideas for achieving a more inclusive school community and promoting service–learning opportunities for students.
■ Begin planning steps to start a peer buddy program at Greenwood.
■ Hear about the experiences and recommendations of teachers who are already implementing similar programs at their school.
■ Enjoy refreshments, good conversation, and meeting new people.

We are looking forward to seeing you there!

"After Latanya's participation in the peer buddy program this year, it has made it easier for me to see her as a part of the community and see her having a more independent life. I am less concerned with her IEP goals than I am with Latanya's having self-confidence and a love of life."

Mr. Shrader
Parent

Indeed, many of the best recommendations for improving the Metropolitan Nashville Peer Buddy Program in Nashville, Tennessee, came not from us, but emerged from brainstorming sessions during advisory board meetings. For example, advisory boards at different schools involved in the program developed solutions for (a) improving recruitment efforts, (b) revising student and teacher peer buddy manuals, (c) expanding peer buddy interactions after school hours, (d) involving students with disabilities and their peer buddies in community-based employment activities, (e) starting a peer buddy club to support peer buddies, and (f) helping general education teachers modify grades and assignments for special education students. Of course, many of these recommendations have been incorporated into this book.

If you are just one **teacher** or school staff arranging for peer buddies to support their classmates with disabilities in one classroom only, it is not necessary to establish an advisory board. However, you need to be certain that you solicit input and feedback from all participants about how the arrangement is working. Later, if you decide to expand the program to additional classrooms, an advisory board can be established to help you in this task.

TABLE 8.2 Reflection Questions for School Staff or Advisory Boards

---

- How well did we meet our goals?
- What was our biggest success? What factors led to that success?
- What was our biggest challenge? How did we respond? What will we take from that experience?
- What school and community activities did students with disabilities and peer buddies participate in together?
- How do these activities align with our goals for the program? Do we need to make any changes to more closely connect activities with goals?
- How do student participants evaluate the quality of their relationships? Are there supports we could provide that would further enhance the quality of these relationships?
- How well did participating teachers, administrators, counselors, and educational assistants communicate with each other? Are there steps we need to take to improve the degree of communication?
- How often and in what ways did teachers communicate with student participants? Did students and teachers feel that this communication was adequate? Were important issues addressed by teachers at the right time? What can we do to improve this communication?
- How did we show program impact? What information have we not been able to obtain or report? Why?
- How did we survey important stakeholders (educators, volunteers, administrators, students, parents) to gauge their satisfaction and seek suggestions for improvement? Have we missed important stakeholders?
- On what topics, how frequently, and in what formats did we offer training or inservice for tutors? Did peer buddies report that they were prepared with a variety of strategies? What issues arose during the year that we could address with training or other support this year?
- How effective was our collaboration? What did each partner do to support and enhance collaboration with one another? How can we improve?
- Did our advisory group and peer buddies play important roles? How can these expand?
- How did we stretch ourselves this year? What was valuable about that experience?
- Given past experiences, where should we focus our energy this year? How can we focus on those objectives?

Source: Adapted from *Beyond start-up: Real answers for established education programs* by Black, A., *Tutor*, Fall 2000, 1-12. Copyright 2000 by Northwest Regional Educational Laboratory: LEARNS Project. Reprinted with permission.

Expanding a Peer Buddy Program

Within a School

Peer buddy programs often start off as the initiative of a single teacher, counselor, or administrator. As word of the success of a program spreads throughout a school, other teachers also will begin to express an interest in becoming involved. As the peer buddy program expands in your school, consider identifying a person to coordinate your growing program. For a smaller program, a special education teacher or counselor can be assigned as the coordinator. For a larger program, the time required to coordinate substantial numbers of peer buddies may be too daunting for just one person. Strategies for addressing considerable program growth include (a) arranging for multiple teachers to assume joint responsibility for the program, (b) establishing release time for a lead teacher, (c) designating an educational assistant or counselor to assume the role of coordinator, or (d) arranging for a parent volunteer to provide assistance to a teacher or counselor.

 As the number of teachers and students participating in the peer buddy program increases, the **counselor's** role in recruiting and assigning peer buddies will become more pronounced. Teachers' time is quickly allotted to interacting with students in their own classes. Although you have many demands on your time as well, you have the advantage of interacting with students from many classes throughout the day. You are likely to know of students who would love to be peer buddies—and likely would be good ones—but just haven't had the chance yet during their high school career. Speak with teachers to find out what their needs are for peer buddies in their classes. If there are teachers who are hesitant to have students participate in the program, you can share with them successes from the peer buddy program in other classes.

Across a District

Once a peer buddy program has been established at your school, you will be in a position to begin helping other schools begin their own peer buddy programs. The successes that you have experienced will serve as the strongest selling point for schools interested in beginning a new program. Share the success stories of your program—such as a student with a disability who became a cheerleader with the support of a peer buddy or a peer buddy who has gone on to become a teacher because of his experiences in the program—in as many ways as possible. Students are often the best promoters of the program. Involve peer buddies and students in spreading the news to other schools. For example, students can share their experiences at local conferences, in front of the school board, or at in-services. If the peer buddy program initially is approved as a credit course within a school district but is on a probationary period awaiting permanent approval, students can provide the school board with a firsthand account of the benefits of the program to encourage its final adoption. A video or portfolio of photographs depicting the program will convey visually to others what a peer buddy program is like.

Schools considering adopting a peer buddy program also will want to know what steps you took to get the program going at your school. If you have developed a peer buddy handbook for teachers and students at your school (see Chapter 5), you can share this resource with interested teachers from other schools. It may also be helpful to develop a list of steps to follow to implement the program in other schools or districts in your state. For example, based on our experiences in Metropolitan Nashville schools, we developed a list of seven steps school staff can use to establish a peer buddy program in their school (see Figure 8.5). These steps can be adapted to reflect local conditions, expectations, and possible constraints.

 As the peer buddy program at your school expands to other schools in your district or state, **administrators** at these schools will want to hear about your experiences with the program. Questions will include how the program works, what are the benefits, what are the risks, how much time does it take to get the program started, and who is responsible for the program. Your testimony as to the successes you have experienced and observed in the program can be compelling evidence for those who are considering program adoption. A strong argument in favor of a peer buddy program will be how well it addresses your school's mission, such as character development and building citizens of tomorrow.

FIGURE 8.5   Seven Steps to Starting a Peer Buddy Program

Step 1: Develop a one-credit course.
- ☐ Incorporate into your school's curriculum a peer tutoring course that allows peer buddies to spend at least one period each day with their partners with disabilities.
- ☐ Begin building a base of support with the administration, school counselors, and teachers in your school for the inclusion of students receiving special education services in general education activities.
- ☐ Follow the established procedures of the local and state educational agencies when you apply for the new course offering.

Step 2: Recruit peer buddies.
- ☐ Actively recruit peer buddies during the first year. After that, peer buddies will recruit for you.
- ☐ Include announcements, posters, articles in the school newspaper and PTA newsletter, videos on the school's closed-circuit television, and peer buddies speaking in school clubs and classes.
- ☐ Present information about the new program at a faculty meeting.
- ☐ Start slowly while you establish the course expectations.

Step 3: Screen and match students.
- ☐ Have school counselors refer students who have interest, good attendance, and adequate grades.
- ☐ Arrange for students to interview with the special education teachers.
- ☐ Have students provide information regarding their past experience with students with diverse abilities and about clubs or activities that they are involved in that their partners could join.
- ☐ Allow students to observe in the classroom to learn about the role of a peer buddy and whether they would be an appropriate match for the class.

Step 4: Teach peer buddies to use instructional strategies.
- ☐ Model the use of prompting and reinforcement techniques.
- ☐ Conduct a peer buddy orientation that includes the concept of "people first," disability awareness, communication strategies, and suggested activities.
- ☐ Communicate teachers' expectations for the peer buddy course including attendance and grading policies.
- ☐ Provide suggestions for dealing with inappropriate behavior, setting limits, and modifying general education curricula.

Step 5: Evaluate the program.
- ☐ Schedule observations and feedback sessions with peer buddies to address their questions or concerns.
- ☐ Provide feedback on their interaction skills, time management, use of positive reinforcement, and activities engaged in with their partners.
- ☐ Have peer buddies keep a daily journal of their activities and reflections, which should be reviewed weekly by the classroom teacher.
- ☐ Establish a peer buddy club, which allows students to share experiences and ideas as well as gives the teacher an opportunity to offer ongoing training and feedback.

Step 6: Hold a Lunch Bunch.
- ☐ Invite peer buddies to join special education students for lunch in the cafeteria.
- ☐ Encourage the peer buddies to invite their general education friends to join the group, increasing social contacts for their partners.
- ☐ Remind general education students who, because of class conflicts, are unable to enroll in the course to join the Lunch Bunch.

Step 7: Establish an advisory board.
- ☐ Develop an advisory board that includes students (peer buddies and partners), students' parents, participating general and special education teachers, administrators, and school counselors.
- ☐ Include community representatives to expand the peer buddy program to community-based activities, such as work experiences.
- ☐ Meet at least once each semester to obtain insight and suggestions for evaluating and improving the program. Thank all members for their participation.

Source: From "They are my best friends:" Peer buddies promote inclusion in high school by Hughes, C., Guth, C., Hall, S., Presley, J., Dye, M., & Byers, C., *TEACHING Exceptional Children, 31*(5), 1999, 32-37. Copyright 1999 by The Council for Exceptional Children. Reprinted with permission.

Summary

Evaluation activities can help you gain a clearer picture of your program's impact on the larger school community. Input from participants can inform you regarding program successes as well as areas needing further investigation or modification. A variety of strategies are available to obtain information from program participants including questionnaires, interviews, and direct observation. Establishing an advisory board is an additional method for obtaining programmatic input as well as additional resources, perspectives, and ideas. Feedback provided by program participants and advisory board members can be the vehicle that assists you in maintaining and building on successes realized during previous semesters of peer buddy program implementation.

CASE STUDY BOX: *Ms. Marantz Goes to School*

The day after freshman orientation, Ms. Marantz sprang into action. She figured there was no point in calling the main office at Hudson Heights High School. She didn't want to be put on hold or told to call back. Instead, she grabbed her peer buddy portfolio—an album of photographs, newspaper clippings, and other momentos she had gathered from her daughter Katie's experiences in the peer buddy program at Randolph Park Middle School—and hurried out the door.

Her first stop after she had passed through security at Hudson Heights High and had been escorted to the main office was the freshman counselor, Ms. McIntyre. As she waited to see the counselor, Ms. Marantz arranged her arguments in her head: (1) Her daughter Katie had "inclusion in general education classes" on her IEP—that was the law! (2) Katie had spoken up many times—including at several IEP meetings—that she wanted to take keyboarding, drama, and several other general education classes taught at Hudson Heights. (3) Throughout both elementary and middle schools, Katie had been included in general education classes as well as several school clubs and extracurricular activities with peer buddies, as could be seen in the pictures and other documentation in the portfolio Ms. Marantz held in her hands. Testimony from Katie's general education teachers as to the success of having peer buddies assist Katie in her classes was included in the portfolio if Ms. McIntyre would like to see it. (4) Ms. Marantz fully intended to have Katie continue to be involved in a peer buddy program in addition to general education classes and activities, and if there was no one at Hudson Heights High School who was willing to start such a program, Ms. Marantz was willing to contribute her time and effort herself to do so. There it was!

Ms. McIntyre listened quietly to Ms. Marantz's arguments. She knew, of course, that Ms. Marantz was right: Special education students were entitled to be included in general education to the maximum extent appropriate. It just hadn't been been done much at Hudson Heights High. And as to a peer buddy program, well, there had never been anything like that. However, peer buddies did seem like a good idea, and Ms. Marantz certainly did present a good case. The pictures and first-person stories she brought spoke for themselves. Besides, Mr. Randazzo, the head principal at Hudson Heights, did say that there was a new initiative on inclusive education in the school district and if having peer buddies could help, it might be worth it.

Right off the bat, Ms. McIntyre could think of several teachers who likely would be interested in participating in a new peer buddy program as well as a few students who had room in their schedules and would likely make perfect peer buddies. Why wait? If Ms. Marantz was willing to help—and she had said she was—and since Katie clearly wanted to participate, why not start with just this one student and see how it goes? If it works, then they could think about expanding it to other students and in other classes. Ms. McIntyre didn't have to deliberate too long. She gave a "thumbs-up" to Ms. Marantz and her peer buddy proposal.

After shaking hands with Ms. McIntyre and arranging for a time to meet again with other school staff to begin looking at the logistics of arranging for peer buddies to support Katie in her general education classes and activities starting in the fall, Ms. McIntrye walked down the hall to the main door of Hudson Heights High School with a smile on her face. It looked like Katie had a promising high school career ahead of her—peer buddies, drama class, and all. Ms. Marantz was certainly glad she had taken the time to go to school that day.

Learning Activities

- Think back to when you first began laying the ground work for your peer buddy program. What goals did you hope that the program would accomplish? Now that your peer buddy program is up and running, make a list of five ways you can determine whether the goals you laid out are being met. After you assess goal attainment, list changes you would like to make in your program to better meet your goals. Also list successes you identified in meeting program goals.

- Arrange to hold focus groups to address particular issues that have arisen during peer buddy program implementation at your school. Choose participants who are knowledgeable regarding the issues to be addressed. For example, if you want to know how well students with disabilities are becoming a part of the classroom community, you could invite a group of peer buddies who accompany these students to their general education classes. In some cases, you may want to have a group of "mixed" participants, such as peer buddies and their classmates with disabilities or a group of teachers and parents, in order to address a topic.

- List three goals that you and your colleagues have for taking your peer buddy program to the next level. Ask other teachers, counselors, and administrators for their input and recommendations. Then, develop a written plan of where you would like the program to be a year from now. Give yourself a timeline and write how you will evaluate if you have reached your goals in a year.

- Make a list of ten people whom you would like to invite to be on your peer buddy advisory board. As you look back over the list, ask yourself: *Is a variety of perspectives represented on this list? Are there any perspectives that are missing? Are these people committed to the program? What will their roles be? What will motivate these people to join the board and to stay on and contribute to program development?*

- You've done a lot of hard work in getting your peer buddy program going as far as it has. Take time to congratulate yourself! List all the accomplishments and success stories you can think of that you've noticed since the program started. Make an album of pictures, student reflections, awards, and anything else to remind yourself and others about the benefits already evident from program participation.

References

Burns, M., Storey, K., & Certo, N. J. (1998). Effect of service learning on attitudes toward students with severe disabilities. *Education and Training in Mental Retardation and Developmental Disabilities, 34,* 58–65.

Carter, E. W., Hughes, C., Copeland, S. R., & Breen, C. (2001). Differences between high school students who do and do not volunteer to participate in a peer interaction program. *Journal of the Association for Persons with Severe Handicaps, 26,* 229–239.

Copeland, S. R., Hughes, C., Carter, E. W., Guth, C., Presley, J., Williams, C. R., & Fowler, S. E. (2004). Increasing access to general education: Perspectives of participants in a high school peer support program. *Remedial and Special Education, 26,* 342–352.

Copeland, S. R., McCall, J., Williams, C. R., Guth, C., Carter, E. W., Fowler, S. E., Presley, J. A., & Hughes, C. (2002). High school peer buddies: A win-win situation. *TEACHING Exceptional Children, 35*(1), 16–21.

Fisher, D. (1999). According to their peers: Inclusion as high school students see it. *Mental Retardation, 37,* 458–467.

Grigal, M., Neubert, D. A., Moon, M. S., & Graham, S. (2003). Self-determination for students with disabilities: Views of parents and teachers. *Exceptional Children, 70*, 97–112.

Helmstetter, E., Peck, C. A., & Giangreco, M. F. (1994). Outcomes of interactions with peers with moderate or severe disabilities: A statewide survey of high school students. *Journal of the Association for Persons with Severe Handicaps, 19*, 263–276.

Hughes, C., Copeland, S. R., Guth, C., Rung, L. L., Hwang, B., Kleeb, G., & Strong, M. (2001). General education students' perspectives on their involvement in a high school peer buddy program. *Education and Training in Mental Retardation and Developmental Disabilities, 36*, 343–356.

Hughes, C., Guth, C., Hall, S., Presley, J., Dye, M., & Byers, C. (1999). They are my best friends: Peer buddies promote inclusion in high school. *TEACHING Exceptional Children, 31(5)*, 32–37.

Individuals with Disabilities Education Act Amendments of 1997, PL 105–17, 20 U. S. C. § 1400 *et seq.* (1997).

Kamps, D. M., Kravits, T., Lopez, A. G., Kemmerer, K., Potucek, J., & Harrell, L. (1998). What do the peers think? Social validity of peer-mediated programs. *Education and Treatment of Children, 21*, 107–134.

Longwill, A. W., & Kleinert, H. L. (1998). The unexpected benefits of high school peer tutoring. *TEACHING Exceptional Children, 30(4)*, 60–65.

Payne, D. A. (2000). *Evaluating service-learning programs and activities.* Lanham, MD: Scarecrow Press.

Peck, C. A., Donaldson, J., & Pezzoli, M. (1990). Some benefits nonhandicapped adolescents perceive for themselves from their social relationships with peers who have severe handicaps. *Journal of the Association for Persons with Severe Handicaps, 15*, 241–249.

Mu, K., Siegel, E. B., & Allinder, R. M. (2000). Peer interactions and sociometric status of high school students with moderate or severe disabilities in general education classrooms. *Journal of the Association for Persons with Severe Handicaps, 25*, 142–152.

Shukla, S., Kennedy, C. H., & Cushing, L. S. (1998). Component analysis of peer support strategies: Adult influence on the participation of peers without disabilities. *Journal of Behavioral Education, 8*, 397–413.

Shukla, S., Kennedy, C. H., & Cushing, L. S. (1999). Intermediate school students with severe disabilities: Supporting their social participation in general education classrooms. *Journal of Positive Behavior Interventions, 1*, 130–140.

York, J., & Tundidor, M. (1995). Issues raised in the name of inclusion: Perspectives of educators, parents, and students. *Journal of the Association for Persons with Severe Handicaps, 20*, 31–44.

Appendix: Resources

Resources Addressing Service Learning

Books and Chapters

Billig, S.H., & Furco, A. (2002). *Service-learning: Through a multidisciplinary lens.* Greenwich, CT: Information Age Publishing.

Boyle-Baise, M. (2002). *Multicultural service learning: Education teachers in diverse communities.* New York: Teachers College Press.

Bringle, R. G., Phillips. M. A., & Hudson, M. (2004). *The measure of service learning: Research scales to assess students' experiences.* Washington, DC: American Psychological Association.

Eyler, J. & Giles, D. E. (1999). *Where's the service in service-learning?* San Francisco: Jossey-Bass.

Eyler, J., Giles, D. E., & Schmiede, A. (1996). *A practitioner's guide to reflection in service-learning: Student voices and reflections.* Washington, DC: Corporation for National and Community Service.

Furco, A., & Billig, S. (2002). *Service-learning: The essence of the pedagogy.* Greenwich, CT: Information Age Publishing.

Gulati-Paree, G., & Finger, W. (Eds.). (1996). *Critical issues in K-12 service-learning: Case studies and reflections.* Raleigh, NC: National Society for Experiential Education.

Hamner, D.M. (2002). *Building bridges: The Allyn and Bacon student guide to service-learning.* Boston: Allyn and Bacon.

Jacoby, B. (Ed.). (2003). *Building partnerships for service-learning.* San Francisco: Jossey-Bass.

Kaye, C. B. (2004). *The complete guide to service learning: Proven, practical ways to engage students in civic responsibility, academic curriculum, and social action.* Minneapolis, MN: Free Spirit.

Kenny, M. E., Kenny, L., Simon, A. K., Kiley-Brabeck, K., & Lerner, R. M. (Eds.). (2002). *Learning to serve: Promoting civil society through service learning.* Boston: Kluwer Academic Publishers.

National Association of Partners in Education. (1999). *Involving youth in the community.* Alexandria, VA: Author.

National Service-Learning Cooperative. (1999). *Essential elements of service-learning.* St. Paul, MN: Author.

Payne, D. A. (2000). *Evaluating service learning activities and programs.* Lanham, MD: Scarecrow Press.

Stephens, L. (1995). *The complete guide to learning through community-service, grades K-9.* Boston: Allyn and Bacon.

Wade, R. C. (Ed.). (1997). *Community service learning: A guide to including service in the public school curriculum.* Albany: State University of New York.

Witmer, J. T., & Anderson, C. S. (1994). *How to establish a high school service learning program.* Alexandria, VA: Association for Supervision and Curriculum Development.

Youniss, J., & Yates, M. (1997). *Community service and social responsibility in youth.* Chicago: University of Chicago.

Youth Service America. (2001). *Effective learning, effective teaching, effective service: Voices from the field on improving education through service learning.* Washington, DC: Author.

Journals

Community Works Journal
  www.vermontcommunityworks.org
NASSP Bulletin
  www.principals.org
Educational Leadership
  www.ascd.org
Journal of Experiential Education
  www.aee.org
Michigan Journal of Community Service Learning
  www.umich.edu/~mjcsl

Middle Ground
    www.nmsa.org
Middle School Journal
    www.nmsa.org
Phi Delta Kappan
    www.pdkintl.org
Principal Leadership
    www.principals.org
The School Administrator
    www.aasa.org
Service-Learning Advances
    www.service-learningpartnership.org

Organizations

American Association of State Service Commissions
    1400 I Street, NW, Suite 800
    Washington, DC 20005-6526
    (202) 729-8263
    www.aassc.org
Compact for Learning and Citizenship
    c/o Education Commission of the States
    700 Broadway, Suite 1200
    Denver, CO 80203
    (303) 299-3600
    www.ecs.org/clc
Corporation for National and Community Service
    1201 New York Avenue, NW
    Washington, DC 20525
    (202) 606-5000
    www.nationalservice.org
Do Something
    423 West 55th Street
    New York, NY 10019
    (212) 523-1175
    www.dosomething.org
National Service-Learning Clearinghouse
    ETR Associates
    4 Carbonero Way
    Scotts Valley, CA 95066
    www.servicelearning.org
National Service-Learning Partnership
    c/o Academy for Educational Development
    100 Fifth Avenue
    New York, NY 10011
    (212) 367-4588
    www.service-learningpartnership.org
National Society for Experiential Education (NSEE)
    9001 Braddock Road, Suite 380
    Springfield, VA 22151
    (703) 933-0017
    www.nsee.org
National Youth Leadership Council
    1667 Snelling Avenue North
    St. Paul, MN 55108
    (651) 631-3672
    www.nylc.org

Points of Light Foundation
    1400 I Street, NW, Suite 800
    Washington, DC 20005
    (202) 729-8000
    www.pointsoflight.org
Youth Service America
    1101 15th Street, Suite 200
    Washington, DC 20005
    (202) 296-2992
    www.servenet.org or www.ysa.org

Resources Addressing Inclusion, Social Relationships, and Peer Support Programs

Books and Chapters

Bauer, A. M., & Brown, G. M. (Eds.). (2001). *Adolescents and inclusion: Transforming secondary schools.* Baltimore: Paul H. Brookes.

Bowe, F. (2005). *Making inclusion work.* Columbus, OH: Prentice Hall/Merrill.

Burrello, L. C. (2001). *Educating all students together: How school leaders create unified systems.* Thousand Oaks, CA: Corwin.

Capper, C. A., Frattura, E., & Keyes, M. W. (2003). *Meeting the needs of students of ALL abilities: How leaders go beyond inclusion.* Thousand Oaks, CA: Corwin.

Cole, S., Horvath, B., Chapman, C., Deschenes, C., Ebeling, D. G., & Sprague, J. (2000). *Adapting curriculum and instruction in inclusive classrooms: A teacher's desk reference* (2nd ed.). Bloomington: Indiana University, Indiana Institute on Disability and Community.

Cushing, L. S., & Kennedy, C. H. (2003). Facilitating social relationships in general education settings. In D. L. Ryndak & S. Alper, *Curriculum and instruction for students with significant disabilities in inclusive settings* (2nd ed.; pp. 206–216). Boston: Allyn and Bacon.

Downing, J. E., & Eichinger, J. (2002). The important role of peers in the inclusion process. In J. E. Downing, *Including students with severe and multiple disabilities in typical classrooms* (2nd ed.; pp. 169–188). Baltimore: Paul H. Brookes.

Doyle, M. B. (2002). *The paraprofessional's guide to the inclusive classroom: Working as a team* (2nd ed.). Baltimore: Paul H. Brookes.

Fisher, D., & Frey, N. (Eds.). (2003). *Inclusive urban schools.* Baltimore: Paul H. Brookes.

Fisher, D., Sax, C., & Pumpian, I. (1999). *Inclusive high schools: Learning from contemporary classrooms.* Baltimore: Paul H. Brookes.

Friend, M. & Bursuck, W. D. (2002). *Including students with special needs: A practical guide for classroom teachers* (3rd ed.). Boston: Allyn and Bacon.

Goldstein, H., Kaczmarek, L. A., & English, K. M. (Eds.). (2001). *Promoting social communication: Children with developmental disabilities from birth to adolescence.* Baltimore: Paul H. Brookes.

Gore, M. C. (2004). *Successful inclusion strategies for secondary and middle school teachers: Keys to help struggling learners access the curriculum.* Thousand Oaks, CA: Corwin.

Gorman, J. G. (2004). *Working with challenging parents of students with special needs.* Thousand Oaks, CA: Corwin.

Hughes, C., & Carter, E. W. (2000). *The transition handbook: Strategies high school teachers use that work!* Baltimore: Paul H. Brookes.

Janney, R., & Snell, M. E. (2000). *Modifying schoolwork.* Baltimore: Paul H. Brookes.

Johnson, D. W., & Johnson, R. T. (1999). *Learning together and alone: Cooperative, competitive, and individualistic learning* (5th ed.). Boston: Allyn and Bacon.

Jorgensen, C. M. (1998). *Restructuring high schools for all students: Taking inclusion to the next level.* Baltimore: Paul H. Brookes.

Kartin, T. J. (2005). *Inclusion strategies that work! Research-based methods for the classroom.* Thousand Oaks, CA: Corwin.

Kennedy, C. H. (2004). Social relationships. In C. H. Kennedy & E. M. Horn (Eds.), *Including students with severe disabilities* (pp. 100–119). Boston: Allyn and Bacon.

Kennedy, C. H., & Fisher, D. (2001). *Inclusive middle schools*. Baltimore: Paul H. Brookes.

Lee, V. E., & Smith, J. B. (2001). *Restructuring high schools for equity and excellence: What works*. New York: Teachers College Press.

Lindsey, R. B., Roberts, L. M., & Campbell-Jones, F. (2005). *The culturally proficient school: An implementation guide for school leaders*. Thousand Oaks, CA: Corwin.

Martin, N. R. M. (2004). *A guide to collaboration for IEP teams*. Baltimore: Paul H. Brookes.

McLaughlin, M. J., & Nolet, V. (2004). *What every principal needs to know about special education*. Thousand Oaks, CA: Corwin.

McLeskey, J., & Waldron, N. (2000). *Inclusive education in action: Making differences ordinary*. Alexandria, VA: ASCD.

Meyer, L. H., Park, H. S., Brenot-Scheyer, M., Schwartz, I. S., & Harry, B. (1998). *Making friends: The influences of culture and development*. Baltimore: Paul H. Brookes.

Nisbet, J., & Hagner, D. (Eds.). (2000). *Part of the community: Strategies for including everyone*. Baltimore: Paul H. Brookes.

Nolet, V., & McLaughlin, M. J. (2000). *Accessing the general curriculum: Including students with disabilities in standards-based reform*. Thousand Oaks, CA: Corwin.

Phillipsen, M. (Ed.). (2000). *Assessing inclusion: Strategies for success*. Bloomington, IN: Phi Delta Kappa International.

Sailor, W. (Ed.). (2002). *Whole-school success and inclusive education: Building partnerships for learning, achievement, and accountability*. New York: Teachers College Press.

Scheurich, J. J., & Skrla, L. (2003). *Leadership for equity and excellence: Creating high-achievement classrooms, schools, and districts*. Thousand Oaks, CA: Corwin.

Snell, M. E., & Janney, R. (2000). *Collaborative teaming*. Baltimore: Paul H. Brookes.

Snell, M. E., & Janney, R. (2000). *Social relationships and peer support*. Baltimore: Paul H. Brookes.

Staub, D. (1998). *Delicate threads: Friendships between children with and without special needs in inclusive settings*. Bethesda, MD: Woodbine House.

Staub, D., Peck, C. A., Gallucci, C., & Schwartz, I. (2000). Peer relationships. In M. Snell & F. Brown (Eds.), *Instruction of students with severe disabilities* (5th ed.; pp. 381–408). Upper Saddle River, NJ: Merrill.

Wehmeyer, M. L., Sands, D. J., Knowlton, H. E., & Kozleski, E. B. (2002). *Providing access to the general curriculum: Teaching students with mental retardation*. Baltimore: Paul H. Brookes.

Journals

American Journal on Mental Retardation
    www.aamr.org
Augmentative and Alternative Communication
    www.isaac-online.org
Assessment for Effective Intervention
    www.unr.edu/educ/ceds
Communication Disorders Quarterly
    www.gsu.edu/~wwwdhh
Disability & Society
    www.tandf.co.uk
Education and Training in Developmental Disabilities
    www.dddcec.org
Education and Treatment of Children
    www.educationandtreatmentofchildren.net
Exceptional Children
    www.cec.sped.org
Exceptionality
    www.leaonline.com
Focus on Autism and Other Developmental Disabilities
    www.dddcec.org
International Journal of Inclusive Education
    www.tandf.co.uk
Intervention in School and Clinic
    www.proedinc.com

Journal of Developmental and Physical Disabilities
    www.kluweronline.com
Journal of Positive Behavior Interventions
    www.proedinc.com
The Journal of Special Education
    www.cecdr.com
Mental Retardation
    www.aamr.org
Preventing School Failure
    www.heldref.org
Remedial and Special Education
    www.proedinc.com
Research and Practice for Persons with Severe Disabilities
    www.tash.org
Rural Special Education Quarterly
    www.extension.usu.edu/acres
Teacher Education and Special Education
    www.tedcec.org
TEACHING Exceptional Children
    www.cec.sped.org

Organizations

American Association on Mental Retardation
    444 North Capitol Street, NW
    Washington, DC 20001
    (800) 424-3688
    www.aamr.org
American Association of School Administrators
    801 North Quincy Street, Suite 700
    Arlington, VA 22203
    (703) 528-0700
    www.aasa.org
American Council on Rural Special Education
    Utah State University
    2865 Old Main Hill
    Logan, UT 84322
    (435) 797-3728
    www.extension.usu.edu/acres
The Arc
    1010 Wayne Avenue, Suite 650
    Silver Spring, MD 20910
    (301) 565-3842
    www.thearc.org
Association for Supervision and Curriculum Development
    1703 North Beauregard Street
    Alexandria, VA 22311
    (800) 933-2723
    www.ascd.org
Association of University Centers on Disabilities
    1010 Wayne Avenue, Suite 920
    Silver Spring, MD 20910
    (301) 588-8252
    www.aucd.org
Autism Society of America
    7910 Woodmont Avenue, Suite 300
    Bethesda, MD 20814
    (800) 328-8416
    www.autism-society.org

Best Buddies
    100 SE Second Street, #1990
    Miami, FL 33131
    (800) 892-8339
    www.bestbuddies.org
Council for Exceptional Children
    1110 North Glebe Road, Suite 300
    Arlington, VA 22201
    (888) 232-7733
    www.cec.sped.org
Federal Resource Center for Special Education
    Academy for Educational Development
    1825 Connecticut Avenue, NW
    Washington, DC 20009
    (202) 884-8215
    www.federalresourcecenter.org/frc
National Association of Secondary School Principals
    1904 Association Drive
    Reston, VA 20191
    (703) 860-0200
    www.principals.org
National Association of State Directors of Special Education
    1800 Diagonal Road, Suite 320
    Alexandria, Virginia 22314
    (703) 519-3800
    www.nasdse.org
National Center on Secondary Education and Transition
    Institute on Community Integration
    University of Minnesota
    6 Pattee Hall
    150 Pillsbury Drive SE
    Minneapolis MN 55455
    (612) 624-2097
    www.ncset.org
National Dissemination Center for Children with Disabilities
    P.O. Box 1492
    Washington, DC 20013
    (800) 695-0285
    www.nichcy.org
National Down Syndrome Society
    666 Broadway
    New York, NY 10012
    (800) 221-4602
    www.ndss.org
National Middle School Association
    4151 Executive Parkway, Suite 300
    Westerville, OH 43081
    (800) 528-6672
    www.nmsa.org
National Resource Center for Paraprofessionals
    Utah State University
    6526 Old Main Hill
    Logan, UT 84322
    (435) 797-7272
    www.nrcpara.org
Office of Special Education Programs
    Office of Special Education and Rehabilitative Services
    U.S. Department of Education

400 Maryland Ave., SW
Washington, DC 20202
(202) 205-5507
www.ed.gov/osers

Parent Advocacy Coalition for Education Rights (PACER) Center
8161 Normandale Boulevard
Minneapolis, MN 55437-1044
(800) 537-2237
www.pacer.org

PEAK Parent Center
611 North Weber, Suite 200
Colorado Springs, CO 80903
(800) 284-0251
www.peakparent.org

Phi Delta Kappa
408 North Union Street
P.O. Box 789
Bloomington, IN 47402
(800) 766-1156
www.pdkintl.org

TASH
29 West Susquehanna Avenue, Suite 210
Baltimore, MD 21204
(410) 828-8274
www.tash.org

Unified Olympics
1325 G Street, NW, Suite 500
Washington, DC 20005 USA
(202) 628-3630
www.specialolympics.org

INDEX